RECEIVING
THE POWER

Also by Long and McMurry

The Collapse of the Brass Heaven

RECEIVING THE POWER

Preparing the Way for the Holy Spirit

Zeb Bradford Long and Douglas McMurry

Chosen Books

A Division of Baker Book House Co
Grand Rapids, Michigan 49516

© 1996 by Zeb Bradford Long and Douglas McMurry

Published by Chosen Books
a division of Baker Book House Company
P.O. Box 6287, Grand Rapids, MI 49516–6287

Printed in the United States of America

Library of Congress Cataloging-in-Publication Data

Long, Zeb Bradford.
  Receiving the power : preparing the way for the Holy Spirit / Zeb Bradford Long and Douglas McMurry.
      p.   cm.
  Includes bibliographical references.
   ISBN 0-8007-9246-7 (pbk.)
    1. Holy Spirit. 2. Baptism in the Holy Spirit. 3. Gifts, Spiritual. 4. Spiritual warfare. 5. Church renewal. 6. Evangelicalism. 7. Torrey, R. A. (Reuben Archer), 1856–1928. 8. Long, Zeb Bradford. 9. McMurry, Douglas. I. McMurry, Douglas. II. Title.
BT123.L66   1996
231'.3—dc20   96-8075

"You shall receive power when the Holy Spirit has come upon you; and you shall be my witnesses in Jerusalem and in all Judea and Samaria and to the end of the earth."

Acts 1:8

"He who has an ear, let him hear what the Spirit says to the churches."

Revelation 2:29

This book is dedicated to Laura and Carla, who have walked with us in this great adventure of growing in the Spirit.

Contents

PART 1

Fresh Challenges from the Spirit of God

A New Movement of the Holy Spirit

Once again God is graciously pouring out His Holy Spirit. None of us deserves it; He is doing it anyway.

Not only have we Westerners done nothing to merit the Spirit of God, but most of us have been denying His power, looking to our own expertise to solve our dilemmas. But God keeps beckoning: "Come to Me. Try Me." In spite of our self-assurance, He has shown more and more evidence of His power. Though many Christians are uncomfortable with such evidence—His power seems to set us to arguing—God refuses to leave us to our own devices.

At the turn of this century, Western countries like ours were enjoying an optimism based on science and a worldview that excluded God. In answer to our fascination with Darwinism and naturalism, God gave the Azusa Street revival in 1905 as part of a worldwide spiritual awakening that spread like a grassfire in (among other places) Wales, Korea, India, South Africa and China.

Zoom ahead to the 1960s, scene of the God-is-dead movement, drug culture and a peace activism whose emblem was the upside-down broken cross. Never was there a time of such spiritual deception and adolescent rebellion against God! God answered by pouring out His Holy Spirit in the Jesus movement and charismatic renewal.

In the '80s we saw the disastrous, well-publicized moral debacles of television Christians, followed by widespread scorn and skepticism directed against Christ and His Church. God has given answer to Western scoffing by pouring out the Holy Spirit again during the '90s.

This latest wave of divine power shows God's heart of forgiveness, His desire to reach out to an imperfect Church and to a warring world. God keeps resurrecting the Church with deeds that none of us deserves—the Promise Keepers men's movement, the Toronto Blessing, laughter in the Spirit, citywide concerts of prayer, prayer summits for pastors, intensive confession of sin around the world (including on college campuses), the A.D. 2000 and Beyond Movement, the Frontier Fellowship push into "hidden people groups" worldwide, the March for Jesus. These are only some of the activities we are seeing.

A Fresh Look-See

The current activity of the Holy Spirit incorporates elements of the Pentecostal and charismatic movements that went before it, but it has its own unique character and distinctive elements. Yes, the Holy Spirit is the same today (just as Jesus Christ is the same today, yesterday and forever). But God never sits still. A changing world scene demands a change in His response to human need. So the Holy Spirit is working in ways few could have predicted.

The following stories, rooted in the 1970s and '80s, exemplify the fruit God plans to harvest in the 1990s and beyond.

Peterson Sozi and Idi Amin

Our first story takes us to Uganda for some surprising developments rooted in the persecutions of Idi Amin. There a friend of ours, Peterson Sozi, struggled with the call of God in a time of great spiritual conflict. Here is the story as described by the Reverend Don Dunkerley:

> "Kill Peterson Sozi!" The order was given to his soldiers by Idi Amin Dada, dictator of Uganda, East Africa, from 1971 to 1979. He tried to turn Uganda into a Muslim state by the mass murder of Christians. By

conservative estimate he killed a half-million persons in a country of then eleven million. Indigenous churches were banned. Soldiers and secret police were given orders to search for underground services and kill everyone.

Peterson pastored such a church. He had been converted by hearing the Scriptures read aloud. The Holy Spirit convicted him of his sins and he could not stop weeping. He wept for three days. Then he knew his sins were forgiven. He did not yet own a Bible, but led many to Christ by his testimony.

His church, which met in a garage, grew rapidly. Soon the congregation overflowed into the yard. The situation was dangerous. Once Peterson had 82 new believers to baptize. "We cannot do this in secret," he said. "We will have to rely on the protection of Jesus. And so that people will know how good His protection is, we will have the baptism in Lake Victoria in the backyard of Amin's palace."

That day, under Jesus' protection, Amin's soldiers searched for secret, hidden, underground church services and paid no attention to the large group of people "swimming" openly in Amin's backyard.

One woman in the congregation did not tell her husband where she and their son went on Sundays because he was a member of the secret police and a persecutor of the Christians. One Sunday Peterson preached on Acts 3, in which the apostle Peter said to the lame man, "In the name of Jesus Christ of Nazareth, walk" (verse 6). The apostle helped him up and the man walked.

After the service the woman's son, a twelve-year-old on crutches, shook the pastor's hand. Remembering the sermon, Peterson said, "In the name of Jesus Christ, walk!" He helped the boy along, who was soon walking. That day the woman went home with a healed son.

Her husband was so thrilled he made his wife disclose the location of the church so he could go worship the God who had healed his son. Soon he told his friends in the secret police, the civil police, the military police and the Marines, who all went to see for themselves what God was doing in the garage. Many were converted there.

Edison Sempa was a Marine who gave his life to Jesus Christ in the garage. Later he was the only born-again Christian on guard duty at Entebbe Airport the night of the Israeli raid. By an amazing series of miracles, though he lost his leg in the raid, he was the only survivor. Today he is an evangelist who walks around Uganda on a prosthesis— living proof of the power of Jesus to deliver.

When the order came to kill Peterson Sozi, the born-again soldiers warned him. He considered fleeing to Kenya but decided to stay and rely on Jesus' protection. He never even moved his home. He was arrested more than once and managed many amazing escapes. Once he held a conspicuous public evangelistic crusade for three days in a major city. The very soldiers who had orders to kill him but had been converted stood, rifles at the ready, and protected the illegal preaching of the Gospel.

When Amin was overthrown in 1979, the churches came out of hiding. Peterson formed the Back to God evangelistic team in Uganda that is both well-known and effective.[1] Today Idi Amin is gone, while Peterson Sozi still preaches the Gospel.

"Are You Presbyterian or Pentecostal?"

In time Peterson found himself hemmed in, not by Idi Amin, but by African Pentecostalism that he felt limited his experience of Christ. Pentecostalism at the time focused on signs and wonders, while little solid teaching based on the Word of God supported Christian discipleship when signs and wonders were not happening. Few asked, "What do the signs point to?" And when faith was based on sensationalism, churches lacked stability and converts fell away.

Peterson became convinced that something important was missing from his experience of Christ. One day he was introduced to the teachings of the Reformed tradition, and began to see that a Reformed understanding of Scripture could help him and his people gain a better foundation for life than what they had experienced. He started a Presbyterian church, the first in Uganda.

His Pentecostal associates warned him against becoming a Presbyterian. When he did it anyway, they waited for the fire of the Holy Spirit to go out. It did not, because the Holy Spirit was still moving in the life and ministry of Peterson Sozi. In 1990, for example, Peterson gained national prominence for his Back to God evangelistic ministry when the feared witch doctor Patrick Kigozi was converted. It became clear that Peterson had not lost the fire of the Holy Spirit in return for gaining the light of the Word of God. We can have both the fire and the light.

Peterson puts it another way: "The Pentecostals have the motor car. The Presbyterians have the instruction manual. Satan keeps trying to keep the motor car and the instruction manual separate, because he knows what happens when the two are brought together.

Therefore he keeps bringing division between the Presbyterians and the Pentecostals. Each thinks it would be a catastrophe if they should have fellowship with the other!"

Today Peterson is responsible for starting eleven Presbyterian churches in Uganda, and he is in the process of forming a presbytery. At the same time, he is the founding secretary of the National Fellowship of Pentecostal Churches in Uganda. Peterson Sozi is trying to run the car according to the instruction manual!

All over the world, God is breaking down walls of pride and fear that have prevented us from seeing what He is doing in traditions other than our own. He is shattering stereotypes that Westerners have been nurturing for centuries—stereotypes about Presbyterians and Pentecostals, for instance (or Baptists or Catholics, for that matter). Maybe we need Africans, Asians and Native Americans to come among us today to bring their fresh perspective about ourselves and about God.

God is showing us that He is bigger than any of us has quite gotten hold of. Every denomination, tradition and ethnic group seems to have a gift placed in it by God, who made us all different. In the Church today God is asking us to open our eyes. He is confronting our tendency to see only the apostasies in other Christians or the weaknesses in other ethnic groups. He is asking us to stop preaching against each other; to learn instead to trade with each other the gifts we have received. What power we could have if we treated one another with love! Like the people of Israel newly arrived in the Promised Land, God is weaning us from tribalism. He wants us to learn to work together. The Holy Spirit is drawn to where the Church works in one accord, and is grieved when the Body of Christ is divided.

God is also showing us (as he showed Peterson Sozi in Uganda) that manifestations of the Holy Spirit are important in bringing God's Kingdom into areas of spiritual darkness.

Confession and Repentance in Monrovia, California

Brad: A second story reveals other ingredients of the current movement of the Holy Spirit.

Two hundred people participating in a leadership training conference[2] in October 1994 reflected the cultural diversity of Monrovia, a city just outside Los Angeles. Pastors attending from Monrovia churches represented denominations from Pentecostal to Presbyterian and backgrounds from African-American to Hispanic to Chinese to Anglo. The crowd was predominantly young. Expectancy filled the air.

After teaching on intercessory prayer, I sensed the Holy Spirit leading us to pray for the churches and city of Monrovia. We started by praying for the pastor of the Foursquare church. As we laid hands on him, words of knowledge came, revealing possible blocks to God's blessing. Prophecies were given showing God's intention to use His Church to advance the cause of Christ in Monrovia.

Suddenly the atmosphere became intense. We sensed we were awaiting a prophetic word or action—what we call a *kairos* moment, when the Spirit of God is moving and preparing to act. Then the pastor of the Presbyterian church stood up and confessed his failure to reach out to the black and Hispanic people of Monrovia. He asked the black and Hispanic pastors there to forgive him. In front of the whole group, these pastors wept together for the way they had been divided.

One astonishing confession led to another. The pastor of one of the Chinese churches came forward, bringing to the front about thirty Chinese Christians. He said that he, too, needed to confess sin on the part of the Chinese community. "Surely we are the most racist of all," he said. "We have thought of ourselves arrogantly as the center of the world. We have enjoyed the benefits of living in America but have kept to ourselves. Many of us were driven here by war or oppression, yet we have often been unwilling participants in the very society that opened its arms to us. Please forgive our arrogance and selfishness."

As this confession was offered, nearly the whole group came forward and gathered around the Chinese conferees to pray for them. An African-American pastor offered a powerfully moving prayer: "Lord, let there just be love."

This powerful time of reconciliation was followed by much more prayer for the empowerment of the Holy Spirit. Many people were filled with the Spirit, and we saw wonderful manifestations of His power. A number of people were set free from evil spirits. Others received emotional healing. Some were healed physically. Some were set free from sexual addictions. Finally the Holy Spirit finished by calling individuals to various forms of ministry and service.

All this had flowed out of a time of confession and forgiveness. It was as though a logjam had burst loose and the River of Life had come flowing out behind it.

Doug: Confession and forgiveness are appearing at a time when our culture has categorically rejected these disciplines. For more than sixty years our universities, with their humanistic climate, have drummed confession and forgiveness out of our consciousness. Some psychologists and helping professionals do not want to acknowledge the reality of sin. Under current politically correct philosophy, it is more acceptable to imagine that every ethnic culture is the center of the world to itself. It is not acceptable for people to confess sins against people of other cultures.

But God knows what we need, and He is again showing us basic biblical truths about confession and forgiveness. He is the ultimate college professor.

Today the Holy Spirit is not just inviting us to experience private renewal, but requiring us to see our corporate sin so that whole people groups can be reconciled under the Lordship of Jesus Christ. Southern Baptist leaders have confessed past racism on behalf of their denomination. The Pope has confessed sin on behalf of the entire Catholic Church. These only begin the list of church leaders confessing sin on behalf of their denominations. Jesus is in the process of uniting all things in heaven and on earth. In a world where ethnic controversies escalate into war and the horrors of ethnic cleansing, the Holy Spirit is cleansing Christians of sin and bitterness so that, as the pastor in Monrovia prayed, love can prevail.

Confession and repentance are far more in evidence today than they were a generation ago in the charismatic renewal, when they were drowned out by the fad of "positive confession." Political correctness is the positive confession of our culture today, but God is showing us how to confess our incorrectness. In a culture that denies the existence of sin, the Holy Spirit is leading Christians to confess deeply personal and corporate faults and failures. The result: a profound lifting of burdens that for generations had been getting heavier.

Prayer for Richmond

Richmond, Virginia, has been a city of great divisions. As capital of the Old Confederacy, the city reflects Old South tradition everywhere you go. Often her traditions have had a divisive, especially racist, impact. Richmond has few mixed-race churches. In addition, denominational tradition and narrowness have carried strong influence. Each denomination tends to stick to itself according to tradition that extends back to when Virginia was an Anglican colony. Until recently Richmond has seen little cooperation or celebration of unity in Christ.

In 1985 Richmond had the second-highest per capita murder rate in the nation, giving it a reputation as the murder capital of the Eastern seaboard. It was also a major drug-trafficking city and supermarket for illegal firearms. With these problems in mind, Pastor Louis Skidmore of St. Giles Presbyterian Church invited the pastors of the community to pray for revival in the city. For several months the pastors met at St. Giles to pray against violence and murder. Often one hundred or more pastors and ministry leaders came together to agree in prayer for the city.

In February 1986, under the leadership of Pastor Wellington Boone of Manna Christian Fellowship, St. Giles hosted a citywide intercessors conference, to which about eight hundred people came. The sanctuary was packed as Gary Bergel, director of Intercessors for America, gave the keynote address. Then eight hundred intercessors bound the spirit of murder in the city, according to Jesus' mandate in Matthew 16:19: "Whatever you bind on earth shall be bound in heaven, and whatever you loose on earth shall be loosed in heaven."

For exactly one month after that, according to a report in the *Richmond Times-Dispatch*—from February 9 (the date of our meeting at St. Giles) to March 10—murders in the city stopped cold. The police were astonished and mystified. Lieutenant W. E. Harver of the Richmond Bureau of Detectives commented, "Whatever forces are at work to keep [the murders] down, I hope they continue."

The gap in the murder rate was a lesson from God. He was reminding us that the evils that beset our cities have a spiritual core. There *are* demonic principalities and powers behind many of our social problems—a fact we choose to forget. Because of this unpleasant reality, solutions that stop at politicians and police never touch the root of our problem.

In Christ we ought to know that nothing can touch that spiritual core of evil but prayer in the name of Jesus Christ. Jesus alone has won the victory over satanic principalities. In our fight against the evils we deplore—including drugs, murder, violence, divorce and suicide—have we not trusted too much in human and political solutions? Jesus put little confidence in these solutions because He knew that only by the power of God can we be redeemed from the power of the evil one. A Lamb would be sacrificed, and God would give the Holy Spirit to those who believe in the Lamb and in the power He won on the cross.

The Holy Spirit is teaching us how to agree in prayer. He is teaching us about spiritual mapping (research to uncover obstacles to revival in our communities) and about spiritual warfare prayer that binds demonic powers. The Holy Spirit is pouring out "a spirit of grace and supplication," as Zechariah prophesied (12:10, NIV) and as that old warrior Martin Luther was fond of quoting. God is inviting Christians once again to learn how to lay hold of the prayer of faith.

Today we are moving beyond simply asking for the gift of tongues and a few other privately enjoyed gifts of the Spirit. God has put all Jesus' enemies under His feet for the sake of the Church, and entrusted her with an awesome responsibility: to bring His Kingdom to our communities. The corporate responsibility of the Body of Christ to prevail in prayer for a lost and depraved world is another dimension of the activity of the Holy Spirit today—a dimension notably lacking in previous moves of the Spirit.

Signs and Wonders

In the current moving of the Holy Spirit, there are signs and wonders, too, as in the previous Pentecostal and charismatic waves of the Holy Spirit.

Doug: For 25 years I considered myself impervious to manifestations of the Holy Spirit like "resting in the Spirit." I can remember several embarrassing moments when I was standing in line for prayer and people dropped to the floor all around, resting in the Spirit, leaving me the only one standing.

But in August 1995 I attended a worship service at the Church of the Nations, a new church in Richmond. At the end of the service, the pastor, the Reverend Tony Fitzgerald, called anyone in full-time Christian service forward to receive prayers of blessing. My wife, Carla, and I went forward, as did six others.

On this particular Monday night in August, no sooner had I gone forward than I began to feel a mysterious power pulling me backward. No one was touching me. The pastor was not standing in front of me or praying for me. Yet it felt as though God had moved the earth's center of gravity by ten degrees, so that gravity itself was pulling me backward. I adjusted my weight by pushing myself forward on my heels, only to be pressed gently backward again. There I was, standing in a line of eight people, rocking back and forth from toes to heels, trying to keep my balance. Finally I gave in and fell backward into the arms of two men waiting to catch me and lower me to the floor.

From the floor I looked up to the ceiling in serenity. Eventually Pastor Fitzgerald stood at my feet and gave a word from the Holy Spirit to encourage Carla and me in our ministries. This pastor was a stranger to me, yet the word he gave about "knives in your back" identified a back pain I have struggled with for years. Apparently God wanted to encourage me about it and about various aspects of our ministry.

In this way I learned about "carpet time," an expression current among certain circles of Christians touched by the Holy Spirit. Why did God put me on the floor? I believe He wanted to get my attention and prepare me to listen to the message He had for us. The floor is a very appropriate place to hear a message from God. It is impossible to be arrogant while lying on your back!

What This Book Is About

We could mention many other ingredients in connection with the current move of the Holy Spirit. We could fill our book with many stories—and we shall have many to tell in due course. But we are not writing a simple book of testimonies. The burden of our hearts is to try to answer two questions people frequently ask. First, how can we understand this move of the Spirit of God so that we can open ourselves to all that is genuine, while closing the door to the counterfeit, the demonic and the merely human? Second, how can we advance the cause of Christ more effectively by relying on the Holy Spirit?

Past movements of the Spirit have been fraught with divisiveness. Yet God seems to be calling Christians today into unity. How can we open ourselves to the Spirit this time around so as to avoid the errors that produced hurt and disharmony in the past? On the other side of things, how can we avoid opening ourselves to the serious dangers of the New Age movement that keeps trying to infiltrate the Church?

If we are to gain perspective to help us with this discernment, we need to get some history under our belts. We offer a tidbit of history in the next chapter like an appetizer to stimulate our appetites for what God will present in the main course.

Healing the Wounds

Brad: The Holy Spirit is calling Christians to stand together to fulfill the Great Commission and, by prayer, to overcome spiritual principalities of wickedness. These callings of the 1990s require us to let go of the hurts, fears and divisiveness that have hindered us in the past.

Yet some of the deepest hurts we have inflicted on one another have happened in the name of the Holy Spirit. Doug and I run into such hurt and anger frequently.

Our purpose in this chapter, then: to analyze divisive elements in the two earlier waves of the Holy Spirit in this century, in the hope of affirming their positive elements and avoiding their weaknesses in future moves of the Spirit.

Tongues: Still a Sore Thumb

For ninety years the gift of tongues has been at the center of the hurts surrounding the Holy Spirit. Two experiences I have had typify the hurt and confusion that result from misunderstanding the gift of tongues.

In one conference where I taught on the empowering work of the Holy Spirit, the people gathered eagerly, for they had grown frustrated trying to do God's work in their own strength. But when my teaching touched on the gift of tongues, I sensed tension in the audience. Some, in fact, looked as though they were about ready to explode with anger and hurt. Knowing I had hit an area of controversy, I stopped my lecture.

"How many of you have received the gift of tongues?" I asked.

About half the hands went up (mine included).

"How many have prayed for that gift but did not receive it?"

Most of the other hands went up.

"How many of you have experienced hurt or were made to feel like a second-class Christian because you did not receive this gift?"

Many of the same hands went up.

In the dialogue that followed, I found that many had been wounded by the implication that if they had never spoken in tongues, they had not received the Holy Spirit—a characterization they found hurtful.

After a time for clearing the air, I presented the baptism of the Spirit not as a second blessing, and not with tongues as initial evidence, but as God's equipping for service. Then we prayed for a healing of the hurts of the past. I listened to prayers from many to forgive fellow believers who had wounded them.

As prayer continued, many of the conferees experienced the Holy Spirit in a fresh outpouring. Hurt was healed, the pressure to prove something by speaking in tongues was gone, and many opened up spontaneously to the gift of tongues that they had resisted for years.

The other situation that stands out in my memory demonstrates how doctrines about tongues have actually blocked people from growing in the empowerment of the Holy Spirit. I was praying for a NASA space scientist who for seventeen years had sought the baptism with the Holy Spirit and always been disappointed because he had not received tongues. As we prayed, it was apparent to me that he was being touched by the Spirit. Still there was no manifestation of tongues, only the assurance of the presence of God and healing from the years of disappointment.

Then, in what must have been a vision from God, I saw light streaming from his eyes and received a clear message: *I have already given him the gift of discernment of spirits.* I spoke these words out. Immediately the man was overcome with emotion and started to shake all over.

"Yes, yes, I knew it all along!" he shouted. "The Lord gave me that gift the first time I asked to be filled with the Holy Spirit. But I didn't think I had the Spirit because I didn't speak in tongues."

Why do confusion and divisiveness so often swirl around the gift of tongues? By mid-century J. Edwin Orr, the well-known evangelist and educator, was already constrained to write: "In my opinion, the greatest hindrance to the progress of spiritual gifts among Evangelical believers is the view that the filling of the Holy Spirit must *always* be accompanied by speaking in tongues."[1]

Doug and I are not purporting that the gift of tongues has little value—far from it. In fact, in chapter 9 we will offer a list of positive effects we have been collecting from 25 years of experience in developing this gift for our own lives and ministries. The problem is not the gift of tongues. Rather, it is the interpretation and doctrines we bring to this gift.

For now let's review the first and second waves of the Holy Spirit in this century. If we can understand how divisiveness behind the spiritual gift of tongues entered the Body of Christ, perhaps we can close off the entry and heal the wound.

The Topeka Revival

To accomplish His gracious purposes, God often chooses what human beings despise as weak and lowly. So it was with the birth of the Pentecostal movement in the first decade of this century. Two men were used by God as the sparks for this revival.

The first was Charles Parham, a lay preacher in the Congregational Church. He later became a Methodist, then joined the Holiness movement, which stressed the sanctifying work of the Holy Spirit. In 1900 he founded a Bible college in Topeka, Kansas. The school was a center not just for academic study but for ministry and teaching.

Parham described life at the school (as quoted by John Nichol in his book *The Pentecostals*):

> No one paid board or tuition, the poor were fed, the sick were entertained and healed, and from day to day, week to week, and month to

month, with no sect or mission or known source of income back of us, God supplied our every need, and He was our all sufficiency in all things.[2]

p. 27

The school, in other words, taught more than academics. It taught reliance on God.

In December 1900 (a significant year, as we will see in the next chapter), Parham had to go to Kansas City. Before leaving, he asked his students to study the book of Acts to see if there was some concrete sign or special witness to the fact that a person had been baptized with the Holy Spirit. Though Parham had apparently experienced many effects of sanctification, he still felt he lacked the power of the Holy Spirit for ministry. When he returned, the students informed him that in apostolic times, when the believers were baptized with the Holy Spirit, they demonstrated the outward manifestation of speaking in tongues. From that moment on, the members of the college determined to pray for such an experience.

On New Year's Eve, after a time of prayer, a Miss Agnes Ozman asked that hands be laid on her for prayer. Parham reflected:

> I had scarcely repeated three dozen sentences when a glory fell upon her, a halo seemed to surround her head and face, and she began speaking in the Chinese language, and was unable to speak English for three days.

Nichol, p. 28

The rest of the students responded by spending days in prayer seeking the same Pentecostal experience. Nearly the whole student body, including Parham, received the gift of tongues.

The First Wave: Azusa Street

The Topeka revival marked the beginning of the Pentecostal movement, but its spread awaited the famous Azusa Street revival in 1906. One of Parham's students, a partly blind African-American named William J. Seymour, went to serve in a Methodist church in Los Angeles. According to one *Los Angeles Times* reporter, Seymour was meek and plain spoken and no orator. He spoke the common language of the uneducated class. He might preach for three-quarters of an hour with no more emotionalism than that there post. He was no arm waving thunderer, by any stretch of the imagination.

Nichol, p. 33

After being kicked out of one church for speaking about his Pentecostal experience, he started his own faith mission on Azusa Street in the industrial section of Los Angeles. Services had no pattern or organization but demonstrated the power of God. In time Azusa Street, with dramatic signs and wonders, became a center for Pentecostal renewal for people from all walks of life and from around the world. One participant of the Azusa Street meetings described her experience:

> A sound like a rushing, mighty wind filled the room, and I was baptized with the Holy Ghost and fire. Rivers of joy and love divine flooded my soul. God gave me the Bible evidence of having received this experience in letting me speak in another language . . . but the greatest joy in my heart was the knowledge that I received power to witness for Christ, power to tell others what great things God can do in a human life.

Nichol, p. 35

From these beginnings, the movement spread all over the world to become what is now the fastest-growing segment of the Body of Christ.

Reaction Sets In

The good news that God was sending a visitation of the Holy Spirit to working class people in Los Angeles was met with scorn in many quarters of the Church. This was, after all, the era when Protestants were laying the cornerstones for modernism and liberalism. The report that the Holy Spirit was moving with powerful signs and wonders did not fit the worldview of the philosophers of the age and was rejected by mainstream Christendom.

At the same time, J. Edwin Orr was right in charging the early Pentecostals with fanaticism and narrowness—a tendency to follow extremes without the balance of the whole counsel of God. "While many choice men of God identified themselves with the leadership of Pentecostalism," Orr concluded, "there was no great scholar like John Wesley to save the movement from its friends. . . ."[3]

Racism and class arrogance might have been part of the mix, too. God in His wisdom chose an African-American to lead this revival in the working class neighborhood of Azusa Street. This choice, while consistent with God's actions in Scripture, offended the established Church, and many rejected what God was doing through William Seymour.

These obstacles could have been overcome, except for the new interpretation that the Pentecostals brought to their very authentic experiences of the Holy Spirit.

History has shown that this experience was a genuine move of the Holy Spirit. As the first sowing of the Pentecostal seed, it has produced over the years some of the most astonishing church growth in history. Today, while mainline churches die on the vine, Pentecostal churches have prospered.

Encouraged by God's answer to their spiritual quest, the Topeka group began to formulate teachings based on their experience—teachings that transmogrified into denominational doctrines. Descriptions became prescriptions. Because of the unique emphasis on tongues as "evidence" of the Holy Spirit, a new theological idea was born in the opening days of this century: the idea that the baptism of the Holy Spirit always includes tongues.

Before then plenty of people had taught on the baptism with the Holy Spirit, but not as an experience of tongues. R. A. Torrey and D. L. Moody (as we will show) had experienced and were teaching a baptism with the Holy Spirit among evangelicals, following the doctrine of Charles Finney, who had two distinct experiences to which he referred as Holy Spirit baptisms. But the Topeka revival redefined the baptism of the Holy Spirit.

As John Nichol summarized in *The Pentecostals:* "Henceforth, for the Pentecostals the evidence that one has been 'filled with the Holy Spirit' is that he will have spoken in tongues" (p. 28).

Pentecostal Doctrine Today

The baptism with the Holy Spirit as an experience of tongues continues as a major element of Pentecostal teaching today. The Holiness Pentecostal Church, for example, holds to the following doctrines (italics added for emphasis):

> 10. We believe that *entire sanctification is an instantaneous, definite, second work of grace*, obtainable by faith on the part of the fully justified believer (John 15:2; Acts 26:18).
> 11. We believe that the Pentecostal baptism of the Holy Ghost and fire is obtainable by a definite act of appropriating faith on the part of the fully cleansed believer, *and the initial evidence of the reception of this experience is speaking with other tongues* as the Spirit gives utterance (Luke 11:13; Acts 1:5; 2:14; 8:17; 10:44–46; 19:6).[4]

While not inherent in the doctrine itself, the gift of tongues has in actual practice often become the sign that you have arrived, not merely at Christian maturity, but at spiritual and moral perfection— "entire sanctification." To be sure, views among Pentecostals diverge on the nature of the baptism of the Holy Spirit as a "second work of grace" or "second blessing." The Assemblies of God, for instance, a denomination founded in 1914 following those early revivals, do not hold to the entire sanctification doctrine, but do believe tongues is the initial evidence of the baptism in the Holy Spirit.

Most Christians believe that by the indwelling of the Holy Spirit we are being sanctified—made into the image of Jesus in order to bear the fruit of the Spirit, chief of which is love (1 Corinthians 13; 2 Corinthians 3:17–18; Galatians 5:16–26). Both Scripture and experience suggest that this process will not be completed until the end of the age, as Paul wrote in Philippians 3:12–15 (NIV):

> Not that I have already obtained all this, or have already been made perfect, but I press on to take hold of that for which Christ Jesus took hold of me. Brothers, I do not consider myself yet to have taken hold of it. But one thing I do: Forgetting what is behind and straining toward what is ahead, I press on toward the goal to win the prize for which God has called me heavenward in Christ Jesus. All of us who are mature should take such a view of things.

In Paul's teaching, maturity in Christ is attainable while moral perfection remains a hope for the future. Sanctification is a process of growth concluded only at the end of the age. In some Holiness teaching, however, sanctification is seen as an instantaneous event, a "second blessing" at which time God confers moral and spiritual perfection. This idea is a stumblingblock to most Protestants, since it suggests a level of present moral perfection that we have found in experience to be unlikely, if not unscriptural.

When "instantaneous sanctification" and a "second work of grace" are combined with the doctrine of "tongues as evidence," these teachings become an insurmountable obstacle for most Christians not indoctrinated early in Pentecostal theology; and connecting these ideas seems to invite spiritual pride more than genuine sanctification. Besides, there is not necessarily a connection between Christian character and the gifts of the Holy Spirit (as we will show in Part 2). Often extraordinary gifts of the Spirit, including tongues, are given to people of relatively immature character, while people of more mature character may show little evidence of spiritual power for ministry.

Nevertheless, the Pentecostal movement, in all its facets and denominational expressions, has been profoundly biblical in relying on the power of God. Hold up their faithfulness in this regard against the vast majority of mainline churches—which have largely rejected the power of God and even challenged the biblical witnesses to that power—and we can see why Pentecostal churches have grown while the mainline churches have been dying. Perhaps God chose Charles Parham and William Seymour, uneducated men like those who first walked with Jesus, to answer the scientific skepticism of higher criticism of the Bible, which blatantly challenged the recorded works of divine power.

The Second Wave: The Charismatic Renewal

Not content with half measures, God sent another wave of the Holy Spirit on the Church in the 1960s. Just at the moment when God-is-deadism was infiltrating mainline seminaries, God made a direct assault on Protestant and Catholic denominations. "Behold, I stand at the door and knock. . . ."

Within the Protestant Church, the charismatic renewal—from the Greek *charisma,* a gift of grace—began at St. Mark's Episcopal Church in Van Nuys, California, in 1959. Spiritual gifts, including tongues, were manifested in a small prayer group in the church. From this group about seventy people began to have similar experiences. They agreed to keep things quiet, for fear their experience might cause controversy.

Word got out, though, and the priest of St. Mark's, the Reverend Dennis Bennett, was forced in April 1960 to make a public statement to his denomination of what had happened. His statement caused controversy and led to his removal by the bishop.

Father Bennett was "exiled" to a small mission church in Seattle, but continued to teach and write on the Holy Spirit. His church grew strong and he encouraged charismatic prayer groups that were springing up in many Protestant denominations. His books became bestsellers, guiding hundreds of thousands of Christians into the baptism of the Holy Spirit.

From this beginning (and others in other denominations), the movement of the Holy Spirit spread around the world.

But not all was sweetness and light. On the one hand, many people got healed and blessed. On the other hand, some churches split right down the middle. Both sides experienced hurt and misunderstanding.

Protestant Charismatics: A Shoot from the Pentecostal Tree

Much of the divisiveness associated with the charismatic second wave came from tongues doctrines borrowed from Pentecostals going back to the Topeka and Azusa Street revivals. While Protestant charismatic teachers tried to distance themselves from old-line Pentecostal thinking, nevertheless they turned to that thinking as the basis for their understanding of the baptism with the Holy Spirit.

Dennis Bennett, for instance, insisted on tongues as a normative part of the baptism. In the following quote from *The Holy Spirit and You*, Bennett answered the question "Can I receive the Holy Spirit without speaking in tongues?"

"It comes with the package!" Speaking in tongues is not the baptism in the Holy Spirit, but it is what happens when and as you are baptized in the Spirit, and it becomes an important resource to help you continue, as Paul says, to "be being (or keep on being) filled with the Holy Spirit" (Eph. 5:18). You don't have to speak in tongues in order to be saved. You don't have to speak in tongues in order to have the

Holy Spirit in you. You don't have to speak in tongues to have times of feeling filled with the Spirit. But if you want the free and full out-pouring that is the baptism in the Holy Spirit, you must expect it to happen as in the Scripture, and to do what Peter, James, John, Paul, Mary, Mary Magdalene, Barnabas, and all the rest did! If you want to understand the New Testament you need the same experience that all its writers had.[5]

"It comes with the package!" is not the same language as the "ini-tial evidence" teaching of the Pentecostals, but it amounts to the same thing. It places tongues above all other spiritual gifts (or at least *before* all other spiritual gifts) by prescribing tongues for everyone. It also makes the assumption that all New Testament Christians spoke in tongues—an assumption we cannot prove.

Larry Christenson, pioneer leader of Lutheran charismatic re-newal, took a similar position. He rejected the doctrine of tongues as initial evidence but saw tongues as normative for the baptism with the Holy Spirit. He wrote of the baptism with the Holy Spirit as a fivefold pattern spelling out *Pilot:*

*P*ower—This is its purpose and result.
*I*nstantaneous—It occurs at a definite moment in time.
*L*ink—A distinct link in the divinely wrought chain which binds
    us to Christ.
*O*bjective—It has an outward manifestation.
*T*ongues—The objective manifestation, wherever mentioned, is
    speaking in tongues.[6]

Despite the efforts of leaders like Dennis Bennett and Larry Chris-tenson to distance themselves from Pentecostal doctrine, tongues were often the identifying mark of Holy Spirit baptism. Protestant charis-matic teaching changed the direction of Pentecostal instruction but, like a sprout from a tree, grew out of pioneering doctrines of the early Pentecostals—doctrines that focused on the gift of tongues.

Catholic Charismatics: A Different Spiritual Tradition

Not so the Roman Catholic charismatic leaders, who did not draw their theology from old-line Pentecostals.

Among Catholics, charismatic renewal broke loose in the autumn of 1966 at Duquesne University of the Holy Spirit in Pittsburgh. A group of lay faculty members gathered for prayer. Feeling they lacked power for effective Christian witness, they began to pray that the Holy Spirit would renew them with power. They started studying the New Testament, especially the first-century Church in the book of Acts. The group also began to read literature describing the empowering work of the Holy Spirit, including, at the beginning, *The Cross and the Switchblade* by David Wilkerson, a Pentecostal.

Then the group decided to take the then-bold step of seeking out an independent Protestant fellowship to see what was happening there. They were impressed by the warm welcome they received and by the spiritual vitality of the group.

Several weeks later, about thirty students and faculty from Duquesne devoted a weekend to prayer and meditation on the first four chapters of Acts. Most of them knew nothing about the manifestations of the Holy Spirit. The weekend was a turning point in the Catholic charismatic renewal. We quote Charles Hummel's narrative of it at length:

> Saturday evening had been set aside for relaxation and a birthday party. Yet one girl felt drawn to the chapel. Soon by ones and twos the others made their way there. As they prayed the Holy Spirit was poured out upon them.
>
> There was no urging, there was no direction as to what had to be done. The individuals simply encountered the person of the Holy Spirit as others had several weeks before. Some praised God in new languages, others quietly wept for joy, others prayed and sang. They prayed from ten in the evening until five in the morning. Not everyone was touched immediately, but throughout the evening God dealt with each person there in a wonderful way.
>
> Throughout the remainder of the spring semester at Duquesne the external gifts and the internal fruit of the Holy Spirit continued to flourish in this little community. They spread the joy of Christ's love to many Catholics in the university area.[7]

From this first outpouring, the movement spread to Notre Dame University and to Ann Arbor, Michigan, where the Word of God Community was founded in 1967. From these beginnings, charismatic renewal spread throughout the Roman Catholic Church with the approval and oversight of the Vatican.

The movement lacked the divisiveness often found in the Protestant renewal, perhaps because Catholic leaders placed a different theological interpretation onto charismatic experience than Pentecostal or Protestant leaders did. Rather than turn to old-line Pentecostal theology to interpret the new experiences, Catholics turned to their own spiritual traditions, which were still vibrant and from which they had not become as alienated.

Among Protestants, modernism had led to the celebration of secularism. The theology of the secular city (the title of a 1965 work by Harvey Cox describing the rise of urban civilization and the collapse of traditional religion) had cut most Protestants off from their spiritual roots. Protestant seminaries had come under what Doug and I call a brass heaven mentality—a sort of geodesic dome stretching from horizon to horizon sealing off the spiritual world.[8]

Among Protestants, therefore, the charismatic renewal felt like jumping into a cool swimming pool after a decade in the desert. For Catholics it was more like moving from one swimming hole to another—not quite the same shock to the system.

Typical of the Catholic response to the second wave was that of Edward D. O'Connor in his book *The Pentecostal Movement in the Catholic Church:*

> It is true that the term, *baptism in the Spirit,* although biblical, has never been much used in classical theology. . . . The Holiness churches in 19th-century America seem to have been chiefly responsible for drawing attention to the term, and their preoccupation with it was one of the main roots of the Pentecostal movement, in which the baptism in the Spirit is thought to be the true introduction to what may be called life in the Spirit, and a phase through which every Christian life is meant to pass.
>
> However, the use of a new term does not create a problem (above all when it is a biblical term!). The important question is whether this new terminology reflects a radically new conception of the spiritual life. As I see it, there is nothing substantially new in what is called the baptism in the Spirit, but there is something new in the circumstances and mode of its occurrence. Substantially, it is an experience of the presence and action of the Holy Spirit. Such an experience is the nor-

mal flowering of the life of grace, a fulfillment of our status as sons of God; it is called for by the very nature of grace, the theological virtues, and the gifts of the Holy Spirit. Once one has taken full cognizance of the New Testament teaching on being born again of the Holy Spirit, and on being the temple in which he dwells, it is not the experience of this great mystery of faith that requires an explanation, but the fact that so many Christians seem to lack this experience.[9]

Catholic interpreters like Kilian McDonnell, Léon Joseph Cardinal Suenens and a host of others who appreciated biblical theology and classical spirituality helped guide this movement into channels that ministered healing and spiritual vitality to millions. Seldom did their teaching emphasize tongues, yet that gift remained one element of the renewal, fully acceptable as part of a long-standing tradition that went back to the "jubilation" mentioned by Augustine and the witness of early Church fathers like Irenaeus. In the 1960s and '70s, you had to read Catholic writings to see the historic roots for the gift of tongues beyond Azusa Street.

Catholic writings were well-balanced on the implications of charismatic renewal. Suenens' book *A New Pentecost?* covered the range of charismatic influences, from liturgical renewal to building vibrant Christian communities to ecumenical relations. Tongues was scarcely mentioned. Nor was it a focus of Kilian McDonnell's book *The Holy Spirit and Power* or of most other Catholic charismatic writings.

Will the Real Culprit Please Stand Up?

What, then, has created the divisiveness and hurt that have often accompanied the work of the Holy Spirit? Not the gift of tongues, but doctrines about tongues—doctrines that defined the baptism of the Holy Spirit as an experience of glossolalia. These doctrines led to the belief that people who speak in tongues are verifiably Spirit-filled or have arrived at a higher plane of spirituality than those who do not. These doctrines have also produced spiritual pride, hurtful condemnation, rejection and divisiveness within the Body of Christ.

Mainline Christians might (apart from this teaching) have been more open to the gifts of the Holy Spirit. After all, what sick person does not want to be healed? What sincere Christian does not want to hear a genuine word from God? What truly God-given gift could harm us? But some of the doctrines surrounding the Topeka and Azusa Street revivals did harm us.

Another culprit, too, lurks in the dark. Intellectual arrogance and class snobbery against Pentecostals inflicted hurts still in evidence today. One reason we believe that Pentecostal teaching about tongues was cast in concrete was the early rejection of Pentecostals by mainline Christians.

I encountered this hurt at the last conference I led before leaving Taiwan as a missionary in 1989. The conference was for Pentecostal missionaries who asked me to share with them my understanding of the Holy Spirit from the Reformed perspective. I was amazed at the invitation, but they had heard that a movement of the Holy Spirit was breaking out among Presbyterians in Taiwan and wanted to know how this could be.

These missionaries received my teaching gladly until I said, "I believe tongues is a good gift. Indeed, I have received that gift, too. But I cannot find clear scriptural support for your doctrine that tongues is the initial evidence of the baptism with the Holy Spirit."

The debate that followed lasted until three in the morning. Finally one of the leaders of the group, an older man, stood up with tears in his eyes and said, "Brother, I suspect you are right in the way you interpret Scripture in regards to tongues. But we Pentecostals have suffered so much for our conviction that the gifts of the Holy Spirit are for today that if we give up the doctrine of the 'initial evidence,' we will be giving up something that has shaped our identity from the beginning."

Then it was my turn to weep, for I was filled with grief for the way we of the mainline denominations had treated him. We knelt and confessed our pride and rejection of one another.

How often pride channels personal experience into legalistic doctrine and denominational narrowness! Groups of Christians hardened by pride have stung other groups with careless or unkind words, necessitating widespread confession and forgiveness.

But after we confess our sins that have grieved the Holy Spirit, what then? We have to grope for teaching that will open the door to spiritual renewal of the Church and to revival in the land. We need sound teaching that will draw us together, not tear us apart.

Happily, we do not need to invent this teaching from scratch. It already exists. One man at the turn of the century drew this teaching from Scripture—though at the time, because of Pentecostal controversies, his teaching was ignored by both Pentecostals and the mainline churches. It is past time to draw up through his very healthy roots the water of the Holy Spirit today.

The Power of God

Doug and Brad: Many Christians avoid talking about the baptism with the Holy Spirit because it has been so divisive. Yet the promise of this baptism is thoroughly biblical and part of our Christian inheritance. Is it not worthwhile to come to a more constructive interpretation of it?

Pentecostal theology is not broad enough to describe the wide range of genuine biblical Holy Spirit experiences among Christians. Many believers, after all, demonstrated the power of the Holy Spirit prior to the Topeka revival. Are we to suggest that these men and women were not Spirit-filled? The present activity of the Holy Spirit around the world requires us to find some other way of interpreting twentieth-century outpourings than by means that exclude everyone but tongues-speakers.

C. Peter Wagner is among those who shun the Pentecostal and charismatic labels but believe nonetheless that evangelicals must recover the power of the Holy Spirit for ministry. Wagner offers this description in his book *The Third Wave of the Holy Spirit:*

> The Third Wave is a new moving of the Holy Spirit among evangelicals who, for one reason or another, have chosen not to identify with

either the Pentecostals or the charismatics. Its roots go back a little further, but I see it as mainly a movement beginning in the 1980's and gathering momentum through the closing years of the twentieth century. Researcher David Barrett estimates 27 million third-wavers in 1988. In it the Holy Spirit is ministering in the same miraculous way but with a different flavor. I see the Third Wave as distinct from, but at the same time very similar to, the first and second waves. They have to be similar because it is the same Spirit of God who is doing the work.[1]

If the third wave is God's appeal to evangelicals that we, too, need the power of God, then we may look to the teaching of R. A. Torrey as foundational.

Reuben Archer Torrey was the first superintendent of Moody Bible Institute (then called Chicago Bible Institute) and dean of the Bible Institute of Los Angeles (BIOLA). He taught the baptism with the Holy Spirit prior to and during the rise of Pentecostalism. He was a world-renowned evangelist and teacher at a time when the Holy Spirit was bringing worldwide revival. Torrey's prayers and preaching were responsible for much of that revival. His writings, especially his teachings on the Holy Spirit, are still disseminated widely among evangelicals.

Grounding in the Power of God

Who was Reuben Archer Torrey and how did God use him? The man's life speaks for itself.

Torrey had vowed as a student at Yale that the one thing he would never do was become a preacher. Perhaps he had heard one too many uninspired sermons in the Congregational churches of his boyhood. But one night he became so depressed with his vapid life at Yale that he seized a razor to slash his wrists.

At that moment God answered the prayers of Torrey's mother, who had been praying (for some reason) that her son would become a preacher. Young Archie decided not to commit suicide but to surrender his life to God, even if it meant becoming a preacher. At that moment deep peace filled him, and he was seized with an inexplicable desire to preach the Gospel.

During the following years, 1875–1889, God worked with Torrey to instill a lifestyle of trust in God's provision and in the power of the Holy Spirit for all Christian ministry. The critical point in Torrey's theological education occurred in Germany. In Leipzig he studied under the famous Old Testament scholar Franz Delitzsch, and in Erlangen under the New Testament scholar Theodor Zahn. His encounter with higher-critical scholarship, which was then emerging in Germany, forced him to a crisis of faith.

Higher criticism, as an approach to biblical interpretation, started with the assumption that the human mind can discern truth, rationally and perfectly, from falsehood. Scientific methods, it claimed, are a surer way of discerning truth than the interpretation the Holy Spirit brings, through faith, to the Word of God.

Torrey decided, after much intellectual struggle, that higher criticism was based on an inadequate philosophical base, and he rejected it. After that he interpreted the Scriptures the way most Protestants had done since the Reformation—by trusting the Holy Spirit to awaken them to the mind and heart.

As he did, he came to believe in the doctrine of inerrancy, not as an invitation to nit-pick over biblical minutiae, but as a conviction that the Bible is an absolutely reliable guide in life when the Holy Spirit is allowed to work. As he said later (quoted by Roger Martin in *R. A. Torrey, Apostle of Certainty*), "I have come to the fork in the road more than fifty times, and in every instance where my reason and common sense differed from the Bible, the Bible has proved right and my reason wrong" (p. 69).[2]

Torrey took up a local church ministry in Minneapolis, which became his school in reliance on the power of God. Married by now and ministering to the poor in a run-down neighborhood, he learned that the power of the Holy Spirit was more available to Christians than most of them thought.

Torrey had three children during his ministry in Minneapolis and found ample opportunity to test God's day-by-day provision and power for a growing family. On one occasion, while he was away from home, his second daughter, Blanche, became seriously ill.

Clara [his wife] cared for her during the night, and in her distress Blanche expressed her yearning for her father to be there to pray for her. Shortly after saying this she felt greatly relieved and fell into a restful sleep. Soon she was completely well and able to return to school. A few days later a letter came from Reuben in a distant city inquiring what was wrong with Blanche. He further noted that he had been deeply impressed to pray for her in the middle of the night. It was later learned that she began to recover at the precise hour in which he prayed.

Martin, p. 71

By reading the life of George Müller, Torrey learned the challenge of relying on God for provision. Müller's life made so great an impact on him, in fact, that he resolved early in his ministry not to climb the ladder of ecclesiastical success to a prestigious church but to go wherever God directed him, for there God's provision would sustain him. In short, he wanted to learn how to rely on God and follow His leadings (a passion similar to that of Charles Parham). God spent several years working with Torrey to help him knead his convictions into his lifestyle. The result: He learned not to go into debt but to cling to God alone for financial provision.

The sum of God's teaching for Torrey at this time was that Christians can rely on the power of God for themselves and their ministries. This became his life message, his philosophy, his divine calling. Is it little wonder, then, that the message for which R. A. Torrey is most remembered is a message about the baptism with the Holy Spirit as the main equipment for Christian ministry?

Basic Equipment

Torrey saw the promise of the baptism with the Holy Spirit as the key to all successful ministry, just as it was for the New Testament Church. Jesus had told His disciples, "You are witnesses of these things. I am going to send you what my Father has promised; but stay in the city until you have been clothed with power from on high" (Luke 24:48–49, NIV).

Here is a biblical command ("Be my witnesses") linked with a biblical promise ("power from on high"). Torrey saw the link, and absorbed into his life and teaching both the command and the promise. To him the baptism with the Holy Spirit was an empowerment for service and witness taught by the Bible for the benefit of all Christians. He could see no exceptions or withdrawals of this biblical promise—one of many that should be appropriated by faith in God's Word.

As he did so for himself, Torrey found God faithful to fulfill it in a way appropriate for him. The baptism with the Holy Spirit became the heart of his ministry of equipping others for Christian witness and service.

Holy Spirit baptism, to Torrey, was not an experience of tongues, though he would later write about tongues and try to reinterpret the Pentecostal experience. Not everyone baptized with the Holy Spirit, taught Torrey, does or should speak in tongues, just as not everyone baptized with the Spirit should become a full-time evangelist or preacher or missionary (another fallacy of that day). Torrey foresaw the dangers in classical Pentecostal teaching and tried to warn the Body of Christ.

But that came later.

D. L. Moody and Holy Spirit Baptism

In 1889 Dwight L. Moody, a former shoe salesman, plunked his Chicago Bible Institute down amid the virulent crime, cattle smells and colorful immigrant population of the Windy City. At the recommendation of his brother-in-law, Fleming H. Revell, Moody tapped Torrey to be the first superintendent of the Institute. Torrey's personality was as far from Moody's as could be imagined; according to biographer Roger Martin, "Moody was brusque, impulsive and uneducated, Torrey polished, logical and scholarly" (p. 89). But they had one thing in common: Both had learned by experience to rely on the promised baptism of the Holy Spirit.

Moody's experience of the baptism had happened more than twenty years before. His work at the YMCA in Chicago during the 1860s, which he loved, had burned him out. He sensed, too, that God was calling him out of organizing for charity work and into evangelistic work. "God was calling me into higher service," he wrote later, "to go out and preach the Gospel all over the land instead of staying in Chicago. I fought against it."[3]

As he resisted God's call, his work increasingly lacked power. Two women in his congregation, Mrs. Sarah Cooke and Mrs. Hawxhurst, discerned Moody's spiritual condition and began not only to pray for him but to speak to him of his need to be filled with the Holy Spirit. Through their influence, Moody started to pray to be baptized with the Holy Spirit. Yet still he refused to accept God's call, which would take him away from Chicago and his beloved work with the YMCA.

The situation changed dramatically during the Chicago fire of 1871, which destroyed not only the YMCA but Moody's home and everything he had built. From the book *Moody: A Biographical Portrait of the Pacesetter in Modern Mass Evangelism* by J. C. Pollock:

> In broad daylight he walked down one of the busiest streets, Broadway or Fifth Avenue, he scarcely remembered which, while crowds thrust by, the clop-clink of cabs and carriages was in his ears and the newsboys shouted. It was then that the last chain snapped. Quietly, without a struggle, he surrendered.
>
> Immediately an overpowering sense of the presence of God flooded his soul. "God Almighty seemed to come very near. I felt I must be alone." He hurried to the house of a friend nearby, sent up his card and brushed aside an invitation to "come and have some food." "I want to be alone," he said. "Let me have a room where I can lock myself in."
>
> His host thought it best to humor him. Moody locked the door and sat on the sofa. The room seemed ablaze with God. Moody dropped to the floor and lay bathing his soul in the Divine. Of this Communion, this mount of transfiguration, "I can only say that God revealed Himself to me, and I had such an experience of His love that I had to ask Him to stay His hand." Turmoil of mind glided into peace, conflict of character snapped into integration. . . . God must lead, and God supply. Moody need never thirst again. The dead, dry days were gone. "I was all the time tugging and carrying water. But now I have a river that carries me."[4]

This moment in the home of a friend changed D. L. Moody dramatically and propelled him into the ministry of mass evangelism for which he became well known.

D. L. Moody + R. A. Torrey = Dynamite

Torrey and Moody shared similar views concerning the Holy Spirit, and worked together to lead young people into the baptism with the Spirit, as revealed in the following typical account:

At three o'clock we gathered in front of Mr. Moody's mother's home; four hundred and fifty-six of us in all, all men from the eastern colleges. We commenced to climb the mountainside. After we had gone some distance Mr. Moody said: "I do not think we need to go further. Let us stop here. I can see no reason why we should not kneel down here and ask God that the Holy Spirit may fall on us as definitely as He fell on the Apostles at Pentecost. Let us pray." We knelt down on the ground; some of us lay on our faces on the pine needles.

. . . The Holy Ghost fell upon us. It was a wonderful hour. There are many who will never forget it.[5]

In chapter 8 we will read of Torrey's own baptism in the Holy Spirit, which had happened earlier in Minneapolis. Suffice it to say, Moody's and Torrey's separate experiences of the Holy Spirit brought them together in a common understanding and empowerment for the task that faced them.

Linked up with Moody at the Institute, Torrey became known for his teaching on the baptism with the Spirit. He felt a special urgency about this, in that Western culture was moving away from reliance on the power of God, and he believed the Church should confront culture rather than give in to the growing trends of rationalism and modernism.

As one might expect, Torrey's basic sermon on the Holy Spirit, in which he challenged people to ask for Holy Spirit baptism, was one of D. L. Moody's favorites. Torrey's biographer writes:

Time and again Moody would tell him, when about to be off on a preaching engagement, "Now, Torrey, be sure and preach on the baptism with the Holy Ghost." Once Torrey asked him, "Mr. Moody, don't you think I have any sermons but those two?"[6]

"Never mind that, you give them those two sermons." And as usual, at the word of Moody, Torrey did as he was told! Moody was the only person who ever dared tell Torrey what to preach.

Martin, p. 116

Several other teachers at the Institute took issue with Torrey's preaching on the Holy Spirit, believing that the power of the Spirit had been withdrawn at the close of the apostolic age, or that the baptism of the Spirit meant simply our inclusion into the Body of Christ ("For by one Spirit we were all baptized into one body," 1 Corinthians 12:13). Moody sat in on some of these discussions and reflected on them later with Torrey:

> Oh, why will they split hairs? Why don't they see that this is just the one thing that they themselves need? They are good teachers, they are wonderful teachers, and I am so glad to have them here; but why will they not see that the baptism with the Holy Ghost is just the one touch that they themselves need?
>
> Martin, p. 118

The Mantle Passes to Torrey

During the final month of the last century—December 12, 1899—Dwight Moody passed away in the middle of an evangelistic campaign. To honor him, the trustees of the Chicago Bible Institute changed its name to Moody Bible Institute.

With the death of this shoe-salesman-turned-evangelist came the passing of an era. For the new century God had new plans, which Dr. Torrey could hardly have guessed at, but which we can see by hindsight. The turn of the century brought the beginning of new global spiritual ferment, the scope of which the world had not yet seen. The West was also due for some unexpected birth pangs—two wars that caught everyone by surprise and soured the optimism of budding faith in science and evolutionary progress. But God was not willing to let the Enlightenment be the last word in the West, and Torrey was to be a star actor on God's stage.

The month after Moody's death, in January 1900, the superintendent of women at the Institute suggested they hold weekly prayer meetings on Saturday nights to pray for worldwide revival. R. A. Torrey acted on the suggestion, and weekly sessions were begun to initiate the new century. Soon attendance at the meetings grew into the hundreds. When asked how long they would keep them up, Dr. Torrey replied, "Until revival comes."

A year later Torrey received an invitation to conduct an evangelistic tour in Australia—an invitation unsolicited and not particularly welcome, since he had enough to do at the Institute and the Chicago Avenue Church, which he pastored. But God impressed Torrey to accept the invitation.

On December 23, 1902, R. A. and Clara Torrey embarked on an evangelistic career that led them around the world many times during the next three years—to England, Scotland, Wales, Ireland, New Zealand, Japan, China and India. In the British Isles alone, more than seventy thousand people registered decisions for Christ.

One writer described Torrey's preaching style:

> He spoke primarily to the conscience and reason rather than to the emotions, and rarely raised his voice beyond a conversational tone. His sermons were so direct and sharp that many expected the audience to get up and walk out *en masse*, but they stayed—and many were converted. It could only be, as one mission leader commented, "that divine gift—undefinable, but unmistakable—'the power of the Holy Ghost.' A gleam from the fire of Pentecost is in his sermons."
>
> Martin, p. 140

Much later Torrey described his life in a nutshell:

> . . . God gave me what I sought, I was baptized with the Holy Spirit. . . . Then I began to tell others of what I had found in the Word of God, first in very small circles, then in larger circles, then in much wider circles, and at last it was my privilege to tell it literally around the globe.[7]

Revival broke out in Wales in 1905 as a direct result of Torrey's presence there, though it was Evan Roberts who would remain in Wales and whose joy-giving presence would linger at the center of the Welsh revival. Revival broke out in India the same year, which in turn inspired Korean missionaries to pray for revival. And in 1905 Torrey's friend Jonathan Goforth helped birth the awakening in Korea. Thousands confessed their sins in public and surrendered their lives to Christ.

The worldwide revival extended well beyond Torrey's personal influence, for it was the result not of personal influence but of prayer.

A Cold Reception

But when Torrey returned home, he ran into trouble (as Jonathan Goforth did when he returned to his native Canada).

During Torrey's absence, God had poured out the Holy Spirit in Topeka and at Azusa Street—part of the answer to the prayers for

worldwide revival. But as God poured out His power, the local leaders of that new American Pentecost developed their own theology
(as we saw in the last chapter), and Torrey was confronted with a definition of the baptism with the Holy Spirit with which he did not
agree. In particular, he rejected Pentecostal theology about tongues:
". . . I saw that the teaching that speaking with tongues was the
inevitable and invariable result of being baptized with the Holy Spirit
. . . was utterly unscriptural and anti-scriptural."[8]

Reactions from mainstream American churches against the "second blessing" doctrine with tongues as initial evidence was so strong
that a backlash formed as well against Torrey's teaching on the baptism with the Holy Spirit. Members of the Moody faculty begged Dr.
Torrey to drop the term *baptism with the Holy Spirit* and limit himself
to speaking of the "fullness of the Holy Spirit." It does not seem to
have occurred to Torrey to check the Greek words for *filled* (as we
will do in a later chapter), but he obviously had a deep sense that
such terminology was ambiguous and unsatisfactory. "The Bible uses
the expression *baptism with the Holy Spirit,*" he said, "and I will use
baptism with the Holy Spirit."

Tension grew at the Institute. Then an invitation to become dean
of the recently founded Bible Institute of Los Angeles (BIOLA) provided Torrey with the solution he needed. He resigned from Moody
Bible Institute without making a public issue of his disagreement
with his faculty, and became dean of BIOLA.

But BIOLA was located not far from Azusa Street: Torrey was jumping from the frying pan into the fire. There, too, he was eventually
asked to stop using the expression *baptism with the Holy Spirit* and to
speak only of "being filled with the Holy Spirit." He resigned from
BIOLA and gave his full energy to Bible conferences, worldwide evangelization and editing the popular "Gist of the Lesson," summariz-
ing the Sunday school studies used in thousands of churches.

His insistence on the phrase *baptism with the Holy Spirit* may seem
picayune to some. But Torrey believed that without a specific appropriation by faith of this biblical promise as equipment for ministry,
the Western Church would slide into self-reliance and worldliness
and lose its spiritual vibrancy. Today Torrey's warnings seem justi-
fied, since to a large degree this is what has happened. On the other

hand, Torrey did not want the term *baptism with the Spirit* to become Pentecostalized. This, too, is just what has happened.

Torrey's "Fundamentals"

Dr. Torrey was unable to convey his message in the midst of an increasingly volatile and controversial atmosphere. In the years before his death in 1928, he formed the World's Christian Fundamentals Association. He wanted to get Christian teaching down to its basic elements in order to present the Gospel to the world more effectively and make disciples in every nation. Unfortunately he lived to see fundamentalism become a narrow, sniping, dogmatizing influence in America, devoid of the power of the Holy Spirit to win an increasingly skeptical, doubting world to Christ.

Dr. Torrey's resignation from two Bible institutes was the harbinger of things to come among fundamentalist and evangelical Christians. Fundamentalism would concentrate not on fulfilling the basics of faith and power to complete the Great Commission, but on gaining political control over seminaries and denominations against the perceived danger of liberalism. Evangelicals, for their part, could not see that it is by the power of God, not political control, that the soul of the Church stays healthy.

In 1905, the very year God was showing His power to be global in scope and relevance, Western culture was increasingly defining that power as abnormal or even fictitious. At the very time R. A. Torrey returned from seeing his teaching vindicated throughout the world, the people who knew him best repudiated his message. The power of God? The baptism with the Holy Spirit? Not today, not for us! In the end, mainstream and evangelical churches repudiated the baptism of the Spirit, while Pentecostals claimed exclusive rights over it.

But the seven fundamentals Torrey believed in are basics we can still recover. He called them "certain steps" and encouraged every Christian to include them in his or her walk with God:

1. Accept Jesus Christ as personal Savior.
2. Repent from all known sin.
3. Make an open, public confession of faith in Christ.

4. Surrender your life fully to Christ as Lord and live a life of obedience.
5. Earnestly desire the baptism with the Holy Spirit as empowerment for witness and service.
6. Pray definitely for it.
7. Accept it by faith, regardless of "initial signs."[9]

These steps (which we will explore in detail in chapter 8) have been proven effective in producing stable, mature Christians who are bearing witness effectively for Jesus and relying on God in ministry. These basics can also heal a church still divided over the Holy Spirit as God pours out fresh waves of spiritual awakening.

PART 2

A Biblical Foundation for the Person and Work of the Holy Spirit

The Holy Spirit "Upon"

Brad: My own spiritual journey led me into an acquaintance with R. A. Torrey's grandson, Archer Torrey. As director of Jesus Abbey in Korea, Archer has had a profound impact on my life—in part by reintroducing to me the teachings of his grandfather. He became my mentor at a time I was struggling to interpret the work of the Holy Spirit in my ministry in Korea and Taiwan.

How Do We Interpret Experiences of Power?

At an evangelistic meeting in Taipei one evening in 1993, the sanctuary was packed with some five hundred people. I had just preached on how to be filled with the Holy Spirit. The sanctuary was bursting with expectation. I could feel it pulsating with the presence of God. But I had no guidance as to what to do next. I pleaded with God to show me His agenda. No leadings came.

Then, from the back of the church, I could see my co-worker Ken Shay making his way to the platform.

"Call the people to come forward," he whispered to me. "I believe the Lord wants to bless them."

I asked the ministry team to approach the front. Then I gave an altar call. Suddenly, like wind catching dry leaves, you could hear a rustling through the crowd. More than half of the people rose to their feet and actually came rushing forward.

We were unprepared for such a response. In fact, the ministry team was pinned against the wall by the mass of people, unable to move. It seemed we were going to be crushed by the crowd surging forward.

Lord, help! I prayed desperately. *These are Your people; You must minister to them.*

I felt the Holy Spirit say to me, *Obey, and I will show My power and glory.*

With this word I felt something like a tingling of electricity. Immediately, although I touched no one, people around me sank to the floor, their faces brightening with joy. I moved forward with my hands outstretched. As I did, everyone I touched or came near dropped to the floor, resting in the Spirit. People were so packed together that some rested against others who also rested. The Lord was not only taking care of a potentially dangerous crowd-control problem, but healing and blessing the people by His Spirit.

By the time I got to the back of the church, that extraordinary power of the Holy Spirit had lifted and people stopped going down with my touch. But God was not finished. Throughout the rest of the evening, we saw physical healings and deliverances from demonic power. As a result of the manifestations of the Holy Spirit, a number of people became convinced of the reality of the Christian Gospel and accepted Jesus Christ as their Lord and Savior.

About one in the morning we finished with ministry and headed for the back door of the church, exhausted and "peopled out." There by the door, a college-age girl on crutches waited, both her legs in iron braces. She dragged herself into my path and asked if we could pray for her. Feeling that the Holy Spirit had lifted, I said I was too tired to pray and that I had to get home. She explained with tears that, crippled, she had been unable to make her way to the front of the church for prayer.

She looked utterly wretched! Torn between exhaustion and compassion, there welled up in me such a love for her that I decided to pray for her. Several of us laid hands on her. This time I had no awareness of empowerment, only the calm assurance that Jesus was going to touch this girl whose life had been wrecked by disease.

As we prayed, her legs began to straighten. Within minutes she was healed. We took off her leg braces. She was weak but she could walk. Her tears gave way to profuse thanksgiving.

But she had not been healed by us. I was tired and had almost turned her aside. She had been healed by Jesus.

This is the kind of experience that forced me to face up to, and deal with, the power and work of the Holy Spirit for today. I am not and never have been a Pentecostal. Doug and I are Presbyterians in both background and viewpoint. We have remained in the Presbyterian Church (U.S.A.) all our lives because God placed us there. We believe, with R. A. Torrey, that God wants all Christians to open their lives to the power of the Holy Spirit, regardless of denomination or doctrinal tradition.

Yet how we think about the Holy Spirit makes a great deal of difference in our openness or closedness to the power of God. Some people think manifestations of the Holy Spirit do not belong in old-line churches. They accept only the more "natural" and "ordinary" ways the Spirit works, and close themselves off from any manifestation that does not fit their denominational tradition and rationalistic Western worldview.

Others erect doctrinal barriers that tell God He cannot do miracles, and that if He does, they will attribute them to the devil. They practically dare God to do works of power, insisting to one another that He works today only through the Bible.

Still others have the Holy Spirit down to a carefully defined series of steps: "First you'll speak in tongues. Then you'll praise Him as you never did before. After that you'll find that God can do through you all the manifestations mentioned in 1 Corinthians 12, if you'll just believe He can."

Our doctrines tend to determine and even limit our experience of the Holy Spirit. They also tend to promote either harmony or disharmony in the Body of Christ. If we are to see the Holy Spirit move through the length and breadth of God's Church, we must have a broadly biblical understanding of His work based on the whole counsel of God.

Archer Torrey "Does Theology"

Archer Torrey helped me come to a more biblical framework of thinking about the Holy Spirit at a time I desperately needed a framework different from the Pentecostal, charismatic or traditional evangelical.

I met Archer at Jesus Abbey in the mountains of South Korea, a place of great spiritual power and renewal for thousands of people who have gone there to seek God's face. This Christian environment was established by Archer and Jane Torrey in 1964.

Archer was called to Korea originally to reestablish the Anglican seminary that had been destroyed during the Korean War. For seven years he rebuilt the institution. He found, however, that the academic context was not an appropriate environment for truly learning how to live the Christian life and minister effectively. The great lack of the seminary was that the life of prayer was neither taught nor modeled.

Archer did not believe we could "do theology" by studying books alone. From them we learn only what certain people think about God, whereas the only place we can learn the ways of God is in practical Christian life and service. There we are forced to live out biblical principles in the practical daily challenge of Christian community.

It was to create such a laboratory that Archer and Jane left the security of the seminary and the financial support of an established mission to found Jesus Abbey high in the rugged mountains of the east coast of Korea. There Archer's extraordinary vision of learning about God through a living community took root and came to fruition.

The purpose of the Abbey: to provide prayer support for world evangelization and discipleship training for lay people. There is now a core community of around sixty members. The life of the community revolves around regular hours of prayer and worship. A small farm, dairy and wood-carving shop generate income to support the community. But basically Archer follows his grandfather in applying the principles of George Müller to depend on God for provision. This makes for some extraordinary adventures of faith.

One bitterly cold winter, for example, the rice ran out, leaving nothing to eat but squash. Consuming squash every day for three meals a day drove the community to its knees in prayer. Finally the squash ran out. Archer was amazingly calm in the face of having to feed more than fifty hungry people. He simply declared that the next day would be a day of prayer with fasting, unless the Lord had other plans. The following morning the fifty residents were astonished to find that someone had left for them a large bag of rice!

Such practical experiences as this teach the power of prayer and learning to rely on God when we do His work. "If God is calling you to do something for His glory that is impossible without a miracle," Archer often says, "just go ahead and obey and expect the miracle." At the Abbey I saw the careful discernment of God's will, radical obedience and then miracles following.

Each year thousands of guests come from all over the world, for various lengths of time, to participate in the life of prayer. Over the years Jesus Abbey has had extensive influence for spiritual renewal in the Korean Church. Its residents have also addressed many issues of social and economic justice (such as land reform) that face the people of Korea.

The Abbey enjoys a kind of oral history of remarkable answers to prayer. There was the time a group of Catholic sisters came for a retreat. As they prayed together on the mountainside one night, the Holy Spirit fell on them, igniting charismatic renewal in the Korean Catholic Church. Or there was the night of a massive demonic attack in which demons swirled around the lonely mountain valley, bringing their darkness into the Abbey itself. Only by the effort of fervent prayer did the evil spirits depart. There was also the man healed of blindness as he walked up the steps—and many other testimonies of healing.

But greater than these remarkable signs and wonders are the hundreds of people whose lives have been changed profoundly by just a few days in this place. In one way or another they encountered Jesus, were filled with the Holy Spirit and found themselves sent back into the world to be witnesses to Jesus.

What I Learned at Jesus Abbey

For me, living at Jesus Abbey was a life-transforming experience. There I came to know Jesus Christ intimately, experienced the empowering work of the Holy Spirit, discovered the power of prayer and was enflamed with a biblical vision of the Kingdom of God.

My experience at the Abbey altered my worldview and understanding of the work of the Holy Spirit. Through my encounters with charismatics in the United States, I had assumed that people interested in spiritual things were not involved in social issues. At Jesus Abbey I found a community that prayed fervently and was also engaged in the social justice issues of the day.

People who spoke in tongues or prayed for healing, I had believed, were anti-intellectual or uneducated. But here at afternoon tea, guests from around the world debated theological and social issues from the standpoint of Christian faith. Residents of the Abbey studied the Bible and theology with greater intensity than I ever saw at seminary, where these had been academic pursuits only. Here was a laboratory of Christian living in which we not only studied the Bible but experienced the realities spoken of in the Bible!

Earlier I had been told that because I did not speak in tongues, I was not much of a Christian. But at Jesus Abbey the issue was not tongues but obedience to all aspects of the calling of Christ, since the promises of God are intimately connected to the commandments of God. Jesus said:

> "If you love me, you will keep my commandments. And I will pray the Father, and he will give you another Counselor, to be with you for ever, even the Spirit of truth, whom the world cannot receive...."
>
> John 14:15–16

In this context I learned much of what Doug and I teach in the following chapters, beginning with Old Testament studies.

"The Spirit Upon" and "The Spirit Within"

There are two major motifs in Scripture, Archer taught, that reflect two different operations of the Holy Spirit. One motif has the Spirit coming "upon" people for power in ministry. A second has the Spirit coming "within" people for salvation and to develop in them skill, wisdom, godly character and maturity in faith and love. Both motifs are equally important and equally biblical.

Archer wrote:

> The Bible consistently distinguishes between the external and internal work of the Holy Spirit. The Holy Spirit upon us, or with us, or

pushing us ("moved"), or leading us, is like the weapons and vehicles which a military unit has to have for its work, but which tell us nothing about the inner attitudes of those who use them.

When the Bible speaks of the Holy Spirit in terms which make it clear the Holy Spirit is in one's inner being, then it also speaks of character, of fruit-bearing, of life, of wisdom to know God's will and the will to do it. These two different roles of the Holy Spirit are quite clear, unequivocal, and distinct in the Bible. . . .[1]

We first see these two ways of describing the Holy Spirit in the Old Testament. He did not suddenly come into existence, after all, with the New Testament. We find Him in the very beginning, moving over the face of the waters on the eve of creation. The psalmist and Job suggest that all life is sustained by the Spirit of God: "If he should take back his spirit to himself, and gather to himself his breath, all flesh would perish together, and man would return to dust" (Job 34:14–15). This is not pantheism but a recognition of the mystery of life created and sustained by God. The power of God is everywhere, if only we had eyes to see it.

We find the Spirit at work elsewhere in the Old Testament, empowering and equipping certain leaders of the people of God—their judges, prophets, priests and kings. The Old Testament speaks of God giving people "the Spirit upon" and "the Spirit within" when He wants to use them in different ways. Below we list several examples of each phenomenon:

The Work of the Holy Spirit in the Old Testament

1. The Spirit falling upon or taking possession = *Dynamic action* (Judges 3:10; 6:34; 14:5–6; 15:14–17; 1 Samuel 16:13)

2. The Spirit falling on people = *Speaking God's word or seeing visions* (Numbers 11:17, 25–26; 1 Kings 18:46; 2 Kings 2:12–14; Ezekiel 1:3–4; 3:22)

3. The Spirit falling on people = *Ecstatic praise of God* (1 Samuel 10:10–13; 19:23–24)

4. The Spirit within = *Wisdom for leadership and skill and craftsmanship to build the Ark of the Covenant* (Genesis 41:38–39; Exodus 31:1–5; Deuteronomy 34:9)

In these places we find our first clues for understanding the present-day working of the Holy Spirit in the Church.

"The Spirit Upon" for Works of Power

The first way the Holy Spirit came upon Old Testament people was to accomplish mighty works to demonstrate His rescuing power.

After the conquest of Canaan, the Hebrews were oppressed and humiliated by various pagan groups that inhabited the land. During these times of trouble, God raised up judges to protect or avenge His people. All the judges had one thing in common: The Spirit of God "came upon them" in power to equip them for mighty acts.

One of these judges, a rogue named Samson, is famous for his superhuman strength—and for his subhuman behavior. The Spirit of Yahweh came upon him repeatedly, resulting in extraordinary physical power. For example: "A young lion roared against him; and the Spirit of the LORD came mightily upon him, and he tore the lion asunder as one tears a kid; and he had nothing in his hand" (Judges 14:5–6).

Samson is usually pictured in children's Sunday school books as a Charles Atlas type with bulging biceps. But why then would he need the power of God? I believe Samson was of average size and strength; he may even have looked like a wimp. His strength came not from his biceps but from the Spirit of God. He lost it not because he forgot to do his workouts but because he frittered away the secret of his strength in a childish game, putting God to the test and taking His power for granted. He paid a high price for disobedience and ungodliness.

Samson, like some Spirit-filled leaders of recent years, reminds us that you can have God's power but lack good character. You can have "the Spirit upon" you for ministry but lack "the Spirit within" you for godliness. Ideally these two dimensions of the work of the Holy Spirit coincide, but they do not have to.

The manifestational gifts, then, are not necessarily a sign of godliness or of long years of walking with God. Sometimes they are purely a sign of God's grace, His unmerited favor, which He chooses to bestow. Often His power does not indicate the credibility of the vessel so much as His simple mercy toward oppressed people. Time and again God showed compassion on suffering persons and had to find someone with a little courage through whom to work deliverance.

"The Spirit Upon" for Prophecy

A second way the Holy Spirit came upon Old Testament people was when God wanted to give a message through someone to someone else. For example:

> The Spirit of God came upon Azariah son of Oded. He went out to meet Asa and said to him, "Listen to me, Asa and all Judah and Benjamin. The Lord is with you when you are with him. If you seek him, he will be found by you, but if you forsake him, he will forsake you."
>
> 2 Chronicles 15:1–2, NIV

Again:

> Then the Spirit of God came upon Zechariah son of Jehoiada the priest. He stood before the people and said, "This is what God says: 'Why do you disobey the LORD's commands? You will not prosper. Because you have forsaken the LORD, he has forsaken you.'"
>
> 2 Chronicles 24:20, NIV

These prophecies came as the result of the Spirit of God falling on people. They manifested God's power not in actions but through the written or spoken word.

"The Spirit Upon" for Praise

A third way the Holy Spirit manifested the power of God upon people of the Old Testament was through ecstatic experiences. King David danced before the Lord as the Ark of the Covenant was brought to its resting place in Jerusalem. David was in an ecstasy of worship, but his wife Michal, observing him coolly from the sidelines, took a more dignified point of view—typical of Western churches today. Ecstatic love removed David's self-consciousness. He was willing to look foolish in the eyes of those who did not love God because the love of God at that moment consumed him.

Saul, too, after his anointing by Samuel, experienced this aspect of the Holy Spirit's work: "When they arrived at Gibeah, a procession of prophets met him; the Spirit of God came upon him in power, and he joined in their prophesying" (1 Samuel 10:10, NIV). This prophesying, although the text gives no indication what the words were, consisted of exalted adoration, dance and songs "with lyres, tambourines, flutes and harps" in which Saul was "changed into a different person" (1 Samuel 10:5–6, NIV).

Westerners tend to look askance at such behavior, dismissing it as a leftover from primitive Canaanite religion. This way of dealing with biblical phenomena reflects our addiction to Western rationalism. Whatever we cannot analyze and understand we dismiss as primitive. But the Bible sees these ecstasies as manifestations of the Holy Spirit. This work of the Holy Spirit continues today and is part of the "Holy Spirit upon" motif.

God Is Not Tame

Perhaps we should say a bit more about ecstasy here, though we will explore it more in Part 3. There is a wild, untamed aspect of the Holy Spirit as He may move us to dance, or be carried off in ecstatic joy in God's presence, or engage in agonizing, travailing prayer.

Brad: The Iona community in Scotland, a renewed community started after World War I by George MacLeod,[2] uses two images to represent the Holy Spirit. The first is the dove, representing the gentle peace of the Spirit of God. The second is the wild goose, representing the wild, creative, ecstatic dimension of the Spirit.

In the sixteenth century, when the Gospel first entered the wild, untrammeled regions of Scotland, it encountered a wild, untrammeled people. Records indicate that the Holy Spirit moved in remarkably un-Presbyterian ways to introduce the Kingdom of heaven to the Scottish clans. Some of the earliest writers about "revivals of religion" were Scottish and Irish pastors who wrote of episodes like this one about a Scottish evangelist in Ireland in 1626:

> And this work appeared not in one single person or two, but multitudes were brought to understand their way, and to cry out, Men and brethren, what shall we do to be saved? I have seen them myself stricken into a swoon with the Word; yea, a dozen in one day carried out of doors as dead, so marvellous was the power of God smiting their hearts for sin, condemning and killing. And of these were none of the weaker sex or spirit, but indeed some of the boldest spirits, who formerly feared not with their swords to put a whole market-town in a fray. . . .[3]

A contemporary example of this wild, ecstatic dimension might be the extraordinary manifestations taking place around the world today—falling to the floor, laughing in the Spirit, shaking, flopping around, roaring and exhibiting other astonishing behavior. (We will attempt to evaluate some of these phenomena in later chapters.) Such manifestations have been characteristic of nearly every major move of the Holy Spirit.

Laughter in the Spirit

Once in 1987, at the home church of Vineyard Ministries in Anaheim, California, I experienced the Holy Spirit falling on more than four thousand people in this way.

That night, after about an hour of praise that exalted Jesus Christ, we went into a period of expectant waiting. Pastor John Wimber said, "Let's wait and see what the Lord wants to do tonight." Suddenly it seemed that there was a wave of spiritual power moving over the crowd. John said something about the Lord calling us to repentance. As he did, repentance started to happen. People began to weep and confess their sins. A sense of brokenness was followed by a proclamation of forgiveness in Jesus Christ, leading to joy and celebration. The Lord then began to heal people in another wave of the Spirit.

After the healing there was a long silence, broken suddenly by a wild, giddy laugh that sounded like the essence of joy itself. "Let's continue to wait upon the Lord," said Wimber. "I think He's going to give us a party tonight." As we waited, several more people started to laugh, then whole groups of people. No one had told a joke. There was no mass psychology happening here. This laughter was more like a ripple or wave of the Holy Spirit moving across specific areas of the crowd.

In fact, a sparkling joy was bubbling up from within the depths of my own being as the wave approached my part of the crowd. It felt like soda water in my stomach. The awareness of the Holy Spirit grew in intensity and I found myself overwhelmed with joy. Soon I was on the floor laughing until tears came to my eyes and my stomach hurt. It was the most refreshing and cleansing laugh I have ever enjoyed. I knew somehow I had been touched by Jesus. It was wonderful beyond words.

Afterward the Holy Spirit "lifted" from me, moving on to those beyond; and they, too, went down with laughter.

"The Spirit Within" for Wisdom

The final operation of the Spirit of God found in the Old Testament is described not by "the Spirit upon" but by "the Spirit within." The cases relate to Joseph, Bezalel and Joshua:

> Pharaoh asked them, "Can we find anyone like this man, one *in whom is the spirit of God?*"
> Then Pharaoh said to Joseph, "Since God has made all this known to you, there is no one so *discerning and wise* as you."
> Genesis 41:38–39, NIV (italics added)

> Then the LORD said to Moses, "See, I have chosen Bezalel . . . and *I have filled him with the Spirit of God, with skill, ability and knowledge in all kinds of crafts*—to make artistic designs for work in gold, silver and bronze, to cut and set stones, to work in wood, and to engage in all kinds of craftsmanship."
> Exodus 31:1–5, NIV (italics added)

> Joshua son of Nun was *filled with the spirit of wisdom* because Moses had laid his hands on him. So the Israelites listened to him and did what the LORD had commanded Moses.
> Deuteronomy 34:9, NIV (italics added)

The purpose of having the Spirit within was to grant special skill or wisdom for a special task. Bezalel, for instance, was equipped by the Spirit within him for skill in craftsmanship to build the Ark of the Covenant. Joseph and Joshua, on the other hand, had the Spirit within them, giving them wisdom and skill for leadership. While these examples of the Spirit's infilling lack the dynamic action of the "the Spirit upon," they are expressions of God's power nonetheless. This aspect of power seems to find expression in a New Testament gift like administration.

After Pentecost the terms *the Spirit within* and *filled with the Spirit* refer not to skill or wisdom in administration, but to the operation of the Holy Spirit in bringing about salvation and changed character.

We Do Not Have to Defend the Power of God

In a culture that denies the power of God and assigns ultimate authority to human science and logic, God pours out His power on people simply to shame the wise and contradict our Western mindset. God has a controversy with a church that clings to the form of religion but denies His power. But during the present century, when the Church *has* denied the power of God, He has chosen to manifest it more clearly than in most other centuries since the apostolic era.

The ecstasies of the Old Testament are still much with us today. God gives "the Holy Spirit upon" us just as He used to among judges, prophets, priests and kings of the Old Testament. Yet we of the Church age have moved beyond the Old Testament era. The ancient writers themselves recognized they had seen but the beginnings of God's power. They prophesied for the present era a broad expansion of the power of God in three ways:

First, they foresaw that the work of "the Holy Spirit upon" would be radically extended to include all God's people, not just a few judges, prophets, priests or kings.

Second, they revealed a completely new operation of the Holy Spirit—"the Holy Spirit within," leading to changed character.

Finally, they prophesied the advent of a Spirit-empowered Messiah who would extend the power of the Holy Spirit throughout the whole earth, as an extension of His Lordship over His creation. He would baptize His people not with water, but with the Holy Spirit; and in that baptism all God's people would take on Jesus' ministry of prophet, priest and king.

Three Prophetic Hopes Fulfilled in Jesus

Brad: The Old Testament prophets were intimate with the Spirit of God. As they were empowered by the Spirit to speak God's words into the crises of their day, they glimpsed His vision for a new covenant with broadly expanded boundaries for the Holy Spirit. They foresaw a new era of the Spirit's work.

Their prophetic expectation is summarized in the chart below:

A New Era of the Holy Spirit's Work

The Spirit will be on all God's people for empowerment (Numbers 11:29; Isaiah 44:3; Joel 2:28–29).

The Holy Spirit will dwell within God's people for new hearts (Jeremiah 31:31–34; Ezekiel 36:25–27).

There will be a Spirit-filled community of faith (Isaiah 43:18–21; Ezekiel 37:14).

A Messiah will come for all nations:
The Spirit will be upon Him for power to fulfill His mission (Isaiah 11:2; 42:1–7; 61:1–3).

The Messiah will baptize His people with the Holy Spirit (Matthew 3:11; Mark 1:8; Luke 3:16; John 1:33).

The Fulfillment of the Promises

Today we recognize that the promises given in the Old Testament are fulfilled in the Person of Jesus Christ, who received the Holy Spirit and conveyed the Spirit to the Church. We summarize this process as follows (italics added to Scripture quotations for emphasis):

Jesus and the Holy Spirit

Jesus is conceived by the Holy Spirit (Luke 1:35).

The Holy Spirit *within Him* gives knowledge of God the Father and shapes His character (Luke 2:48–49; Hebrews 5:8–10).

The Holy Spirit *falls upon* Jesus, empowering Him for mission, in continuity with the Old Testament judges, prophets, priests and kings (Luke 3:21–22; 4:18–19; Acts 10:38).

Jesus performs mighty works because He is empowered by the Holy Spirit and obeys the Father (John 5:19–21; Luke 4:17–18).

Jesus baptizes His people with the Holy Spirit that they may continue to do His work (Luke 9:1–2; 24:48–49; John 1:33; Acts 1:8).

Through the Holy Spirit, Jesus and the Father are present and active (John 14:16, 20, 23).

As we look more closely at the ministry of Jesus, we find that He fulfilled all of the prophecies having to do with the Holy Spirit. Let's look at three of them.

1. The Spirit "Upon" Is No Longer for the Few but for the Many

In the Old Testament God raised up great judges, prophets, priests and kings who were empowered by the Spirit. These Old Testament figures were few and far between. But some of the prophets looked to an era when the Spirit would fall on the common people without distinction.

Such a democratization of the Spirit would have been shocking and unacceptable to the people of those times, especially the religious leaders. The idea that an ordinary person could receive spiritual powers from the Creator—that God should so profligate Himself!—would have been considered almost blasphemous. Yet those Old Testament prophecies stand out to this day as a shining example of the risk-taking love of a God with big plans.

Moses' Unwitting Prophecy

We see hints of this prophetic expectation when Moses was overwhelmed with the responsibilities of leadership. He complained to God that the burden of leading Israel was too heavy for him. In response, God commanded him to gather seventy elders to share the burdens of leadership:

> "I will come down and speak with you there, and I will take of the Spirit that is on you and put the Spirit on them. They will help you carry the burden of the people so that you will not have to carry it alone."
>
> Numbers 11:17, NIV

Notice the word *on* (or *upon)*—speaking, apparently, of empowerment for the task of judging disputes. When the Spirit fell upon the seventy, He also fell upon two others in the camp, who began to prophesy as the seventy had done. Joshua objected, asking Moses to forbid these unauthorized enthusiasts.

> But Moses replied, "Are you jealous for my sake? I wish that all the LORD's people were prophets and that the LORD would put his Spirit on them!"
>
> verse 29, NIV

What an amazing response from Moses, who (perhaps without realizing it) grasped God's intentions far into the future!

Joel

The hope of Moses was expressed more fully in the time of Joel. That prophet was speaking God's word to the tragic events of his day, when a message about the new work of the Holy Spirit burst into his writings:

> "Afterward, I will pour out my Spirit *on all people*. Your sons and daughters will prophesy, your old men will dream dreams, your young men

will see visions. Even on my servants, both men and women, I will
pour out my Spirit in those days."

                              Joel 2:28–29, NIV (italics added)

It was to this prophecy that the apostle Peter referred to interpret
the events he was witnessing at the birth of the Church on Pentecost.
For him this prophecy became a promise of empowerment to anyone in the Church who wants to receive it, regardless of age, sex,
social class or educational level. What a shocking idea to the religious leaders of Jesus' day! We read in Acts 4:13: "When they saw
the courage of Peter and John and realized that they were unschooled,
ordinary men, they were astonished and they took note that these
men had been with Jesus" (NIV).

It is easy enough to say that Jesus sent the Holy Spirit "upon" ordinary Christians. But when we turn to the reality of life among ordinary Christians today, we may be tempted to question whether God
really knew what He was doing!

When I was in Toronto, I heard much criticism from pastors about
the spiritual awakening at the Airport Christian Fellowship. Some of
their discernment was on track, for there were excesses. But several
pastors were upset that uneducated people, people from the lower
classes, even people who had never known Christ, were experiencing God's power, often in ways that they themselves had not experienced. Groups of young people would stand outside the door drink-
ing beer, smoking and enjoying the commotion. Then they would
step into the meeting, sometimes to gawk at or make fun of the goings-
on. The Holy Spirit would draw them in and touch them with power
in some way. That God would be so indiscriminate offended the pastors who had never been swept off their feet by the Holy Spirit.

The same may be said for all major revivals. A great "offense" of
the Azusa Street revival was that the Holy Spirit fell on uneducated,
working-class people, including many African-Americans. Sometimes the elder brother still resents the returning prodigal. At other
times Gamaliel still counsels his Sanhedrin to wait and see. But God
reserves for Himself the right to make no distinctions, and He makes
no apologies for the revelations of His power. Since no one deserves
it, no one may feel cheated when God glorifies Himself in or through
someone else.

2. A New Idea: "The Spirit Within"

The Holy Spirit coming on ordinary people for power in ministry is dramatic and exciting enough. The second aspect of the Spirit's work foretold by the prophets is even more astonishing: that God would maintain His Law not by political structures and social pressure alone, but by His Spirit, whom He would send *within* people to write His Law on their hearts.

Through Abraham and Moses, God had established a covenant with the Hebrews. He would be their God; they would be His people. But God said they must obey His Law given through Moses and the prophets.

The Hebrews broke the covenant. They rebelled against His commandments and forgot His promises. The problem was not that they did not know the Law, nor that they lacked prophets to remind them of it. It was a problem of the heart and will. Humanity needed something radically new and powerful in order to be restored to God.

Through the prophet Jeremiah, God promised a new covenant. He would, He said, write His laws on the hearts of His people and put His Spirit within them:

> "Behold, the days are coming, says the LORD, when I will make a new covenant with the house of Israel and the house of Judah, not like the covenant which I made with their fathers when I took them by the hand to bring them out of the land of Egypt, my covenant which they broke, though I was their husband, says the LORD. But this is the covenant which I will make with the house of Israel after those days, says the LORD: *I will put my law within them, and I will write it upon their hearts;* and I will be their God, and they shall be my people. And no longer shall each man teach his neighbor and each his brother, saying, 'Know the LORD,' for they shall all know me, from the least of them to the greatest, says the LORD; for I will forgive their iniquity, and I will remember their sin no more."
>
> Jeremiah 31:31–34 (italics added)

Another audacious vision! All the more so when we remember that the Hebrew word for "to know" does not mean intellectual knowing, but deeply intimate knowing, as between a man and a woman in sexual intercourse. Jeremiah used the same word the book of Genesis used in describing Adam and Eve: "Adam knew Eve his wife, and she conceived and bore Cain" (4:1).

Out of this inner knowing would come changes of character, in preparation for an eternal relationship. These changes would not occur through social pressure or human teaching in high schools or colleges. They would be the result of a new way the Holy Spirit would work in the new era. Out of the Old Testament prophets was emerging a new way of speaking of the Holy Spirit—"the Spirit within." (We saw only the briefest use of this expression in Genesis 41:38–39, Exodus 31:1–5 and Deuteronomy 34:9 in the previous chapter, but it had to do with skill, not salvation or sanctification.)

Jeremiah did not say specifically that this would be the work of the Holy Spirit. It was Ezekiel who added that bit of prophetic information:

> "I will sprinkle clean water on you, and you will be clean; I will cleanse you from all your impurities and from all your idols. *I will give you a new heart and put a new spirit in you;* I will remove from you your heart of stone and give you a heart of flesh. And *I will put my Spirit in you* and move you to follow my decrees and be careful to keep my laws."
>
> Ezekiel 36:25–27, NIV (italics added)

This work of the Spirit coming within us was, in Jesus' day, outrageously new. It was surely what Jesus referred to when He said: "Truly, I say to you, among those born of women there has risen no one greater than John the Baptist; yet he who is least in the kingdom of heaven is greater than he" (Matthew 11:11).

Again and again the New Testament confirms the promise of the Spirit within as a promise for all followers of Jesus Christ, as we showed at the beginning of this chapter. What would the "Spirit within" do to a person? How would this be different from the Spirit "coming upon"?

Doug: I had the pleasure of hosting Frank Worthen during a recent visit to Richmond. Frank founded Love In Action, a ministry to homosexuals in San Rafael, California, and he is one of the early founders of Exodus International. The present exodus of

Christian men and women from homosexuality, as well as Frank's testimony itself, are good examples of the work of the Spirit "within" a person:

My pastor took me into his office and said, "Frank, you are a homosexual." Being only thirteen, I needed him to explain same-sex attraction. He did. Then he added that homosexuals were different from other people.

I'd been called different before! When my mother took me to kindergarten, my teacher told her, "Your boy is very different from the other boys." And she was right; I'd detached from my family's constant arguing by hiding in the attic and creating my own fantasy world. In response to my patterns of isolation, my peers called me names (which I later learned meant "homosexual").

When I was ten, I began taking piano lessons. My piano teacher knew the Lord in a powerful way. She was ecstatic when, three years later, I accepted Him. She took me to her church, where I began to study organ.

My father died that year. The pastor took an interest in me, assuming the "father" role in my life. He was everything I looked for in a father! But in my heart, I hoped he was wrong about me being a homosexual. Certainly, I was different; I had no friends, I wasn't into sports, and I devoted a lot of time to music. Still, I hoped that I was just late in developing opposite-sex attractions.

When I turned eighteen, I met a young lady. We went together for about a year. It was very exciting to think, "Thank God, I'm normal! I love this woman and I want to marry her." So I proposed. She answered, "There are only two things that I love: horses and other women." Crushed, I returned to my pastor, who told me that I'd been attracted to my girlfriend's masculinity. He reasoned, "I've been telling you for years that you are a homosexual." I left the church that day, making the decision to accept my homosexuality. Since "God's man" had convinced me that I was homosexual, I hoped that God would accept me.

I entered the gay life-style at that time. By accepting my homosexuality, I believed I'd found where I belonged. The male homosexual life-style, however, is built on youth. And so, by the time I was 40, it was pretty much over for me. The only steady lover I could find wasn't even really homosexual—he just stayed with me for the money! But even then, we both cheated on each other. It was very depressing.

The business I owned required me to travel around the world a great deal. During one of my trips, the manager of my biggest store hired a "hippie" boy. Though I didn't want Michael there at all, the manager promised to keep him out of the customers' sight if I'd let him work in the stock room. I agreed, reluctantly.

Returning from another trip, I was startled to see Michael with short hair, properly washed, and working at the front counter. He was efficient, the customers loved him, and he smiled all the time. Finally, after a week of watching him, I asked, "What in the world happened to you?"

He answered, "I accepted the Lord." I wondered if Michael's Christianity would last. During the following year, his life kept getting brighter and brighter. I began to wonder if God could change me the way He had changed Michael. But I told myself, "No. God has never changed a homosexual person." I vacillated between hope and despair.

One day, the Lord spoke to me, saying, "Today I want you back." I knew, without a doubt, that this was the voice of God. I ran to the store and located Michael, gasping, "I've just heard from God, I don't know what to do." I was beside myself. Michael suggested that we go over to his church to pray. Michael had me kneel on the altar's marble steps as he led me through a 20-minute sinner's prayer!

When the prayer ended, the Lord's Spirit came alive in my heart. I came out of the church a changed person!

When I went to Michael's church, the people expressed love for me. Later I learned that they'd spent two years praying for "Michael's gay boss." And for the next year and a half, people from that church came to see me every day! That accountability kept me from going back to the homosexuality.[1]

This year Frank celebrated his tenth wedding anniversary with his wife, Anita. He comments about his marriage: "It has been far better than our greatest expectations. The honeymoon continues." Today thousands are finding release from homosexuality as God touches hearts by the Spirit within and leads ex-gay people into accountable relationships with other Christians.

The promise of the Spirit within opens up a truly liberating possibility: that we can learn the ways of God without being scolded, pressured, manipulated or threatened. It sets church life, Christian relationships and pastoral ministry on a new and refreshing footing. The basic work of the Holy Spirit within is to give us a new nature that leads to eternal salvation, which grows up in the "fruit of the Spirit"—Christian character.

3. Not Just for the Jews

At the center of the Old Testament prophetic hope was the promise that a Messiah would come, born in the lineage of David, who would bring obedience not just to Israel, but to all the nations of earth:

> "It is too light a thing that you should be my servant to raise up the tribes of Jacob and to restore the preserved of Israel; I will give you as a light to the nations, that my salvation may reach to the end of the earth."
>
> Isaiah 49:6

How would the Messiah perform His mission? As we have already seen, the Spirit of God would rest upon Him:

> There shall come forth a shoot from the stump of Jesse, and a branch shall grow out of his roots. And *the Spirit of the LORD shall rest upon him*, the spirit of wisdom and understanding, the spirit of counsel and might, the spirit of knowledge and the fear of the LORD.
>
> Isaiah 11:1–2 (italics added)

> Behold my servant, whom I uphold, my chosen, in whom my soul delights; *I have put my Spirit upon him*, he will bring forth justice to the nations.
>
> Isaiah 42:1 (italics added)

> *The Spirit of the Lord GOD is upon me*, because the LORD has anointed me to bring good tidings to the afflicted; he has sent me to bind up the brokenhearted, to proclaim liberty to the captives, and the opening of the prison to those who are bound; to proclaim the year of the LORD's favor, and the day of vengeance of our God; to comfort all who mourn. . . .
>
> Isaiah 61:1–2 (italics added)

The language here, "Spirit upon," denotes empowerment for ministry. The Messiah, in continuity with the Old Testament, was to draw into Himself the prophetic, priestly and kingly powers of the Old Covenant in Israel. But while His first ministry in the Spirit's power would be to "the lost sheep of the house of Israel" (Matthew 15:24), He would bring that power well beyond those limits because "I have other sheep that are not of this sheep pen" (John 10:16, NIV).

The new Messiah would not only have the Holy Spirit upon Him to fulfill His own mission, but He would pour out the Spirit on His people. John the Baptist, the last of the Old Testament prophets, spoke of a radically new thing—that the One to come would "baptize you with the Holy Spirit and with fire" (Luke 3:16). Here is another concept unknown to any Old Covenant person (except John the Baptist). Old Testament prophecy, in other words, pointed to a Messiah who would involve Himself in new ways with the Holy Spirit, and enable those who follow Him to experience the Spirit in new ways.

The new era of the Holy Spirit, glimpsed by Old Covenant prophets, hinged on the coming Messiah who would first receive the Holy Spirit for Himself, then baptize His disciples with the Spirit.

Where Did Jesus' Power in Ministry Come From?

The New Testament understanding of Jesus is based on the Old Testament verses we just looked at, which picture Jesus receiving the power of the Holy Spirit for ministry.

Evangelical Christians have often seen the miracles of Jesus as evidence of His divinity. The apostle John taught this when he quoted Jesus as saying, "Believe me when I say that I am in the Father and the Father is in me; or at least believe on the evidence of the miracles themselves" (John 14:11, NIV). Clearly John saw the works of power as signs of Jesus' divinity:

> Jesus did many other miraculous signs in the presence of his disciples, which are not recorded in this book. But these are written that you may believe that Jesus is the Christ, the Son of God, and that by believing you may have life in his name.
>
> John 20:30–31, NIV

That the works pointed to His divinity, however, does not imply that His power came *from* it. The apostle Paul was clear about this in describing Christ Jesus "who, being in very nature God, did not consider equality with God something to be grasped, but made himself nothing, taking the very nature of a servant, being made in human likeness" (Philippians 2:6–7, NIV).

The American Standard Version says Jesus "emptied himself." This emptying began at Jesus' birth but continued during His life on earth.

In the face of human limitations and pain, Jesus had to empty Himself again and again—to subordinate His divinity to His humanity.

In the wilderness, Satan tempted Jesus (freshly filled with the Holy Spirit) to fall back on His divinity, rather than operate as a Man empowered by the Holy Spirit, with His will subordinated to the Father's will. Satan's temptations began with the taunt "If you are the Son of God. . . ." The Father willed that Jesus empty Himself of all divine power, taking on Himself the weakness of the human race, then submit Himself voluntarily to the Father and receive the Holy Spirit to accomplish only the works that the Father wanted Him to do. Jesus' "power ministry," in other words, did not flow from His divinity, but from His submission to the Father, and from the Holy Spirit.

Later, in the Garden of Gethsemane, Jesus struggled in the face of the terrors of death and judgment, still having to empty Himself and rest in the Father's will and in the Holy Spirit's power.

When Peter cut off the ear of the high priest's servant, Jesus healed the ear but said to Peter:

> "Put your sword back in its place. . . . Do you think I cannot call on my Father, and he will at once put at my disposal more than twelve legions of angels? But how then would the Scriptures be fulfilled that say it must happen in this way?"
>
> Matthew 26:52–54, NIV

Jesus retained authority as the Son of God, yet subordinated it to His Father's will to take on human weakness and, as the Son, to die on the cross for us. He chose not to exercise power flowing from His own will. Instead He chose weakness, submission, humility, the cross. The works of power came not from His divinity but from the Spirit of God, who fell on Him ("The Spirit of the Lord is upon me. . ."). Then He bestowed the Holy Spirit upon His disciples.

The disciples themselves taught this, for they attributed the power of Jesus not to His divinity but to the Holy Spirit. Peter preached in the house of Cornelius, for example, that "God anointed Jesus of Nazareth with the Holy Spirit and with power; . . . he went about doing good and healing all that were oppressed by the devil, for God was with him" (Acts 10:38).

We Can Have the Same as Jesus

To believe that Jesus' works came from His divinity, rather than from the Spirit of God on Him, could have one of two results for us.

First, we could believe that only Jesus can do those works, because He is the only begotten Son of God. We, by contrast, are perfectly helpless to accomplish any such works because we are not the Son of God. But this flies in the face of the clear teaching of Jesus that "he who believes in me will also do the works that I do" (John 14:12).

There is a second option in this scenario—the Gnostic, neo-pagan option as presented by the New Age movement today that Jesus was able to do mighty works of power because of the "spark of divinity" within Him, and that you and I can do those same works because of the spark of divinity within us.

It was to get Christians to believe in this option that the false, Gnostic gospels of the second and third centuries were devised. They show Jesus doing all sorts of miracles prior to His baptism with the Holy Spirit. These gospels are designed to obscure the truth that Jesus' power for ministry came *entirely* from the Holy Spirit through the will of the Father. Jesus gave up His own will voluntarily, as we have seen, and emptied Himself.

Look at the experience of the apostles Paul and Barnabas, who were used by the Holy Spirit to heal a man lame from birth at Lystra. The townspeople started bowing down and sacrificing to the apostles, believing them to be gods. Paul, however, was following Jesus, who had always emptied Himself, bringing glory to God the Father. So Paul had to empty himself, too. "We too are only men," he replied, "human, like you" (Acts 14:15, NIV).

If Jesus the Son of God repudiated divine power, how much more must we repudiate the "spark of divinity" teaching that flows from paganism!

We will have more to say about this in a later chapter, for Christian churches are being tempted at this moment to listen to New Age, neo-pagan, Gnostic teaching. Enough for now to point out that Jesus received the power of the Holy Spirit when He was baptized by John; then He bequeathed that power to the Church. Today Jesus baptizes people with the Holy Spirit who are willing to do as He did and find empowerment for ministry through their willingness to submit to the Father's will.

What Does It Mean to Be "Spirit-Filled"?

Brad and Doug: The distinction between "the Spirit upon" and "the Spirit within" forces us to reexamine the way we talk about the Holy Spirit, as we see in the following conversation between Ben and Mark.

"Did you hear there's a new Spirit-filled church in town?" Ben comments one day.

Mark, a member of a thriving Christian & Missionary Alliance church, has heard the term *Spirit-filled* one too many times. He has accepted Jesus Christ as his Savior and knows his denomination is faithful to the Great Commission—to go out and make disciples of all nations. He believes he himself is Spirit-filled but does not identify with the charismatic label or theology. He decides to challenge Ben's use of the term.

"Spirit-filled, you say? In what sense?"

"Well, you know. I mean, they. . . ."

Silence.

"They what? Speak in tongues? Raise their hands in worship? Talk about being baptized in the Holy Spirit?"

Ben, suddenly awkward, does not know how to respond.

What Ben and Mark are discovering is that the language we use is loaded with innuendo. We speak words that hurt other Christians in the Body of Christ because we use them in unbiblical ways and often without the whole counsel of God.

The phrase *Spirit-filled* is like that. The expression itself is biblical. But the way we use it may divide Christians by promoting a false idea about the Holy Spirit.

It helps, in describing the work of the Holy Spirit, to not only stick to biblical expressions but use them in ways God intended. This is our best hope of avoiding some of the divisive speech that has swirled around past moves of the Holy Spirit. The Bible—which preserves apostolic teaching that all Christians can and must embrace—provides the anchor to stabilize the Church amid waves that would otherwise capsize us. So overwhelming are the winds of doctrine blowing around us that we need the Bible more than ever to keep us right-side up.

We have been describing the two main biblical motifs of the Holy Spirit, "the Spirit upon" and "the Spirit within." Scripture uses three other expressions to describe the work of the Spirit: *receiving the Holy Spirit, being filled with the Spirit* and *being baptized with* [or in] *the Spirit*. Whatever movement of the Holy Spirit may be current, these terms persist because they are biblical ways God has given us to talk about the work of the Spirit. We may balk at one or more of them (perhaps because of hurts we have endured), yet for the sake of the Body of Christ, let's use them, rather than invent our own. Let's try to work through to a deeper, broader understanding of these expressions.

In this chapter we will dig into the first two expressions, *receiving the Holy Spirit* and *being filled with the Spirit* (and save the third one, *being baptized with the Spirit,* for the next chapter).

What Does It Mean to "Receive the Holy Spirit"?

Brad: Half-truths tend to divide us in half. And because they divide, they are dangerous.

In some circles the charismatic renewal tended to focus on "the Spirit upon" for power in ministry, almost to the exclusion of "the Spirit within" for wisdom and character formation. Too many charismatics identified "the Spirit upon" as "the full Gospel." Tongues or power ministry was evidence that people had received the Holy

Spirit. Evangelicals, on the other hand, tended to focus almost exclusively on "the Spirit within" for salvation and Christian character, to the neglect of the empowering work of the Spirit.

But the Bible uses the phrase *receiving the Holy Spirit* more comprehensively than that. To reflect the full Gospel, the idea of receiving the Holy Spirit must include both "the Spirit upon" and "the Spirit within." The following chart covers the first of these two elements (italics added to Scripture quotations for emphasis):

---

1. Receiving the Holy Spirit = "The Spirit Upon" for Empowerment

Example: "[Peter and John] laid their hands on them and they *received* the Holy Spirit" (Acts 8:17).
Manifestation: Not reported, but in verse 18 Simon the Sorcerer saw something.

Example: "'[These people] . . . have *received* the Holy Spirit just as we have'" (Acts 10:47).
Manifestation: "The Holy Spirit fell on all" (verse 44). "They heard them speaking in tongues and extolling God" (verse 46).

Example: "[Paul] said to them, 'Did you *receive* the Holy Spirit when you believed?'" (Acts 19:2).
Manifestation: "The Holy Spirit came on them; and they spoke with tongues and prophesied" (verse 6).

Each of these contexts includes a power manifestation of the Holy Spirit. We infer this because each case showed an immediate result—some visible evidence of the power of God that others took as an outward sign that He had indeed given His Spirit.

Not so with the next group of Scriptures on the next page. These verses have to do with godly character growing in the life of a believer (italics added to Scripture quotes for emphasis).

These verses relate to the work of the Holy Spirit to recreate in us the image of Christ—the operation we are calling "the Spirit within."

So the idea of receiving the Holy Spirit in Scripture is used to describe our initiation to both "the Spirit upon" and "the Spirit within."

> **2. Receiving the Spirit = "The Spirit Within"**
> **for Salvation and Godly Character**
>
> "You did not *receive* a spirit that makes you a slave again to fear" (Romans 8:15, NIV).
> "We have *received* not the spirit of the world, but the Spirit which is from God . . ." (1 Corinthians 2:12).
> "Do you not know that your body is a temple of the Holy Spirit, who is in you, whom you have *received* from God" (1 Corinthians 6:19, NIV)?

What Does It Mean to Be "Filled with the Spirit"?

The second expression the Bible uses, *filled with the Holy Spirit*, is more complicated, but it, too, can be understood in the context of the inner and outer work of the Spirit.

When the New Testament speaks of people being "filled with" or "full of" the Holy Spirit, the Greek word reveals one of two concepts. English translations (or Korean or Portuguese or Chinese, for that matter) use the same words for both Greek concepts and do not reflect the difference. One Greek term, *pleitho*, is used consistently for the outer work of the Holy Spirit and usually refers to a brief, temporary filling. Another Greek word, *pleiroo* (or its cognate *pleires*), is used consistently for the inner work of the Holy Spirit and usually refers to something that gets fuller and fuller until it is saturated. This refers to a state of being.

The distinction between *pleitho* and *pleiroo* is more or less consistent, whether they speak of being filled with the Holy Spirit or with anything else.

"Filled" for Action

The filling referred to by the word *pleitho* is temporary and followed immediately by action. It corresponds to *upon* or *fell upon*.

One evening I was scheduled to preach at a church on the healing ministry of Jesus. It was to conclude a series of talks that we all felt should lead to a culmination of God's power for healing. But before the talk I became violently ill. I was in no condition to preach, let alone minister to dozens of people. I showed up at the church out of sheer obedience.

The service started. I kept feeling sicker and sicker. The choir sang an anthem that went on and on, and I felt I was going to embarrass myself in front of everybody before they finished.

After what seemed an eternity, the singing ended, the pastor introduced me and I crawled into the pulpit. On the way I prayed, *Lord, if You want me to preach this evening, You'll have to fill me with Your Spirit, 'cause there isn't anything in me. I can't do it.* Then I prayed silently in tongues.

As I opened my mouth to preach, I felt the Holy Spirit come upon me. The nausea lifted. Words came with power. The crowd was deeply moved. I concluded my talk, sat down and immediately felt sick again. I left the church, threw up and spent the next two days violently ill.

The ministry team returned to the hotel later that evening excited about the way God had used my talk to bring people to believe in the healing power of Christ. Some that night had been healed.

The power I had experienced in ministry was decidedly episodic, as it always is. God gives the Spirit's power in order to meet an immediate need. When the need is met, the power is lifted. That's how it is when God gives "the Spirit upon."

Take a look at the following Scripture quotes (to which italics have been added to emphasize the filling and subsequent action):

Examples of *Pleitho* Not Used for the Holy Spirit

". . . took a sponge, *filled* it with vinegar . . . *gave* it to him to drink" (Matthew 27:48).

". . . *filled* both the boats, so that they began *to sink"* (Luke 5:7).

". . . all in the synagogue were *filled* with wrath. And they *rose up* . . ." (Luke 4:28–29).

Examples of *Pleitho* Used for the Holy Spirit

"Elizabeth was *filled* with the Holy Spirit and she *exclaimed* . . ." (Luke 1:41–42).

"Zechariah was *filled* with the Holy Spirit, and *prophesied* . . ." (Luke 1:67).

Those people were still under the Old Covenant. The following were under the New Covenant:

> "They were all *filled* with the Holy Spirit and began to *speak* in other tongues . . ." (Acts 2:4).
> "Then Peter, *filled* with the Holy Spirit, *said* . . ." (Acts 4:8).
> "They were all *filled* with the Holy Spirit and *spoke* . . ." (Acts 4:31).
> "'Brother Saul, the Lord Jesus . . . has sent me that you may regain your sight *and be filled* with the Holy Spirit.' And immediately something like scales *fell* from his eyes and he regained his sight. . . . And in the synagogues immediately he *proclaimed* Jesus . . ." (Acts 9:17–18, 20).
> "Saul, who is also called Paul, *filled* with the Holy Spirit, *looked* intently at him and *said* . . ." (Acts 13:9–10).

This kind of filling happens again and again, just as a sponge may be refilled many times (see Matthew 27:48). It comes and goes, just like the power given to Samson or Saul or Elijah, and it prepares for and results in dynamic action. So, too, the disciples were not filled with the Holy Spirit only once on Pentecost, but many times thereafter. Whenever the Lord wanted to reveal His power anew, they received "the Spirit upon them for power" in a fresh new outpouring. The presence of the Holy Spirit is constant, but the expression of the power is episodic.

"Filled" as a State of Being

Doug: The other Greek word for being filled with the Holy Spirit, *pleiroo* (or its derivative *pleires*), describes something becoming fuller and fuller. The filling does not happen at distinct times but is a slow, progressive saturation, like yeast permeating dough, and describes a state of being. Usually there is no reference to dynamic action.

When I was in college, I saw the film *American Graffiti* and laughed hysterically all the way through it. Twenty years later I rented the video, remembering how funny it was and wanting to treat myself and my family to a little nostalgia.

Instead I grieved at the cursing, grossness and immorality that pervade that film. Suddenly I realized how much I had changed. I

WHAT DOES IT MEAN TO BE "SPIRIT-FILLED"?

had become more Spirit-filled without realizing it. It had not happened by conscious effort, human teaching or manipulation by family or society. Though I live in a culture that has relaxed its moral standards, mine have tightened up. This change was as much a surprise to me as to anyone. It was a work of the "Spirit within."

Examples of *Pleiroo* and *Pleires*
Not Used for the Holy Spirit

"The child grew and became strong, *filled* with wisdom . . ." (Luke 2:40).

"The house was *filled* with the fragrance of the ointment" (John 12:3).

"May the God of hope *fill* you with all joy and peace in believing, so that by the power of the Holy Spirit you may abound in hope" (Romans 15:13).

"He who descended is he who also ascended far above all the heavens, that he might *fill* all things" (Ephesians 4:10).

"A sound came from heaven like the rush of a mighty wind, and it *filled* all the house where they were sitting" (Acts 2:2).

"'Ananias, why has Satan *filled* your heart . . . ?'" (Acts 5:3).

"'You have *filled* Jerusalem with your teaching. . .'" (Acts 5:28).

Examples of *Pleiroo* and *Pleires*
Used for the Holy Spirit

"Jesus, *full* of the Holy Spirit, returned from the Jordan, and was led by the Spirit for forty days in the wilderness, tempted by the devil" (Luke 4:1–2).*

"Pick out from among you seven men of good repute, *full* of the Spirit and of wisdom . . ." (Acts 6:3).

"They chose Stephen, a man *full* of faith and of the Holy Spirit . . ." (Acts 6: 5).

"[Stephen], *full* of the Holy Spirit, gazed into heaven and saw the glory of God . . ." (Acts 7:55).*

"[Barnabas] was a good man, *full* of the Holy Spirit and of faith" (Acts 11:24).

"The disciples were *filled* with joy and with the Holy Spirit" (Acts 13:52).

"Be *filled* with the Spirit, addressing one another in psalms and hymns . . ." (Ephesians 5:18–19).*

On the previous page, look at the chart of Scripture quotes that exemplify this second kind of infilling. (Italics have been added for emphasis; and the asterisks seem to describe both an action and the mature character of the person.)

Two Ways of Being Spirit-Filled

Brad and Doug: We can summarize these findings simply. God wants us to be filled with the Spirit in two distinct senses of the word. He wants us, on the one hand, to be open to all the inner workings of the Spirit in our character, preparing us for eternity and yielding the fruit of the Spirit, especially love. On the other hand, He wants us to be open to occasions when we can minister in His power through the gifts of the Spirit.

In the first instance, we "have" the Holy Spirit. He is described as being "in" us to change our character. Christian character arises from the slow, percolating work of the Holy Spirit. It increases with age; it shows itself in mature wisdom, skill in handling relationships, trust in God, growth in prayer and understanding of God's Word.

In the second instance, the Holy Spirit "has" us. He chooses to use us in a moment to accomplish a ministry by His power. At no time does the Bible indicate that you or I can "have" the power of God in the same way a New Ager tries to get spiritual power to use for good or evil. This kind of power for service comes and goes. Recall Elijah, at one moment confronting hundreds of pagan prophets, and the next moment seeking refuge in a cave, powerless, depressed and discouraged.

The Christian Church is not divided into congregations that "have" or "have not" the power of God. God's empowerment for ministry in a Christian's life is episodic, not permanent.

Content with Half-Measures?

Those who want to experience the full Gospel and the whole counsel of God will seek both kinds of infilling. Seeing God manifest His power through immature and even immoral people is a stumbling-block to unbelievers. Samsons abound. Equally perplexing is the vision of whole congregations of Christians who have attained godly character but who manifest no power in ministry. American churches house many sweet, godly people with no effective ministry in bringing others to a saving knowledge of Jesus Christ.

Too many Christians are content to be only half-filled with the Holy Spirit. They are "filled" (*pleitho*) but not "filled" (*pleiroo*), having "the Spirit upon" but not "the Spirit within," or vice-versa. Half-measures.

How do we account for this incongruity?

Grieving Leads to Quenching

As bitter experience has shown, "the Spirit upon" for gifts and power may occur to great effect, but if there is no parallel growth in the inward work of the Spirit, there can follow a loss of power leading to disaster. The history of failed ministries—despite signs and wonders and great preaching and many people converted—is long and dismal. Many a large church or impressive evangelistic ministry has been swept away because the preacher or evangelist neglected the inward work of the Holy Spirit, growing proud and unaccountable. He or she fell into sin, received private warnings from the Holy Spirit and from loved ones, ignored them, then received more. In the end the ministry was destroyed and many were left confused and broken.

This is the tragic result of ignoring, over a long period of time, the inner work of the Holy Spirit in favor of the glamour of spiritual power in public ministry. Those who grieve the Spirit (Ephesians 4:30) invariably end up quenching Him (1 Thessalonians 5:19). A want of the fruit of the Spirit will eventually destroy His gifts of power.

Quenching Leads to Ineffectiveness

An opposite but equally tragic situation afflicts the Church when there is growth in the inward work of the Holy Spirit but rejection of the outward work. In this case a believer may pursue moral living, altruistic works, concise exposition of the Word and genuine Christian fellowship, but demonstrate no spiritual power to set people free from bondage or fulfill the task of evangelism and making disciples. This lack results in a failure to bring in new believers, to set demonized people free, to heal the wounded, to give hope to the hopeless or to bring the Kingdom of God on earth as in heaven. He or she has no power to change anything, except for the power the world already has—that of science and the rational mind and a human sort of love.

This half-full Christianity is as scandalous as the other. The world scorns a powerless church as much as it scorns an immoral one. Many people are secretly hungry for a touch from God, for some evidence of His love. When they come to church and do not find it, they are deeply disappointed.

Surely the answer to both dilemmas is that we open our lives to both kinds of infilling, to the work of "the Spirit upon" and "the Spirit within." Let us seek with our whole hearts to receive the Holy Spirit according to the whole counsel of God.

Balance between Inner and Outer Works

The power gifts of the Holy Spirit are like ornaments on a Christmas tree. They are given from outside. They can be put on and pulled off and rearranged. The inward fruit of the Spirit is more like the fruit of a fruit tree. It grows gradually and comes not from outside but through the life of the tree itself.

The following drawings help to illustrate the point that in the mature Christian life, both the inner and the outer operations of the Spirit are to be in balance.

Keeping Our Balance

Brad: One of the most dramatic instances I have experienced of the contrast between these two kinds of infillings was during a preaching trip to Taiwan in 1995.

That mission trip, sponsored by Presbyterian & Reformed Renewal Ministries International, concluded with two days of meetings in the southern port city of Gau Shung. If there is a controlling principality over that city, it surely must be lust.

We were working in a Baptist church where several hundred people had gathered for leadership training. But for two nights during the conference, we were lodged in a hotel down the street that was an active site for prostitution. Not only were such activities going on all night, but hard-core pornography was piped into the rooms on TV.

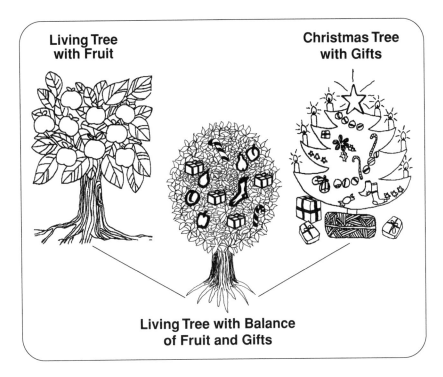

Living Tree with Fruit

Christmas Tree with Gifts

Living Tree with Balance of Fruit and Gifts

The first night in our hotel rooms threw us into a real battle. The men on the team had to deal with temptation to sexual lust. The women felt the exploitation and abuse of women. We were all uncomfortable and vulnerable.

On that first night, we prayed for God's cleansing of the rooms and ourselves, and submitted ourselves to be accountable to one another. Sharing rooms helped in this. We pleaded the blood of Jesus for protection, at the same time wrestling with our humanity. Then we went over to the prayer service, where we saw the power of God at work setting captives free. As a brutal reminder of the consequences of sin, I prayed with a number of men who were tormented by sexual lust and whose marriages had been destroyed because they were unable to resist the lure of the very kind of place where we were staying.

On the second night I was having a serious battle with sexual temptation. It was hard to keep the TV turned off. I rationalized that I was just checking the world news on CNN. Distracted by the porn, I never got to the news. Yet back at the prayer meeting, the Holy Spirit was upon me for power in ministry. I experienced firsthand the possibility of having the inward and outward working of the Holy Spirit functioning at different levels. Outwardly there was great power, as the Holy Spirit fell on those I prayed for. Yet inwardly the pornographic images I had glimpsed on TV clouded my mind. I was thoroughly ashamed of myself, yet the Holy Spirit did not stop working to bless other people through me.

At that moment I was tempted to delude myself into thinking I could simply move on two unrelated tracks, experiencing the power of God while giving in to the lust of the flesh. I was being enticed to "continue in sin that grace may abound" (Romans 6:1).

But on that second night, as I was getting onto the elevator to return to my room, I met one of the prostitutes. She was not more than twenty, with an attractive figure. I was assaulted with a thought like a flaming arrow: *You're fluent in Chinese. Just speak to her. Ask her up to your room. Your roommate won't be back for another hour.*

Then my eyes caught hers, and instantly the lustful temptation was quenched by the weight of sadness I saw there.

O God! I thought. *How lonely she is! How desperate the message of her eyes!*

It seemed that a beam of darkness and resignation and even despair shone from her face. She lowered her head with a look of embarrassment and slipped past me into the night.

Not knowing what else to do, I prayed for her—and thought about my two pretty daughters at home who, just like this girl, were created to be loved and honored, not used and abused. The Holy Spirit was showing me the consequences of lust while allowing me the freedom to make choices. But He was not permitting me to give in to temptation without a struggle. He was working to make me Spirit-filled, both in the public prayer meetings—with the episodic power for ministry—and in my hotel room, to keep my character growing.

God kept all the team members in accountable relationships to resist and flee from the devil. (That the Holy Spirit does an inner work of character transformation does not mean we get the character of Jesus instantly or miraculously. He appeals to our wills. That is why the fruit of the Spirit is not "Spirit-control" but "self-control.")

By the power of the Holy Spirit, we stayed faithful to the Kingdom of God and resisted the other reality reaching out to us in the hotel.

At the end of our stay, I overheard the women at the desk asking our Taiwanese co-worker, "Who are these Americans who have been staying with us? There's something different about them. They've been kind to us. What business are they in?"

George was able to say, "They're Christians, here in Taiwan to do the work of Jesus."

The next question was, "Jesus? Who's that?"

Because we had chosen to live in the reality of the Kingdom of God and resist the temptations of darkness swirling around, George was able to share the good news of the Gospel with the women at the desk.

Seeing this, I realized again that to do the work of Jesus Christ and to advance His Kingdom on earth, we must grow in both "the Spirit upon" and "the Spirit within."

7

Is There a Baptism with the Holy Spirit?

Brad: One promise about the Holy Spirit anchors itself exclusively in the Person of Jesus. In the words of John the Baptist, "He will baptize you with the Holy Spirit" (see Matthew 3:11; Mark 1:8; Luke 3:16; see also John 1:33). Because of past controversies associated with this unique promise, many Christians who believe in the gifts of the Spirit for today nonetheless tend to avoid speaking about a baptism with the Holy Spirit, though it lies at the core of New Testament hope for every Christian.

Doug and I realize that this promise gets us into hot water with some believers. When you talk about a baptism with the Holy Spirit, their eyes glaze over and they think, *You must be Pentecostal.* But this promise has nothing to do with being Pentecostal and everything to do with following Jesus. It is not Pentecostals who baptize with the Holy Spirit, after all, but Jesus. If we follow Jesus, shouldn't we find out what He can do for us according to this promise?

Holy Spirit baptism (we use a noun for convenience, but it is always a verb in the Bible—a process, not a possession) is so central to the promise about Jesus listed in all four Gospels that we wish to recover it for all Christians, as R. A. Torrey tried to do. Because he laid the groundwork, we will simply rebuild his foundation, adding some insights from Archer Torrey and backing them up with a few illustrations.

Four Propositions about the Baptism

R. A. Torrey liked to cite a number of Scriptures, then summarize their contents in a proposition. Torrey challenged all Christians to accept four propositions about the baptism with the Holy Spirit:

1. There is a diversity of terms but the same experience.
2. The baptism with the Spirit is a definite experience.
3. The baptism with the Spirit is distinct from salvation and sanctification.
4. The baptism with the Spirit is primarily for witness and Christian service.

Let's explore each of these propositions.

1. Diversity of Terms, One Experience

In *What the Bible Teaches about the Holy Spirit*,[1] Torrey asserted that several expressions "are used in the New Testament to describe one and the same experience" (p. 270): *baptized with the Holy Spirit, filled with the Holy Spirit, the Holy Spirit fell on them, the gift of the Holy Spirit was poured out, receive the Holy Spirit, "I send the promise of my Father upon you," endued with power from on high.*

Torrey's supportive texts (Acts 1:5; 4:8; 10:44–46; 11:15–17; 19:2–6; Hebrews 2:4; 1 Corinthians 12:4, 11, 13; Luke 24:49) show God urging His Church to trust Him for power in ministry.

In Acts 1:5, for example, Luke makes clear that what happened on Pentecost was from Jesus, who was fulfilling the promise of John the Baptist. Some people have taught that the baptism with the Holy Spirit was a one-time, nonrepeatable experience, in which the whole Church, and not individual Christians, was initiated into power ministry.

This idea seems plausible until we get to Acts 11. Here Peter explains the outpouring of the Spirit in the house of Cornelius:

"As I began to speak, the Holy Spirit fell on them just as on us at the beginning. And I remembered the word of the Lord, how he said, 'John baptized with water, but you shall be baptized with the Holy Spirit.'"

Acts 11:15–16

Peter was seeing that his own initiation into power ministry was being repeated in the household of Cornelius. He concluded that the Gentiles were being baptized in the Holy Spirit, passing through a gateway of their own.

The other verses Torrey listed, especially those in the book of Acts, describe similar gateways into power ministry for believers, although other expressions were used to describe them. All these expressions, Torrey asserted, refer to the power of the Holy Spirit coming upon them for ministry:

"They were all *filled [pleitho]* with the Holy Spirit . . ." (Acts 2:4).
". . . they *received* the Holy Spirit" (Acts 8:17).
". . . be *filled [pleitho]* with the Holy Spirit" (Acts 9:17).
". . . the Holy Spirit *fell on* all . . ." (Acts 10:44).
". . . the Holy Spirit *came on* them . . ." (Acts 19:6).

It seems clear that Jesus initiated His followers into power ministry and that this initiation is not just a one-time experience for the Church as a whole, but for individual believers.

2. A Definite Experience

"The Baptism with the Holy Spirit," declared Torrey, "is a definite experience of which one may and ought to know whether he has received it or not" (*What the Bible Teaches,* p. 270). He based this proposition on the fact that whenever New Testament believers were initiated into the power of the Holy Spirit for ministry, a discernible change occurred. From the brief descriptions given, we do not always know what that change was, but others could confirm it.

A key passage is Acts 19:1–6 (NIV):

While Apollos was at Corinth, Paul took the road through the interior and arrived at Ephesus. There he found some disciples and asked them, "Did you receive the Holy Spirit when you believed?"

They answered, "No, we have not even heard that there is a Holy Spirit."

So Paul asked, "Then what baptism did you receive?"

"John's baptism," they replied.

Paul said, "John's baptism was a baptism of repentance. He told the people to believe in the one coming after him, that is, in Jesus." On hearing this, they were baptized into the name of the Lord Jesus. When Paul placed his hands on them, the Holy Spirit came on them, and they spoke in tongues and prophesied.

Paul assumed that receiving the Holy Spirit is not just a theological doctrine to be believed but an event that happens to people, an experience about which they can answer, "Yes, it happened," or, "No, I don't know what you're talking about."

The issue is not whether the Ephesians spoke in tongues and prophesied, but that Paul discerned they had not experienced the empowering of the Holy Spirit, and asked them as much. He did not see evidence of the Holy Spirit upon them, and wanted them to receive everything a Christian should rightfully claim. His conversation with the Ephesians implies that the baptism with the Holy Spirit makes an observable difference in the life of a believer.

We run into trouble when we try to codify what sign will "prove" that one is initiated in power ministry. Nevertheless, from the biblical evidence, the experience should make a noticeable difference. A person can know that he or she has received the promise. God gives assurance and confirmation as He chooses.

3. Distinct from Salvation and Sanctification

The sanctifying work of the Holy Spirit in building Christian character is equally important, as we have seen, but the baptism with the Spirit does not refer to that. It is an initiation into power ministry distinct from salvation, regeneration, justification, sanctification or any other work we would classify as "the Spirit within."

Wrote Torrey:

A man [or woman] may be regenerated by the Holy Spirit, and still not be baptized with the Holy Spirit. In regeneration there is an impartation of life, and the one who receives it is saved; in the Baptism with the Holy Spirit there is an impartation of power, and the one who receives it is fitted for service.

What the Bible Teaches, p. 271

Thus, we are dealing with "the Spirit upon," a promise intended for all Christians, to be received by faith for empowerment. The Scottish theologian Thomas Smail expressed the point more recently:

> In the New Testament the essential content of the expression to be "baptized in the Spirit" is the experience of the released power and energy of the Spirit. Those to whom it happens are regenerated men [and women], who confess Christ as Lord, have their sins forgiven and are accepted as sons [and daughters], and in all that the Spirit has been at work. But to say that they are baptized in the Spirit refers not specifically to any of that, but rather to the release of the Spirit in power and love and charismatic manifestation within and through them.[2]

Confusion about the Word *Baptism*

Two points need to be addressed before we move on.

First, why is the term *baptism* used? Doesn't this create confusion and entangle us in debates about the sacrament of water baptism?

We understand the word *baptism* to signify an initiation. Just as water baptism is the initiation into Christ, Holy Spirit baptism is the initiation into the power of the Spirit. Because it is a beginning, we do not speak of being "baptized with the Holy Spirit" every time God uses us in some new manifestation of the Spirit. *Baptism with the Spirit* refers to the *first* time we sought the Lord and He answered our prayer with power. It is a gateway into power ministry.

Second, the work of "the Spirit within" can be mingled experientially with that of "the Spirit upon," but scripturally they are two distinct dimensions of the work of the Holy Spirit. Torrey observed:

> The steps by which one ordinarily receives the Baptism with the Holy Spirit are of such a character, and the Baptism with the Holy Spirit makes God so real, that this Baptism is in most cases accompanied by a great moral uplift, or even a radical transformation, but the Bap-

tism with the Holy Spirit is not in itself either an eradication of the carnal nature or cleansing from an impure heart. It is the impartation of supernatural power or gifts in service. . . .

What the Bible Teaches, p. 273

The Ripple Effect

Because the promises of God may be poured out indiscriminately, some call a conversion experience the baptism in the Holy Spirit, or receive both in one fell swoop. Others, at the same time that they receive power for service, experience deep forgiveness from God, or find that the fruit of the Spirit has ripened into mature Christian character because of a fresh awareness of God's love.

The following chart shows the ripple effect of the baptism with the Holy Spirit. The essence is empowerment. But, as Torrey said, there may be some very positive side effects. This is partly because the experience itself builds faith, and also because the inward and

Ripple Effects of the Baptism with the Holy Spirit

Empowerment for witness
Acts 1:5, 8

Sealing
of the Holy Spirit

Holiness

Joy (holy laughter)

The primary purpose of the baptism with the Holy Spirit is empowerment, but it may have other effects.

outward operations of the Holy Spirit are connected. The ripple effect helps to explain why different terms have historically been applied to this initiation.

Bearing in mind this ripple effect, we are ready to look at Torrey's fourth proposition about the baptism in the Holy Spirit.

4. For the Purpose of Christian Service

Let's go back to Jesus. At the time of His baptism in water by John, the outpouring of the Holy Spirit upon Him by God the Father marked a radical turning point in Jesus' ministry. Suddenly "evidence" started pouring out of His life: "They were amazed at his teaching, because his message had authority" (Luke 4:32, NIV). "All the people were amazed and said to each other, 'What is this teaching? With authority and power he gives orders to evil spirits and they come out!'" (Luke 4:36, NIV). "The power of the Lord was present for him to heal the sick" (Luke 5:17, NIV). And so on.

Jesus Himself attributed these works of power to the Holy Spirit when He quoted Isaiah 61:1–2 as a prophecy about Himself: "The Spirit of the Lord is upon me, because he has anointed me to preach good news to the poor . . ." (Luke 4:18).

Before His baptism, Jesus already had the Holy Spirit within to "[learn] obedience through what he suffered" (Hebrews 5:8). The Spirit was apparently working within Jesus from the time of His conception, to bring extraordinary wisdom in interpreting the Scriptures, a surrendered heart, humility and love. But not until Jesus was initiated into the power of the Holy Spirit for ministry did the Spirit fall *on* Him for mighty works.

So, concluded Torrey:

> The Baptism with the Holy Spirit is an experience connected with and primarily for the purpose of service. . . . The Baptism with the Spirit is not primarily intended to make believers happy nor holy, but to make them useful. In every passage in the Bible in which the results of the Baptism with the Holy Spirit are mentioned, they are related to testimony and service.
>
> *What the Bible Teaches,* p. 272

A Point of Crisis

Doug: The baptism with the Holy Spirit is a threshold across which we may pass into the works of God, just as Jesus did at age thirty. It involves us in a personal and spiritual crisis in which we give up a life based only on rational certainty and surrender our desire for personal control. We yield to God our natural or worldly ways of making decisions and reevaluate our relationships with people as to their usefulness to God.

Jessie Penn-Lewis, writing in the wake of the Welsh revival at the turn of the century, described this crisis:

> The baptism with the Holy Spirit is a crisis in the life of a Christian, which none but those who have gone through it in experience, can fully understand. It means that the Spirit of God becomes so real to the man [or woman], that his [or her] supreme object in life is henceforth implicit "obedience to the Holy Ghost." The will is surrendered to carry out the Will of God at all costs, and the whole being is made subject to the powers of the unseen world. . . .[3]

In this crisis we have grown weary of our self-reliance, the shallowness of our church programs, the meager results of our academic professionalism, the paralyzing effect of our rational analysis of problems, the futility of our political programs. All these hopes appear like chaff, straw and stubble, barely attaining the status of wood and stone, much less the gold, silver and precious stones described by Paul in 1 Corinthians 3:12. Must we spend the rest of our lives groveling in trivialities and works that will surely burn up after we die?

It is not an experience of tongues (or of carpet time, or of holy laughter) that we yearn for in the midst of this crisis. These signs may be part of God's answer, but they are not integral to the baptism with the Holy Spirit, nor to the crisis that produces it. Rather, we long for significance in the Kingdom of God, power to bring the Kingdom here on earth "as it is in heaven." Confidence in human endeavor, nurtured by humanistic educational institutions, has worn thin. We are ready to agree with the prophet Zechariah to work "not by might, nor by power, but by my Spirit" (4:6); to seek the purpose only God can give, the works that only God can do, in the hope that He can use us, even us, to accomplish His great plan.

For such a privilege, we are willing to pay the price of a surrendered life, to embrace the cross and go where Jesus says. We will gladly sacrifice our need to be in control of our futures, our desire to run our lives and the lives of everyone in our families and churches. We have seen at long last that we have not the power to give ourselves a high purpose for living. The purposes we give to ourselves amount to nothing. We seek God to show His purposes to us, for we are "created in Christ Jesus for good works, which God prepared beforehand, that we should walk in them" (Ephesians 2:10). We are ready to listen to Him for those good works, to receive His vision for our lives. We will resist the bit and bridle no longer.

By bringing us to such a crisis, God has prepared us to receive "power from on high" (Luke 24:49). Before the crisis, we were not ready to receive such power. The power of the Holy Spirit for ministry is for those willing to be tested in the wilderness, as Jesus was after He was baptized with the Holy Spirit. It is for those who seriously want to accomplish a work of God, not just a work for God. The world is full of people doing works for God. Many of these works are well-intended but badly managed. Some of the worst disasters in history have happened because people wanted to "do it for God."

But now this crisis has brought us to a place where we are tired even of working *for* God. We want to do something that is *of* God.

Some Who Passed through This Gateway

Brad: We want to tell the stories of three Christians who passed through this crisis.

"I Feel So Empty of Christ's Love"

Ashbel Green Simonton was caught up in a revival movement that overtook the College of New Jersey (now Princeton) in 1849–50. As a result of awakening to the regenerative power of Christ, he committed himself to a life of Christian service. He wrote in his prayer journal:

I am now resolved in God's promised strength to go forward and endeavor to serve him, whether a bright light shines around my path or not; to confess before men my desire and resolution to forsake the world and seek an interest in the atoning blood of Christ.[4]

He entered seminary and, as a result of an anointed sermon by Dr. Charles Hodge, decided on the mission field. He wrote:

The little success apparently attending missionary operations had operated to dissuade me from all thought of the work, but I see I have been wrong. That the heathen are to be converted to God is clearly revealed in Scripture, and I am convinced that day is coming rapidly.[5]

Attending the concerts of prayer that were proliferating in 1858–59, Simonton became convinced God was leading him to Brazil. In 1859, before he could even learn Portuguese, he followed that leading and sailed to the country of God's choice. There he was to found the Presbyterian Church of Brazil.

But when we look in on him (through another translation of his journal, here and following[6]) after 53 days in his new land, we find him struggling with powerlessness in ministry:

I have had new experiences of my own weakness and lack of ability and the need of divine grace. I seek a deeper experience of spiritual things. I must cultivate my own sanctification or I will not be able to do anything for others. I feel so empty of Christ's love and hate for sin that I fear that I am not doing what I should, and feel that I will be able to accomplish little here. God is Holy and I am a sinner. Can it be that He will use such an instrument?

Here was the crisis. A year and a half later, on January 20, 1861, Simonton wrote:

I observe that the lack of privileges for growth in grace, common in Christian lands, appears in my spiritual neglect, the coldness and formality of my prayers and the little joy I find in reading the Scriptures. More than anything else, *I need the baptism of the Holy Spirit*. If in this hour, in the imminence of actively beginning the preaching of the Gospel of Christ, *I should receive the gift of the Spirit to prepare me for this work,* how happy I would be! I want to be able to preach Christ more from experience, to be able to speak of that which I know because Christ has revealed it to me. I cannot imagine a higher calling than being filled with Jesus daily, having intimate communion, to work day by day to bring the same happiness to an entire nation.

I have not been able to find a report of Simonton's experience of being baptized with the Holy Spirit. But later journal entries reveal that something had happened to him, something he wanted to pass along to the Brazilian people by means of fervent prayer:

> I spent the week in prayer. I hope that God's people everywhere have sent up fervent petitions for the descent of the Holy Spirit, so that the Kingdom of God may be established in the land in these troubled times. I explained the plea to pray this week to the Brazilians who came to worship, and it made a very good impression on them.

The result of the crisis Ashbel Green Simonton passed through was equipping for the work of ministry. Brazilian Presbyterians do not remember him as a member of the frozen chosen trying to foist Reformed tradition onto an unwilling populace. They remember his ministry as a fruitful one full of the power of God. Comments Joao Marcos Pacheco:

> Historians have attributed to the Rev. Mr. Simonton these principal characteristics: love, faith, obedience, courage, the desire to serve and the constant wish to be completely controlled by the Holy Spirit. The results included: a Sunday School and a church in Rio de Janeiro, a newspaper—"*Imprensa Evangelica*" (Evangelical Press), a seminary, a presbytery, as well as a number of sermons and poems in Portuguese.[7]

For Simonton, the baptism with the Holy Spirit came as the result of a yearning for a more effective ministry. As a member of a mainline denomination, he shows us the value of this promise for all Christians who want to dedicate their lives to the work of God.

A Step of Sheer Obedience

The baptism with the Holy Spirit is not a "one-size-fits-all" sort of glove. The Spirit opens people up in a great kaleidoscope of experiences, all genuine but no two alike.

When Archer Torrey was a student at Davidson College, he followed his grandfather's approach: Ask in the name of Jesus for the baptism with the Spirit, receive in faith, then step out in obedience as the Lord leads.

At the time Archer saw no effects of his prayer, either outward or inward—neither tears nor joy. He did not speak in tongues until twenty years later. But God had given him the faith that if he asked for something according to God's will, He would give it to him. Archer knew without a doubt that God willed to give him the baptism.

Later he began to receive clear daily guidance from the Holy Spirit—evidence that he had indeed received new power for witness. It started after his initial prayer:

> Several weeks later I was asked to supply preach at a nearby church. The only contact I had with anyone in the church was with an elder who told me which bus to take to get there. When I was preparing, I asked the Lord what he wanted me to preach on. The Lord said, "What you like best," which at that time was worship.
>
> After the service many of the people came forward and asked me, "Who told you about our church?" God had used me to speak directly to a crisis in their church!
>
> That was a manifestation of the power of the Holy Spirit—a word of prophecy that I was not even aware of speaking.[8]

Some will find this testimony disappointing. What? No tongues? No healing? Nothing dramatic? Yet it was the beginning of a life of service and powerful witness. I have already described how Jesus Abbey, as a laboratory for Christian living, has brought spiritual awakening throughout the world and helped thousands come to know Jesus Christ in the power of the Holy Spirit.

Archer's testimony shows that the baptism in the Spirit does not necessarily involve emotion, inner transformation, signs, wonders, tongues, ecstasy or anything that has come to be associated with it. It is, pure and simple, empowerment for service. All else is frosting.

"Some Precious Jewel Buried within Me"

My wife, Laura, entered this experience differently from Archer, but through a distinct crisis that led her to seek and ask for the promise.

Like me, Laura grew up in the Presbyterian Church, accepting Christ in grade school. During college, while attending an Episcopal church, God called her to seminary, where we met and married. Two years later we went to Korea as short-term missionaries. She reflects:

My year in Korea was extremely difficult. Brad was right at home there, knew many people and spoke some Korean, but for me it was an alien culture. Our living situation was difficult. That winter we were cold all the time and had no running water or plumbing for four months. The market was a mile down the mountain. Seoul, where we had a few English-speaking friends, was an hour's bus ride away.

As a woman in a very chauvinistic culture, I was often treated as a non-person. I got used to not being looked at or spoken to. Brad received compliments on what a wonderful wife he had because I was so quiet. I had little choice, of course, because I couldn't speak the language!

While in America, I had been turned off by the charismatic movement. Occasionally we had attended prayer meetings in Richmond out of curiosity. But in Korea, perhaps driven by our spiritual need, we spent a lot of time in the homes of Presbyterian missionaries who had a vibrant faith and spoke often about the role of the Holy Spirit in their successful mission work.

A couple of months after Brad was dramatically baptized with the Holy Spirit at Jesus Abbey, I reached a low point. Besides the hardships of the place, I questioned whether I could ever be an effective minister. I was really broken and searching.

Thankfully, about that time we were able to attend a monthly prayer meeting with Protestant and Catholic missionaries from all over Korea. That night I was sitting in the circle, listening to the singing and praying. In the security of that fellowship, I noticed that my tongue was moving. I just let it go. It felt comfortable and right to do so. I do not think anyone noticed anything happening to me, and I told no one about the experience.

The next morning I awoke with the most wonderful sense that God had given me a gift. It was as though there were some precious jewel buried within me that had not been there before. This marked a turning point for me. The things of the Spirit became suddenly very real. For the first time I found the courage to share my faith with others. And I began quietly to grow in the gifts of the Holy Spirit for ministry.

Laura never sought tongues as an experience. It was simply a free gift to help her get through a crisis—a gift she continues to receive for her own edification, as Paul says in 1 Corinthians 14:4. The main result of her "gateway": She became equipped for the pastoral and teaching ministry she has been doing ever since. God reassured her that He did want to use her and that she could learn to rely on Him for power, wisdom, pastoral discernment, the ability to speak His will into the lives of others, and leading them to maturity in Christ.

Maybe *you* desire not only to work for God, but to do the works of God. If so, keep reading, as we turn to the practical question of how a Christian can walk through the gateway that is called the baptism with the Holy Spirit.

How to Pray for the Empowerment of the Holy Spirit

Brad and Doug: We are now ready to ask the practical question, How do we open ourselves to the empowerment promised to those who follow Jesus?

To answer this question, let's pick up the strand we left dangling in chapter 3. At the end of that chapter we discussed seven fundamentals that every person who accepts Christ should include in his or her walk with the Lord, according to R. A. Torrey. (We have added one additional step.)[1]

1. *Accept Jesus Christ as personal Savior* (Acts 2:38; John 14:15–17).
2. *Repent from all known sin* (Acts 2:38; John 16:8; 1 John 1:5–10).
3. *Make an open, public confession of faith in Christ* (Mark 8:36–38; Romans 10:9–10).
4. *Surrender your life fully to Christ as Lord and live a life of obedience* (Acts 5:32).
5. *Earnestly desire the baptism with the Holy Spirit as empowerment for witness and service* (Psalm 63:1; John 7:37–39).
6. *Pray definitely for it* (Luke 11:13; Acts 4:31; Acts 8:15–16).

7. *Accept it by faith, regardless of "initial signs"* (Mark 11:22–24; Galatians 3:13–14; 1 John 5:14–15).

8. *Step out in obedience to follow the leading of the Holy Spirit* (Acts 5:32; Galatians 5:25).

Let's look at these steps one by one.

1. Accept Jesus Christ as Savior

"The first step toward receiving the Baptism with the Holy Spirit," wrote Torrey in *The Person and Work of the Holy Spirit*,[2] "is that we rest entirely upon the finished work of Jesus Christ on the Cross of Calvary, upon His atoning death for us, as the sole ground of our acceptance before God" (p. 158).

Doug: Jesus is a Promise-Maker. The gift of the Holy Spirit is but one of many promises Jesus gave. They can be fulfilled nowhere but in Him. Our Lord and Savior paid a price for the blessings He showers on us, and we must come to Him alone to receive them. Go to anyone else and you will get a cheap counterfeit—or worse.

Trusting Jesus as Savior requires us to change how we deal with common, ordinary, everyday problems. Now we can bring them to Jesus, who is our Savior. We can trust His power to shepherd us through this life and into the next. We can study His promises—and how His commandments interact with them, for promise and command fit together into a whole picture, the New Covenant. It is in the context of trusting Jesus that we ask Him to baptize us with the Holy Spirit. And when praying with others for the baptism, we should make sure they understand the basics of faith in Christ and have embraced Him as Savior.

Why is this so important? We live in a day of spiritual deception. The Bible prophesies that in the last days, the evil one will come on the world with signs and wonders, and that he aims "to deceive even the elect—if that were possible" (Matthew 24:24, NIV). Counterfeiting spirits can and do masquerade as the Holy Spirit. Self-professing pagans speak as though they have received the Holy Spirit and think they know what they are talking about.

Against all this we must insist on the words of Jesus:

"If you love me, you will obey what I command. And I will ask the Father, and he will give you another Counselor to be with you forever—the Spirit of truth. The world cannot accept him, because it neither sees him nor knows him. But you know him, for he lives with you and will be in you."

John 14:15–17, NIV

The Holy Spirit is for followers of Jesus, not for "the world" who "cannot accept him." If people who do not follow Jesus have received a spirit, they have received not the Holy Spirit but a counterfeit spirit. Only in Jesus are the inward and outward works of the Holy Spirit joined.

In *War on the Saints* Jessie Penn-Lewis put it this way:

The word "deceived" is, according to the Scripture, the description of every unregenerate human being, without distinction of persons, race, culture, or sex. "We also were . . . deceived" (Titus iii. 3), said Paul the Apostle, although in his "deceived" condition he was a religious man, walking according to the righteousness of the law, blameless (Phil. iii. 6).

Every unregenerate man first of all is deceived by his own deceitful heart (Jer. xvii. 9; Isa. xliv. 20), and deceived by sin (Heb. iii. 13); the god of this world adding the "blinding of the mind" lest the light of the gospel of Christ should dispel the darkness (2 Cor. iv. 4).[3]

Jesus is the only One who can accurately see the spiritual world and the God who reigns from there. "He who comes from above is above all; he who is of the earth belongs to the earth, and of the earth he speaks; he who comes from heaven is above all" (John 3:31). Jesus' testimony about spiritual things is faithful and true. He is our only hope for wading through the shoals and currents of spiritual deception all around us. He alone can show us how to minister power without being corrupted by it. He alone saves us from the power of the evil one. He alone knows the pathway to God. He alone baptizes with the Holy Spirit. He is our protection from the phony and clever counterfeits of Satan, from the way that leads to death, from deceitful doctrines about the spirit world, and from everything that would destroy our potential in the Kingdom of God.

Without the precondition of a relationship with Jesus Christ, praying with someone to receive the Holy Spirit will more likely lead to spiritual deception than to useful service for God. So before suggesting that anyone pray to be filled with the Spirit, pray first that he or she will be brought to faith in Jesus Christ as the only basis of God's forgiveness and acceptance, and to rest in His teaching, power and pattern for living.

To be sure, Brad and I have seen the Holy Spirit fall in power even upon non-Christians, bringing healing and manifestations like resting in the Spirit. But such experiences are expressions of God's grace and are intended to lead people to Jesus.

2. Repent from All Known Sin

At Pentecost the crowd of Jews under the conviction of the Holy Spirit cried out,

> "Brethren, what shall we do?" And Peter said to them, "Repent, and be baptized every one of you in the name of Jesus Christ for the forgiveness of your sins; and you shall receive the gift of the Holy Spirit."
>
> Acts 2:37–38

As we start the Christian life, we dare to begin a relationship with a holy God. This God, our Creator, has provided a way for us to approach His throne of grace, even though we do not possess the necessary condition for doing so: holiness, perfection, sinlessness. For "in him is no darkness at all" (1 John 1:5). In us, on the other hand, there is. So we approach the throne of grace acknowledging our need for mercy. This awareness leads us into confession and repentance. It can lead us nowhere else.

The Holy Spirit is called many things according to His many tasks—for example, "the Spirit of truth" (John 16:13) and "the Spirit of adoption" (Romans 8:15, KJV). But most often He is called the *Holy* Spirit, because He wishes to prepare us for eternity with a holy God.

Consistently, during seasons of revival and awakening, we see Him bringing conviction of sin and a supernatural longing to confess sin, even in public. During these times of profound spiritual revival, we see what is also true at other times (but less obviously)—

that the Holy Spirit wishes to clean us out through confession of sin and repentance. "He will convince the world concerning sin and righteousness and judgment" (John 16:8).

Sincere repentance weaves a pathway between the false security of believing, on the one hand, that we have achieved perfect sanctification, and, on the other hand, that we are unworthy to receive the Holy Spirit and therefore should not ask. On the one hand, we deceive ourselves into thinking we have everything we need already, so why ask for anything more? On the other hand, we think we cannot receive what we know we need.

Rather, let us become like Peter who, after denying Jesus, went out and wept bitterly. Later, on the beach at the Sea of Galilee, he accepted Jesus' recommissioning in the question and command "Do you love me? . . . Feed my sheep" (John 21:17). Peter knew he had not arrived at perfection, but he also knew Jesus had forgiven him and chosen him for a work, despite his imperfections.

The apostle John instructs us to "walk in the light" (1 John 1:7). This means, first, to let the searchlight of the Holy Spirit explore the secret places in us. Second, it means to respond to that searching by confessing and repenting of sin, then receiving forgiveness and cleansing from Jesus.

Brad: The willingness to deal honestly with sin begins at our initiation into the Christian life but becomes a permanent feature of our lifestyle. I have found that if I am to continue receiving the "Holy Spirit upon" me, I must make confession a regular spiritual discipline. Here the inner and outer work of the Holy Spirit are brought together.

Again and again before going into power ministry, I have prayed, *O Lord, fill me with Your Holy Spirit. Empower me to do Your work.* Nearly every time, the Lord impresses on me some area of sin in my life or some area I have been refusing to surrender to Him. Each time, confession and repentance have been followed by the Holy Spirit falling on me for power.

I will never forget my feelings of helplessness before conducting the first "Prayer Mountain" for Presbyterian & Reformed Renewal Ministries. I had no idea how to lead a three-day prayer event. All I knew was, God had led me to issue a call for Christians to gather in Montreat, North Carolina, to do the work of intercessory prayer for the Church and the world.

For two weeks before the event, I spent every evening until late at night in prayer. I struggled with God, asking Him to bless the event and fill me with the Holy Spirit, that I might be empowered to lead it. Each time I went into prayer, I got the same deep nudging: *Go be reconciled with your predecessor, Brick Bradford.*

That was the last thing I wanted to do. I was angry and hurt over the way I felt he had handled some aspects of the transition from his leadership of PRRMI to mine. Each night I held out against these leadings of the Holy Spirit, but I knew deep down that my rebellious attitude would prevent God's power from working through me. Finally, the day before leaving for the event, my pride caved in and I obeyed. I confessed my sin of rebellion to God; then I called Brick and asked him to meet me for lunch. I confessed my attitudes and we were reconciled.

The next day I flew off to North Carolina, where the Holy Spirit anointed me not only to lead the prayer retreat, but also to lay hands on many people to see them baptized with the Holy Spirit. This first Prayer Mountain launched a whole series of PRRMI Prayer Mountains that continue to impact the Church.

A repentant heart, I believe, is a precondition for receiving—and for continuing in—the power of the Holy Spirit for ministry. Paul wrote:

> Do not grieve the Holy Spirit of God, in whom you were sealed for the day of redemption. Let all bitterness and wrath and anger and clamor and slander be put away from you, with all malice, and be kind to one another, tenderhearted, forgiving one another, as God in Christ forgave you.
>
> Ephesians 4:30–32

Ironically, the Bible tells us we "put away" these things not by trying to hide them in some dark closet, but by getting them out into the open. This passage also tells us that putting away our sin—casting it off through confession and repentance—keeps us from grieving the Holy Spirit of God, which in turn keeps the power and wisdom of God flowing through us to bless others.

Complete honesty is rare in Christian circles these days, yet without that honesty and trust, heartfelt repentance is difficult. Ideally, all who open themselves to the Holy Spirit will have a growing number of confidants—listening, caring brothers and sisters to whom they can confess struggles with sin and with whom they can work out repentance.

3. Publicly Confess Faith in Christ

Doug: The Western nations are full of closet Christians. It is as though we are ashamed of who we are. R. A. Torrey resisted this tide of shame by insisting that people make an open, public declaration that they have changed sides in their allegiance, that they no longer serve the prince of this world but the King of heaven—following the words of Jesus:

> "Whoever is ashamed of me and of my words in this adulterous and sinful generation, of him will the Son of man also be ashamed, when he comes in the glory of his Father with the holy angels."
>
> Mark 8:38

It is clear, isn't it, that if we are to receive the Holy Spirit for witness and service, we must cast off shame about being a Christian. Since Jesus baptizes with the Holy Spirit to equip us for witness and service, our reluctance to make public a decision for Christ cannot coexist with the baptism of the Spirit. All of us in some way or other are to be witnesses for Christ. This is the top priority with the Holy Spirit, and why we must stand up and say publicly that we are for Christ. Until we break out of the closet, our ministry for Him will be hindered.

4. Surrender Your Life to Christ as Lord

Full surrender, like repentance, is an initial decision that we must renew each day for the rest of our lives. We begin the Christian life full of self-centered passions and desires. We want our own way; we love to control not only our own lives but the destinies of others. We feel, when it comes down to it, that God should jump when we say, "Jump," and that He should see things just as we do.

This attitude begins to change when we realize that our attempts to control God and everyone else have destroyed the fabric of our relationships, given us ulcers, wrecked our ministries and robbed us of our joy and peace. Only then can we begin to yield our lives to God, letting Him carry us where He wills.

Catherine Marshall spoke eloquently in the 1970s about "the prayer of relinquishment." Unfortunately other teachers in the Church appealed to the gross selfishness of the American dream by suggesting we could "possess" whatever we "confessed." Relinquishment became the forgotten ingredient and the cross dropped out of the Christian lifestyle. These teachers viewed faith as a pathway to successful living and did not define *success* by the standards of Christ. Their teaching brought discredit to the work of the Holy Spirit.

How refreshing to rediscover the teaching of R. A. Torrey:

> The heart of obedience is in the will. The whole essence of obedience is the surrender of the will to God. It is coming to God and saying, "Oh God, here I am. Thou hast bought me with a price and I acknowledge Thine ownership. Send me where Thou wilt, do with me what Thou wilt, use me as Thou wilt." THIS IS ONE OF THE MOST FUNDAMENTAL THINGS IN RECEIVING THE BAPTISM WITH THE HOLY SPIRIT, THE UNCONDITIONAL SURRENDER OF THE WILL TO GOD.
>
> More people miss the Baptism with the Holy Spirit at this point, and more people enter experimentally into the Baptism with the Holy Spirit at this point than at almost any other.
>
> *The Person and Work of the Holy Spirit,* p. 168

R. A. Torrey's insistence on full surrender is essential to any sustained movement of the Holy Spirit. When it comes to power for ministry, we don't "get" the Holy Spirit. The Spirit "gets" us. This is why a surrendered life is essential.

But what does full surrender mean?

First, full surrender does *not* mean we sit in an enclosed room like a medium at a séance, waiting to be taken over by a spiritual power who will move our limbs or cause us to speak God's words involuntarily. Rather, full surrender means giving up our personal ambitions in favor of the purposes and goals of Jesus. It means listening to Him for instructions, spending time seeking His will, letting Him have first say in how we use our time, develop relationships, make our money, spend our money and conduct ourselves in private.

No sooner have we abandoned our will to Christ than He gives it back to us. He opens up the Scriptures to us and invites us freely to obey them. The Holy Spirit does not bring Spirit-control (as we pointed out at the end of chapter 6) but self-control (see Galatians 5:23). He shows us how to choose the things Jesus wants, and He makes our will and conscious thinking part of the equation.

This is important to understand because demonic powers can do just the opposite with a life surrendered to them. Satan enslaves people, takes away their wills, removes their right to choose, fills them with obsessions and compulsions, takes over their personalities. No such thing happens when we surrender our hearts to Christ. The Holy Spirit begins to "breathe upon the word," enlivening it to our minds and hearts so that we want to obey it. "God is at work in you," wrote Paul, "both to will and to work for his good pleasure" (Philippians 2:13).

God wants people with their wills intact, people who freely choose Him, people who can think clearly and make good decisions—which is how He made us to be.

5. Earnestly Desire the Baptism with the Holy Spirit

Brad: "If any one thirst," said Jesus, "let him come to me and drink. He who believes in me, as the scripture has said, 'Out of his heart shall flow rivers of living water'" (John 7:37–38). Jesus was referring, John wrote, to the Holy Spirit.

Spiritual thirst begins with an intense desire for intimacy with God, as the psalmist wrote: "O God, thou art my God, I seek thee, my soul thirsts for thee; my flesh faints for thee, as in a dry and weary land where no water is" (Psalm 63:1). Then it develops into an awareness of our inadequacy to do the works of God in our own strength. R. A. Torrey put it like this:

> Just as long as we think we can get on some way without the definite Baptism with the Holy Spirit, we are not going to have it. Just as long as we are seeking to accomplish by new tricks of oratory, or by a skillful use of words, or by all sorts of psychological and other trick meth-

ods, to influence people, we are not going to have the Baptism with
the Holy Spirit; but when we come to the place that we realize our
utter need of the Baptism with the Holy Spirit if we are to do effective service for God, and long for it at any cost, then it will be ours,
and not till then.

The Person and Work of the Holy Spirit,
pp. 176–177

For a long time I did not thirst for the Holy Spirit because, through
my education, I thought I had all I needed to do the work of ministry. But when I became a missionary in Korea, I found that my education and skills were more or less useless in dealing with the desperate need I encountered. People came to me wanting healing or
help from afflicting evil spirits. At seminary no one had ever taught
about demons, much less showed how to cast them out.

One night at the U.S. 8th Army retreat center in Seoul, I talked
with a young married Christian soldier who was waging a daily battle against lust and the temptation to seduction in the brothels that
surrounded the military post. In desperation he said, "I'm losing! Is
there no help in Christ for me to resist the temptations that are consuming me?"

I was appalled at my inability to offer any more than words of
comfort or mere advice to encourage his willpower. *Surely there is
some power in our faith,* I told myself. *But where?* Again I saw the impos-
sibility, in my own strength and understanding, to provide any help.

Finally my sense of competence and educational completeness
died. In me was birthed a desperation for the Holy Spirit. I could do
nothing useful as a missionary or minister, I realized, unless the Holy
Spirit empowered me. Thirst for the power of God finally forced me
past all my stereotypes to seek the Holy Spirit urgently.

How do you get this thirst that drives you to God?

First, pray for it. Thirst itself is a gift given by the Holy Spirit, who
already dwells within believers, drawing us to a place of need where
we may be reduced to praying for everything He wants to give us.

Second, if Jesus Christ is your Lord, take the risk of following Him
wherever He calls you. Before long you will find yourself in some
situation where you crash up against impossibilities. You do not have
to go to the mission field to be reduced to this state of dependence.

Just try to bring a non-Christian to Jesus Christ or minister to someone with problems. Sheer powerlessness will lead you to dependence on Jesus, who will, if you ask Him, give you the power of the Holy Spirit.

6. Ask Definitely

For many of us, our God is too small, and our expectations of the Christian life microscopic. We have limited and tamed God by our fears, worldview and lack of knowledge. We do not really expect anything to happen in church except to meet a few friends, hear a pleasing sermon, sing some familiar hymns, contribute to an offering and go home to a good Sunday dinner. In our lives we expect God to do little, except perhaps bless our homes and our children and get us through the day. Many of us sincerely hope that nothing much else *will* happen! And because we expect little, God does little.

Expectancy, on the other hand, is a dimension of faith in God that prepares us to receive His gifts and be involved in all He has for us:

> Now to him who by the power at work within us is able to do far more abundantly than all that we ask or think, to him be glory in the church and in Christ Jesus to all generations, for ever and ever. Amen.
>
> Ephesians 3:20–21

God has decided, in normal circumstances, to work in the world in cooperation with us as free, responsible agents. He has given us the capacity for faith that interfaces between the material and spirit realms. Without faith it is not only impossible to please God, but impossible for God (by His own self-limiting decision) to work in or through us.

This proved true even of Jesus when He visited His hometown. The people's expectancy of who Jesus was and what He could do was limited by their knowledge of Him only as their neighborhood carpenter. As a result, Jesus was unable to do any great works in their midst.

To build expectancy in you of what God can do and what He may wish to give you, dwell on the book of Acts. This is the "can do" book of the New Testament. It shows vividly what the Holy Spirit can do in the lives of ordinary Christians. Read, too, the reports of past revivals in which God showed the possibilities of His power. We recommend Jonathan Edwards' *A Faithful Narrative of the Surprising Work of God* or his *Life and Diary of David Brainerd; The Memoirs* of Charles Finney; *By My Spirit* or *When the Spirit's Fire Swept Korea* by Jonathan Goforth; *Mr. Pentecost,* the biography of David du Plessis; and *The Great Revival in Wales* by S. B. Shaw.

Even better, take the risk! Swallow hard and just go to some Pentecostal miracle service, Vineyard fellowship or someplace you hear that the Holy Spirit is moving. Our PRRMI Dunamis Project conferences can help, especially for people from a Presbyterian or Reformed background. Let firsthand experience stretch your worldview and expand your expectations of what God can do. Seek out those you trust who may have had such experiences, and find out more. Putting yourself in a place where the Holy Spirit is moving in power is often the first step to increasing your faith.

Pray that all this will nurture in you an attitude of abandonment to God and to the vastness of who He is and all that He does. Cultivate an attitude of expecting great things from God and an outrageous willingness to attempt great things for Him. Such expectancy is an expression of faith in Jesus Christ and part of the preparation for being filled with the Holy Spirit.

Filled with expectancy, you are in a position to ask. As Jesus said:

> "I tell you, Ask, and it will be given you; seek, and you will find; knock, and it will be opened to you. For every one who asks receives, and he who seeks finds, and to him who knocks it will be opened. What father among you, if his son asks for a fish, will instead of a fish give him a serpent; or if he asks for an egg, will give him a scorpion? If you then, who are evil, know how to give good gifts to your children, *how much more will the heavenly Father give the Holy Spirit to those who ask him!*"
>
> Luke 11:9–13 (italics added)

The reformer John Calvin affirmed the need to ask in faith, whatever the biblical promise:

> Therefore we see that to us nothing is promised to be expected from the Lord, which we are not also bidden to ask of him in prayers. So

true it is that we dig up by prayer the treasures that were pointed out by the Lord's Gospel, and which our faith has gazed upon.[4]

It matters not what words you use; there are no formulas. What matters is the intent of your heart. Urgent yearning born of helplessness will give you all the words you need. This may take the form of a simple but effective prayer: "Lord, there's no way I can do this in my own strength. Help! Please empower me. Fill me with Your Holy Spirit." Or the simpler form: "Lord, help!"

How Not to Do It

Often we make the infilling with the Holy Spirit more complicated than we should.

While Laura and I were missionaries in Korea, we became close to the Reverend and Mrs. Ko. Mrs. Ko became a good friend to Laura and came over to our little apartment several times a week to teach us Korean.

In mid-February 1976 Laura and I returned from Jesus Abbey. I had just had a tremendous experience of being filled with the Holy Spirit. Mrs. Ko, who was hungry spiritually, noticed that something had happened to me. So during our next few language lessons, Laura and I spent the whole time answering questions about the Holy Spirit.

Finally Mrs. Ko said in a voice full of emotion, "My heart's deepest desire is to serve Jesus Christ. But I am just a woman, my husband is a professor and I am nobody. I am mostly invisible on this campus. I must be baptized with the Holy Spirit if I am to be useful for Jesus. How can I receive the Holy Spirit?"

I did not know what to say. Though I had read one of Torrey's books on the Holy Spirit, I did not understand his steps. So I offered the only response I could think of.

"Take the train to Tong Ni," I said, referring to an eight-hour, all-night trip, "then the bus to Hunagji; then, if there is no rain or snow, the bus to Hasami." (That was another two- or three-hour trip.) "At Hasami get off the bus, wade across the river, continue along the dirt Jeep trail up the mountain for about thirty minutes, and you will arrive at Jesus Abbey. Then ask Archer and Jane Torrey to lay hands on you for prayer to be baptized with the Holy Spirit."

Mrs. Ko's countenance fell. So I started to set up a way for her to make the trip. But nothing seemed to work, either with her schedule or for the Torreys.

Several months went by. All the while Mrs. Ko's hunger deepened, as did her knowledge of the teaching of Scripture on the Holy Spirit. Finally one day she said, "I cannot wait any longer to go to Jesus Abbey. Here in Luke 11 it says that the Father will give the Holy Spirit to anyone who asks. So I am just going to ask."

I doubted anything could be that simple, but I said, "Fine. I'll pray that God answers your prayer."

Early the next morning she showed up at our door. One look told us that her prayers had been answered. She was radiant, bursting with excitement and overflowing with praise of Jesus.

She had gone home, she told us, locked herself in the bathroom (the only room in their small home where she could be alone) and said, "Jesus, I love You and want to serve You. Please fill me with Your Holy Spirit."

As for the rest of what happened, neither her English nor our Korean was adequate to describe it. But it must have been glorious! Along with overflowing joy, Mrs. Ko received an awareness that she was somehow called to witness.

"I knew God was giving me the Holy Spirit," she told us, "just like what happened to you at Jesus Abbey. I was hoping He would let me be a missionary. So I asked the Lord whether He wanted me to go to India or to one of the islands. Instead God told me that my mission field is to go to my in-laws who are not Christians. I said, 'Lord, it would be much easier to go anywhere but to them!'"

Nevertheless, within two months Mrs. Ko had led seventeen members of her husband's family to the Lord and brought them into the church. Her evangelistic method was simple: She went to each of them, asked them to forgive her for anything they might have against her and told them about Jesus.

Mrs. Ko has continued to grow, having the Holy Spirit not just upon her but also within her. Her witness and service have affected her family and church greatly. And all this blessing began because she asked in faith.

I do not send people to Jesus Abbey anymore. I just tell them to ask Jesus.

Some Tips in Praying

Many find it helpful to have hands laid upon them. This has good biblical precedent and may support a person's faith (Acts 9:17; 19:6).

Also, because of the episodic nature of the Holy Spirit's power, we may ask to be filled with the Spirit as often as needed. The baptism is our initiation into power for ministry, but many Christians (like Charles Finney) have felt the need to seek a renewing of God's power later when they sensed a waning of it, or when they faced a greater challenge or new responsibilities. We may ask for God's power again and again, whenever we face new hurdles in ministry.

7. Accept the Promise by Faith

Receiving the baptism with the Holy Spirit is not necessarily an emotional experience. In fact, it does not have to be an experience at all (although it may lead to experiences). It is entry into the power of God for ministry, to be received by faith. Often we know we have been baptized with the Holy Spirit by what God does through us *after* we have asked.

Paul asked the Galatians, "Does he who supplies the Spirit to you and works miracles among you do so by works of the law, or by hearing with faith?" (Galatians 3:5). Again: "Christ redeemed us from the curse of the law . . . that we might receive the promise of the Spirit through faith" (verses 13–14). And again:

> This is the confidence which we have in him, that if we ask anything according to his will he hears us. And if we know that he hears us in whatever we ask, we know that we have obtained the requests made of him.
>
> 1 John 5:14–15

The emphasis on appropriating the baptism with the Holy Spirit by faith (the unique emphasis of R. A. Torrey) is biblical, fully

respects the sovereignty of God and avoids the gimmicks and manip-
ulations (like tarrying meetings or pressuring people to speak in
tongues) that have marred our joyful reception of God's free gift.
Torrey explained in his book *The Holy Spirit: Who He Is and What He Does:*[5]

> You have taken all the other six steps, and you have come to God
> and asked Him definitely to baptize you with the Holy Spirit (or, to
> fill you with the Holy Spirit, as the case may be). Then ask yourself,
> "Is this petition of mine according to His will?" You know that it is
> because Acts 2:39 and Luke 11:13 say so. Then read I John 5:14,
> "This is the confidence that we have toward Him, that, if we ask any-
> thing according to His will, He heareth us." Then say, "I asked for
> the Baptism with the Holy Spirit, I know that is according to His
> will because God says so in Luke 11:13 and Acts 2:39, therefore, I
> know He has heard me." Then read the fifteenth verse [of 1 John 5],
> "and if we know that He heareth us, whatsoever we ask, we know
> that we have the petitions which we have asked of Him." The peti-
> tion I asked was the Baptism with the Holy Spirit, I know He has
> heard me, I know I have what I asked, I know I have the Baptism
> with the Holy Spirit. And what you thus take upon naked faith in
> the word of God, you shall afterwards have in actual experimental
> possession.
>
> p. 189

It was by accepting the Word of God in "naked faith" that R. A.
Torrey himself received the baptism with the Holy Spirit. This is the
way he told the story:

> I had been a minister for some years before I came to the place where
> I saw that I had no right to preach until I was definitely baptized with
> the Holy Ghost. I went to a business friend of mine and said to him
> in private, "I am never going to enter my pulpit again until I have
> been baptized with the Holy Spirit and know it, or until God in some
> way tells me to go." Then just as far as I could, I shut myself up alone
> in my study and spent the time continually on my knees asking God
> to baptize me with the Holy Spirit. As the days passed, the devil tried
> to tempt me by saying, "Suppose Sunday comes and you are not bap-
> tized with the Holy Spirit, what then?" I replied, "Whatever comes,
> I will not go into my pulpit and preach again until I have been bap-

tized with the Holy Spirit and know it, or God in some way tells me to go; even though I have to tell my people that I have never been fit to preach." But Sunday did not come before the blessing came. I had it more or less definitely mapped out in my mind what would happen; but what I had mapped out in my mind did not happen. I recall the exact spot where I was kneeling in prayer in my study. I could go to the very spot in that house at 1348 N. Adams St., Minneapolis. It was a very quiet moment, one of the most quiet moments I ever knew; indeed, I think one reason I had to wait so long was because it took that long before my soul could get quiet before God. Then God simply said to me, not in any audible voice, but in my heart, "It's yours. Now go and preach."

The Holy Spirit, p. 198

The results were immediate:

I went and preached, and I have been a new minister from that day to this. I was then the pastor of a very small and obscure church. . . . But from that time my field began to wonderfully enlarge until at last I had preached the Gospel around the world and had seen, I suppose, hundreds of thousands converted to Christ.

The Holy Spirit, p. 199

Torrey's greater effectiveness in witnessing to Jesus Christ in a way appropriate to his calling is the one sure mark that the Holy Spirit had indeed started falling upon him.

Later he did have an experience with an emotional dimension:

Some time after this experience (I do not recall just how long after), while sitting in my room one day, that very same room, I recall just where I was sitting, before my revolving bookcase, I do not know whether I was thinking about this subject at all, I do not remember, but suddenly, as near as I can describe it, though it does not exactly describe it, I was struck from my chair onto the floor and I found myself shouting (I was not brought up to shout and I am not of the shouting temperament, but I shouted like the loudest shouting Methodist), "Glory to God, glory to God, glory to God," and I could not stop. I tried to stop, but it was just as if some other power than my own was moving my jaws. At last, when I had succeeded in pulling myself together, I went downstairs and told my wife what had happened. But that was not when I was baptized with the Holy Spirit. I was baptized with the Holy Spirit when I took Him by faith in the naked Word of God. . . .

The Holy Spirit, pp. 199–200

Our Contrasting Experiences

Doug: My gateway into the power of the Holy Spirit for ministry was the result of several years of frustration, seeing poor results flow from everything I did. I had been trained to honor the helping professions, and I followed them more than I followed Jesus. I had received an award from my seminary given to one student each year for an additional post-graduate year of study in Europe. I used that year to do practical work as a psychiatric social worker, to observe how the real professionals bring healing to troubled people.

That was the beginning of my disillusionment. The awareness dawned on me that professionalism does not really have the answers to the deep depravity and evil lodged in human nature.

After moving to Oregon to begin pastoral ministry, my disillusionment and frustration increased. In response to the personal testimony of a woman in my congregation, I began to suspect that the promises of the Bible might be true. I focused especially on the promised Holy Spirit, because my issue at that moment was powerlessness in ministry. At the end of a nine-month, highly rational study of this biblical promise, I gathered a few other Presbyterians and we all asked Jesus to baptize us with the Holy Spirit.

Little happened that night to confirm that God had answered our prayer. Tongues was part of the fulfillment of this prayer, but more important to me was the completely new way of life I began to learn—a life dependent on the guidance and power of the Holy Spirit, empowering me to love people who were hard to love and pray for miracles in their lives. My preaching became more autobiographical—sharing simply with other people the lessons God was teaching me. Others saw authenticity in my life and preaching and became interested.

In other words, the Holy Spirit was showing me how to witness for Christ. It was simple and effective—overcoming by the word of my testimony (see Revelation 12:11).

As I continued to walk by faith, I began also to see signs and wonders, especially healing, flowing from my ministry. But those experiences came some months after I began the walk of faith.

Brad: Some of us may follow the path of receiving the Holy Spirit in raw faith. But for me (and I suspect many others), some immediate evidence of the Holy Spirit's empowerment is graciously given to bolster our faltering faith.

When I asked Archer Torrey to pray that I be baptized in the Holy Spirit, I had little faith that God would do anything. (If anyone had faith, it was Archer and the others who gathered around me to pray.) Later that night came an incredible experience of the power of the Holy Spirit that, when matched with God's Word, helped me understand that God was doing something new in me. This was my gateway, my initiation, into power ministry.

Since then, I have prayed many times for the Holy Spirit to fall on me. Mostly I experience no emotion, just a deep-down certainty that God will indeed put the Holy Spirit on me for power as He promised. It often happens as I stand before a sanctuary full of people or in a power ministry situation. I offer a quiet, confident prayer: *Lord, this is Your work! Please fill me with Your Holy Spirit.* Usually I have no time to take my spiritual or emotional temperature; I must move into the action of preaching, teaching, inviting people to accept Christ, casting out demons or praying for people. I simply go forward expecting the Holy Spirit to do His part.

I have yet to be disappointed. Usually I am astonished and delighted at the results.

So ask and receive in faith. Then step out in a life surrendered to the obedience of faith.

8. Obey!

Doug and I feel the need to add one more step to those elaborated by R. A. Torrey. Acts 5:32 says that the Holy Spirit is given to those who obey God. We also see from Galatians 5:25, which speaks of keeping in step with the Holy Spirit, that after we have asked for His power, the Spirit requires of us practical steps of obedience. We experience His power only when we respond to His leadings.

Like Peter raising up the lame man at the Gate Beautiful, or Elizabeth responding to the Holy Spirit when the birth of her child was announced, there are many ways the Spirit may invite you to action. You may be called to speak in tongues, give a prophetic word, do an act of mercy, witness to a stranger or contribute a gift of money. You may be led to lay hands on someone who is sick or pray for a nation in trouble. Obey and you will see results.

When George Hsu, my co-worker in Taiwan, asked for the baptism with the Holy Spirit, nothing appeared to happen. He received in faith. Several weeks later George and I were ministering at a Presbyterian church not far from the Taipei International Airport. Suddenly a woman fell onto the floor in the grip of an evil spirit. I saw George hesitate, so I shouted to him to come and help. He told me later that as I said, "Come," he made a decision to obey not just my call, but a command of the Holy Spirit to come fling himself into a supernatural power encounter with an evil spirit. As George ran to the woman, he suddenly received a prayer language. I stood back in astonishment and watched him conduct his first deliverance with the power of God on him.

God's power manifests itself as we obey.

In the following chapters, we will explore some of the results of following the Holy Spirit in obedience. One of these results may be tongues. So in the next chapter, we will take a closer look at the role of tongues in the life of a believer. If we do not receive tongues as the "evidence" of the Holy Spirit, what good is this peculiar gift? We believe it brings great value to our walk with Jesus.

What's So Special about Tongues?

Brad: By now I have prayed with hundreds, perhaps thousands, of people to be filled with the Holy Spirit, with many diverse results. Some people weep; others fall to the floor or shout. Some speak in tongues or praise God with great joy. Others prophesy or shake all over or begin to laugh in the Spirit. For many others, nothing observable happens at all.

There is great diversity in the way the Holy Spirit works. Doug and I celebrate this diversity. But some people prefer to reduce the working of the Spirit to one feature we can easily lay hold of and even predict ahead of time. Then we can say, "There! That's the sign of the Holy Spirit. Now you've received the baptism for sure." Such a sign becomes a kind of passport into the fellowship of the truly Spirit-filled.

The gift of tongues, selected by some as the passport, has taken on a taint of controversy it does not deserve. First, tongues are just one manifestation of the Holy Spirit among many in the New Testament (see Mark 16:17–18; 1 Corinthians 12:4–11, 27–31). Second, the book of Acts reveals diverse evidences of "the Holy Spirit upon." Prophecy could have been chosen as the initial evidence just as well as tongues, not to mention extolling God. Here are some evidences recorded:

Manifestation	Incident
Rush of a mighty wind, tongues as of fire, other tongues.	Acts 2:1–4
No sign recorded, but Simon saw something happen.	Acts 8:14–24
Scales fell from Paul's eyes; he preached Jesus as the Son of God. (We know he received the gift of tongues, but there is no mention of his receiving it at this time.)	Acts 9:10–22
Gentiles spoke in tongues, extolled God.	Acts 10:44–48
Ephesian disciples spoke in tongues, prophesied.	Acts 19:6

Getting Past the Controversy

In conferences I often find people open to any gift of the Spirit that God wants to give them—except one. Their feelings about tongues can be traced (as I suggested in chapter 2) to hurtful experiences in which they could not show their ticket into the Spirit-filled life. They were too honest to pretend to have it and too hurt to keep trying to get it when they felt they were not succeeding, and were made to feel ostracized and unworthy among people who did have the ticket. They were not sure whom to blame for this—a cruel God prejudiced against certain people, or other Christians who had something wrong with their teaching.

Doug and I recommend allowing free expression to such buried hurts, and stress our conviction that tongues were never meant to be the only initial evidence of the Holy Spirit. This releases most people from the pressure to perform, takes tongues out of its legalistic light and presents it as a good gift from God.

Why Tongues?

Scholars often point out varieties of tongues in the New Testament. We review these in the following summary:

1. *An actual foreign language* (Acts 2:4)
2. *A heavenly language, a language of prayer* (1 Corinthians 13:1; 14:2, 14–15)
3. *A form of praise* (1 Corinthians 14:15a–17)
4. *When interpreted, a form of prophecy* (1 Corinthians 12:10; 14:13)

The gift of tongues is not evidence *for* the saints but edification *of* the saints—a sort of vitamin for the spirit that, once taken, extends a subtle but healthful influence over many parts of our spiritual lives.

What exactly are these subtle and healthful influences? Doug and I have collected a list of nine benefits from 25 years of experience in using this gift in our own lives and ministries. Here it is, for anyone who questions the value of tongues or wants to seek that gift:

1. Tongues has proven to be *a simple way of learning to obey the leading of the Holy Spirit.* The Spirit works by invitation, not manipulation. He invites you to "yield . . . your members to God as instruments of righteousness" (Romans 6:13). In this the Holy Spirit differs from demonic spirits, who tend to take over our personalities and enslave our wills. The gift of tongues, by contrast, has a voluntary dimension to it in which an inner desire wells up in us to speak in an unlearned language—but we have to go along with it, to be willing to speak out what appears to be childish nonsense, trusting God to form the sounds into words pleasing to Him. Thus a tongue is not "initial evidence" but it can be "initial obedience." It is a good way to learn how to obey God in little things to prepare us for obedience in bigger things.

2. Tongues is *an invitation to enter the Kingdom of God like a child.* It forces us to crucify our need to be intellectually respectable, properly "adult" and worldly wise. God uses tongues to bring us into child-like faith through a doorway of humility—"for to such belongs the kingdom of heaven" (Matthew 19:14).

3. Tongues is *a trans-rational way to let the Holy Spirit pray through us.* When we do not know how to pray for a situation and can find no words in our learned language, we can pray in tongues, as Paul counseled: "We do not know what we ought to pray for, but the Spirit himself intercedes for us with groans that words cannot express" (Romans 8:26, NIV). Though this passage refers to travailing prayer (groaning and weeping in the Spirit), it applies just as well to praying in tongues. Sometimes, for example, Doug or I have been overwhelmed with a tongue that sounds for all the world (as our friend Bob Whitaker puts it) "like a Jewish mama scolding her little children." We sense at times like these that the Holy Spirit is rebuking

demonic spirits, and we do not need to understand what is being said in order for it to be effective.

4. The gift of tongues provides *an inner melody or flow of life that keeps us in touch with God at an intimate level* more or less continuously. Surely this is what Paul meant when he wrote that tongues "edifies" a believer (1 Corinthians 14:4). It is as though my spirit is singing or praying in the inner nature while my outer nature is involved in more mundane pursuits. Tongues enables us to maintain that inner sense of intimacy with God—sometimes more so than with rationally understood prayer.

5. Accordingly, tongues is *the only way we know to pursue Paul's admonition to "pray without ceasing"* (1 Thessalonians 5:17, KJV). It is a great boost to our prayer lives when we arise at 5 A.M. and try to start our morning quiet time. It primes the pump of prayer when our thought processes are still asleep in bed!

6. In healing prayer, counseling ministry or leading groups or congregations, the gift of tongues *opens us up to the influence of the Holy Spirit,* sensitizing us to His leadings. It gets the current flowing not only in prayer, but for other ministries as well.

7. Tongues are *an effective means of spiritual warfare,* especially when we are under spiritual attack or involved in deliverance ministry. Many times, when an evil spirit is holding on and refusing to let go of a person or situation, we gain the victory when we pray at length in tongues. Here the Holy Spirit is using our tongue to win a victory we do not understand. Why God should require or invite prayer of this sort we do not understand, but it is surely what Paul referred to when he told us to "pray at all times in the Spirit" (together with prayers in our natural language) after we have put on the whole armor of God (Ephesians 6:10–18).

8. When spoken out in a public meeting and interpreted by someone, a tongue takes on *a prophetic purpose to edify the Body of Christ* (see 1 Corinthians 14:5). Since a message in tongues is often spoken by the Spirit in praise to God, true interpretation will most likely be addressed to God as a way of pulling the congregation into deeper worship (see verse 2). In this, tongues differs from strict prophecy, which is addressed to people, not God.

9. In evangelism, tongues can *help us cross a language barrier* (see Acts 2:7). Several times while preaching in Mandarin Chinese (which

I labored long and hard to learn), the Holy Spirit has helped me speak that language far more articulately than I learned. This was confirmed by my co-workers, who told me how I suddenly started speaking Mandarin perfectly, where before (and since) I floundered.

How Do We Know It's Tongues?

Doug: What is it like to receive the gift of tongues? Misconceptions prevail. Most people seem to assume it will come—*whomp!*—like a block of language suddenly downloaded into our beings from above.

During our conferences, in which large numbers of people have already opened themselves to the gift of tongues, about half say they experienced some powerful sign or confirmation that the language they were speaking was tongues. The language of the Spirit came rushing out in an unmistakable way or was accompanied by joy, elation or a sense of release. This was Brad's experience.

The other half seem to have had an experience more like mine.

My initial experience of tongues came as a result of a purely rational inquiry into all the Scriptures surrounding the gift of tongues, praying in the Spirit and singing in the Spirit (Acts 2:1–13; 10:46; 19:6; 1 Corinthians 12:10, 30; 13:1; 14:1–40; Ephesians 6:18; Jude 20). This gift, I found, was recommended by the apostle Paul for a variety of reasons. Since I was learning to seek the promises of God and lay hold of them by the prayer of faith, this promise seemed worthy to pray for, along with many others I had discovered in the Bible. It seemed even more worthwhile after I researched the matter back to Augustine's "jubilation" and to the early Church fathers, who mentioned the gift of tongues in the first and second centuries. I decided the gift was for real and that I could profit from it.

So I went to a Pentecostal home prayer group, where a woman prayed for me to be baptized with the Holy Spirit and speak in tongues. She attempted a "repeat-after-me" approach to encourage me to speak in tongues, probably hoping I would speak some syllables to confirm that I was now baptized with the Holy Spirit. This effort yielded no fruit, but I was relieved that she did not grab hold of my tongue and wag it with her hand (which happened to a friend of mine)!

Later a small group of fellow Presbyterians gathered to seek the gift of tongues. During that time I felt an inner urge to speak unknown syllables. It was impossible to tell whether this was self-deception or a genuine move of the Holy Spirit. I had no sensation of divine glory nor any rush of Spirit-language.

I was willing to believe, however, that God wanted to give me a good gift, so as time passed I pressed on, letting my tongue go with whatever syllables came to me. All the while, during my personal quiet time, I was evaluating this experiment to see what good might come of it. All I had to go on was my study of the Scriptures, the early Church fathers and a few testimonies I had heard and read.

After several weeks I began to feel that something real was happening, that my tongue was forming real prayers that took on a life of their own. I could never be sure that what I was speaking was a "tongue of angels" or a real language spoken somewhere on earth. But I did feel it was becoming a good thing for my prayer life and relationship with God. On this basis I kept developing it and was encouraged to believe I had gotten hold of something genuine.

Under the influence of my faith in God's Word, my prayer language has branched out to become the many-sided wonder that Brad and I have described in the preceding pages. These positive and confirmed results have convinced me it is from the Holy Spirit.

Brad: As I prayed for the baptism with the Holy Spirit in Korea, I was seeking intimacy with Christ and empowerment for service. The last thing I wanted was tongues! But it was as if Jesus were right there pouring buckets of liquid love all over me. It was wonderful and delicious. I was caught up in praise and holy laughter. At the same time I started to pray spontaneously in a language I did not know. With my consent but without my volition, I let my tongue go and it fluttered gently by itself. With this there came sounds and words I did not understand. It was as if my joy and desire to speak to God, in order to be expressed adequately, had to transcend the English language. My spirit was being freed from the limits of the rational mind. I knew this was the gift of tongues.

This spontaneous way of receiving tongues is consistent with my personality, for I am a spontaneous sort of person. Doug is more rational and self-controlled, and his way of opening up to tongues is more consistent with his personality.

Many people miss the gift of tongues because they require it to come to them in just the way it came to me. They are unwilling to step out in a prayer of faith, as Doug did, for fear of "making it up."

But even spontaneous people have to will consciously to speak in tongues sooner or later. The rush of exhilaration lasts only a moment; the command to "pray in the Spirit" is a command for always. Like any other kind of prayer (except some satanic prayer), speaking or praying in tongues requires a decision of the will, an act of faith. The old saying is true: God can steer a moving car more easily than a stalled one. Just as it took an act of faith for most of us to learn to pray to God in English, so it takes an act of faith to learn to pray to Him in tongues.

How to Begin

Once we have cleared away misconceptions, looked into what the Scriptures say and examined our motives for wanting the gift of tongues, how can we open ourselves to it?

Let's make it as uncomplicated as we can. We recommend this simple approach:

1. Ask for the gift. Will God give a stone to His child who asks for bread?
2. Stop talking or praying in English or some other learned language. You cannot pray in English and in tongues simultaneously.
3. Wait on God to put in you the *urge* to speak in an unlearned language. A gentle urge is a mark of the genuine leading of God—more so than an overpowering compulsion you cannot resist.

Often people do not open up to this gift at the time they pray or are prayed for. The first person I prayed for to receive tongues was a Chinese student named Helen. When we prayed, nothing happened. We were both disappointed, of course. But she was awakened at two in the morning praying in tongues.

So it is with many. God does not want us to use tongues to impress others. For most of us, tongues is a language most appropriate for private prayer. Accordingly God often gives this gift when we are in our prayer closets with no one else around. There we are free from the pressure of the crowd, the need to please people, the false motives that tug at our hearts and the history of past disappointments. We have only God. We are able to concentrate on Him and offer our tongues to Him in the intimacy of our love for Him.

What if obstacles remain to receiving this gift? Here is a list of ten guidelines for those seeking to open themselves to the gift of tongues, or to those helping others to do so:

1. The gift of tongues requires divine-human cooperation. God gives but we must act (see Acts 2:4).

2. Personalities differ. Some receive spontaneously, others by an act of will.

3. There are a variety of ways of receiving: with the laying on of hands, in worship, while alone in prayer, while in ministry, etc. There is no one way to receive.

4. Respond in obedience to the prompting of the Spirit: Open your mouth and speak.

5. Do not block the gift by speaking your own language. If the Spirit moves you to speak, offer whatever "nonsense" the Spirit gives.

6. Some people find tongues-speaking an emotional experience. For others there is no emotion at all.

7. This gift, like all spiritual gifts, is given in God's sovereign timing, not ours.

8. The Holy Spirit respects our freedom and will. We are in control of our response (see 1 Corinthians 14:32–33).

9. Follow the principles given by Paul in 1 Corinthians 12–14 for the use of tongues and prophecy.

10. Keep growing in the Spirit! The manifestations of the Holy Spirit are not a sign that one has arrived, but a beginning of growing in service in the Kingdom.

Next we will discuss three views of the work of the Holy Spirit in believers.

A Summary: Three Views of the Holy Spirit

Brad and Doug: Now let's see where we have arrived in our understanding of the work of the Holy Spirit in believers.

There are three main ways we can put Scripture together with regard to the empowerment of the Spirit for Christian life and ministry: the traditional Holiness-Pentecostal view, the traditional evangelical view, and what may be called the neo-evangelical view developed from the teaching of R. A. and Archer Torrey. The table on the following page expresses and differentiates among these three views.

The Traditional Holiness-Pentecostal View

The Pentecostal view of the work of the Holy Spirit, which developed primarily after the turn of the century, emphasizes personal holiness and empowerment for service and witness. In these it has made a great contribution to the worldwide Body of Christ. Further, the doctrine of tongues as the initial evidence of the infilling of the Holy Spirit has built expectation that when a person is filled with the Spirit, he or she will see actual, supernatural manifestations. When

Three Views
of the Empowering Work of the Holy Spirit

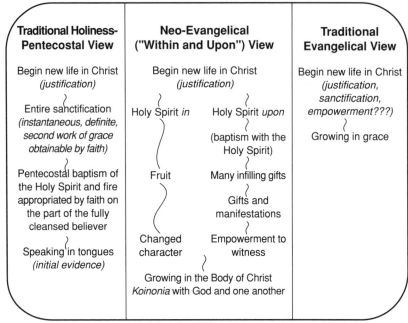

Traditional Holiness- Pentecostal View	Neo-Evangelical ("Within and Upon") View	Traditional Evangelical View
Begin new life in Christ *(justification)*	Begin new life in Christ *(justification)*	Begin new life in Christ *(justification, sanctification, empowerment???)*
Entire sanctification *(instantaneous, definite, second work of grace obtainable by faith)*	Holy Spirit *in* Holy Spirit *upon* (baptism with the Holy Spirit)	Growing in grace
Pentecostal baptism of the Holy Spirit and fire appropriated by faith on the part of the fully cleansed believer	Fruit Many infilling gifts Gifts and manifestations	
Speaking in tongues *(initial evidence)*	Changed Empowerment to character witness Growing in the Body of Christ *Koinonia* with God and one another	

these evidences come, faith is built and the believer is prepared for obedience to God.

But theorizing a "second blessing" that brings a person into "entire sanctification" (see chapter 2), and adding the "initial evidence" of tongues, runs the danger of seeming to create classes or levels of Christians and producing hurt and schism in the Body of Christ. The second-blessing teaching also suggests that something needs to be added to the already completed work of Jesus on the cross.

Look at the chart from the bottom up. If a person speaks in tongues, a Pentecostal may assume that he or she has received Holy Spirit baptism, as well as the second blessing of entire sanctification. The manifestation of tongues is the badge of arrival at both empowerment and the height of sanctification.

Some Pentecostals take it farther. One outspoken woman voiced this steel-trap logic: "Romans 8:9 says, 'Any one who does not have the Spirit of Christ does not belong to him.' If you've never spoken in tongues, you don't have the Spirit, so-o-o. . . ."

Pentecostal and charismatic teachers with more pastoral sensitivity have tried to soften the implications of the view of tongues as initial evidence. But without a theological basis, and without giving up the doctrine itself, they end up sounding as though they are backpedaling, which offers no real resolution.

To put it bluntly, if you believe Pentecostal doctrine about initial evidence, it is difficult to argue against this woman's logic. Such reasoning implies, however, that virtually all Christians who lived prior to 1903 were not real Christians. In these pages, we are trying to find the way out of this simplistic thinking.

The Traditional Evangelical View

The traditional evangelical view has the great strength of emphasizing the completed work of Jesus Christ for our salvation and recognizing Scripture as the sole rule for faith and practice. The evangelical doctrine of the Holy Spirit, grounded firmly in the Reformation teachings of John Calvin and Martin Luther, has focused almost entirely on the Spirit's role of bringing us to Jesus.

Much recent evangelical teaching on the empowering work of the Holy Spirit seems to have been formulated in reaction to the "second blessing, tongues as initial evidence" doctrine of the Pentecostals. The British theologian John Stott (whose teaching is summarized by the third column in the chart) has been a prominent proponent of the evangelical view in recent years:

> In light of all this biblical testimony it seems to me clear that the "baptism" of the Spirit is the same as the promise or gift of the Spirit and is as much an integral part of the gospel of salvation as is the remission of sins. . . . When sinners repent and believe, Jesus not only takes away their sins but also baptizes them with his Spirit.[1]

This view regards the baptism with the Spirit simply as conversion rather than as a gateway to empowerment. It affirms the scriptural truth that there is only one baptism, and that nothing further needs to be added to the finished work of salvation in Jesus Christ. The task of the Christian is to grow in grace—that is, to become more

Christlike. The Spirit's work of empowerment is left ambiguous or assumed to grow out of the process of sanctification.

Those who hold this view understand very well the inner, saving and sanctifying work of the Holy Spirit, but they often seem to neglect the distinctive empowering operations of the Spirit for witness and service.

The tendency of the traditional evangelical view—and its weakness—is to leave a person content with what he or she received at conversion. There is nothing more to be attained (in this view) by a specific appropriation of faith for power in ministry and service. Also, this approach does not adequately account for the biblical witness to the Spirit's empowering work as distinct from His sanctifying work.

By reacting against the Pentecostal view, evangelicals try to assuage the hungering and thirsting of a believer to receive more love and power with a meager diet of doctrine. "You already have it all" may be true in theory—legally, positionally and biblically—but we scarcely notice, apart from a severe crisis, that it is not yet true *in our lives.*

A Neo-Evangelical View: "Within and Upon"

In the third understanding, the Holy Spirit takes up residence within us when we accept Christ's finished work on the cross, and the inner *and* outer operations of the Spirit are available to us from that time on. We are baptized in the name of the Father, Son and Holy Spirit (Matthew 28:19) to indicate we have begun a relationship with all three Persons of the Trinity.

But neither the inner nor outer tracks—"the Spirit within" and "the Spirit upon"—develops automatically. Both involve human cooperation, the obedience of faith (Romans 1:5). A Christian must search the Scriptures, find what God has revealed and seek the fulfillment of His promises in his or her life. We need to grow along both tracks.

We are challenged to ask for intentionally and to appropriate by faith the outer empowerment of the Holy Spirit. The biblical term *baptism with the Holy Spirit* is a legitimate expression to describe the first time this conscious appropriation takes place. Clearly Jesus intended that we rely not on our ability and insights in Christian ministry, but on His power.

The neo-evangelical view sees the empowering dimension of the Holy Spirit's work not as connected with sanctification, but as episodic and available for all Christians. While it is true that some believers are more open to having "the Spirit upon" for power, this does not imply that they are more sanctified than those who are less open.

So it is incumbent on all Christians (since we do not do this naturally) to rely on the Holy Spirit. This is as true of the inner work of the Spirit as it is of the outer. We cannot make ourselves more loving or patient by trying, but in prayer we can seek the power of God for greater purity, love and power in ministry.

In this conception, Christians are not divided into two classes, the "Spirit-filled" and the "non-Spirit-filled." We are all one in Jesus, and by definition all Christians are Spirit-filled. But we open our lives in varying degrees to the different impulses and workings of the Spirit of God. Those who have matured in the character-building virtues of Christ but lack the power gifts in ministry can learn from those who have developed the power gifts, and vice-versa. Rather than defend ourselves against each other, why not learn from each other?

God wants us all to grow in both the character of Christ and in power ministry. A proper understanding of the biblical model (as we have tried to show) will help each of us in the Body of Christ retain balance in the things of the Spirit.

PART 3

Discerning the True from the False

The Ministry of Jesus as Prophet

Brad and Doug: You cannot grow in the inward and outward works of the Holy Spirit without opposition in the spirit realm. Satan the deceiver comes in to thwart the power of God or steal and use it for his own purposes. Jesus Himself, after receiving the Spirit, was led into the wilderness to be tempted by the devil. He was modeling for us the life of a spiritual warrior of the Kingdom of God opposing the kingdom of the prince of this world.

Being filled with the Holy Spirit, therefore, is no risk-free proposition. It does not make us suddenly impervious to the demonic, as many suppose. If anything, we become more of a threat to the evil one than before. So we should seek discernment to distinguish the true from the false in the spiritual realm.

Is the Baptism with the Holy Spirit Dangerous?

Jessie Penn-Lewis, writing from her experience with the Welsh revival in the early years of this century, became painfully aware of the dangers in the baptism with the Holy Spirit. She discusses these in her book *War on the Saints:*

... There are others, who may be described as the advance guard of the Church of Christ, who have *been baptized with the Holy Ghost,* or who are seeking that Baptism; honest and earnest believers, who sigh and cry over the powerlessness of the true Church of Christ, and who grieve that her witness is so ineffective; that Spiritism and Christian Science, and other "isms," are sweeping thousands into their deceptive errors, little thinking that, as they themselves go forward into the spiritual realm, the deceiver, who has misled others, has special wiles prepared for them, so that he might render ineffective their aggressive power against him.[1]

Penn-Lewis mentioned especially the following dangers:

- A narrow, fanatical spirit
- A spirit of literalism and legalism based on Scripture (for Satan knows the Scriptures well!)
- A lack of balance in spiritual gifts
- A want of humility and love that arises from spiritual pride
- An openness to deceptive teaching and cult communities
- Harsh judgment toward other Christians who do not have the same experience of the Holy Spirit

Most of these tendencies amount to a lack of balance between the inner and outer work of the Spirit. Consumed with the power of God for ministry, the novice neglects issues that relate to the heart and to the character of Christ. He or she, having become "spiritual," grows arrogant, hard, judgmental, fanatical and full of darkness that everyone except he or she can observe.

These tendencies, taught Penn-Lewis, come from the evil one, and are a means by which the adversary destroys the Church of Jesus Christ. They are counterfeits designed to keep Christians, in the name of the Holy Spirit, from manifesting both the power and the love of Jesus to a lost and hurting world. They manifest a spirit from which the world shrinks because it is repulsed by it. "If that's God," people say, "I want no part of Him."

Those who have recognized these dangers during past movements of the Holy Spirit may be tempted to give up on the baptism with the Spirit as a bad idea, or lay aside the gifts of the Spirit as just too dangerous to use. But to give in to this temptation is to fall for the very strategy the evil one has devised. He intends that no one find the power of the Holy Spirit, so he can reign on earth unopposed as long as possible until Jesus comes back to unseat him.

To gain a mature appreciation of what the Holy Spirit seeks to accomplish in us, we must turn to Jesus, whose threefold ministry of Prophet, Priest and King models the parameters within which the Spirit works today. By looking to Jesus, we can distinguish the work of the Spirit from that of our own nature or the counterfeits of the evil one.

Let's turn now to Jesus, who will help us understand the Spirit's work as broadly as God understands it, but no more so than He has designed.

Jesus as Prophet, Priest and King

The Holy Spirit is the power ministry of Jesus flowing through the Church. As Jesus Himself said:

> "Believe me when I say that I am in the Father and the Father is in me; or at least believe on the evidence of the miracles themselves. I tell you the truth, anyone who has faith in me will do what I have been doing. He will do even greater things than these, because I am going to the Father."
>
> John 14:11–12, NIV

In the context of this passage, Jesus was going to the Father to send the Holy Spirit. We may also infer from it that the Spirit wants to reproduce in us the ministry of Jesus. The Spirit glorifies Jesus by taking what belongs to Him and giving it to us—which is probably why the apostles called the Holy Spirit "the Spirit of Christ" (Romans 8:9; 1 Peter 1:11) and the "Spirit of Jesus Christ" (Philippians 1:19). Jesus helps us see the work of the Holy Spirit in all its fullness, while teaching us to reject the demonic.

In order to reveal the fullness of God's power on earth, Jesus fulfilled three Old Testament offices:

1. The *prophet,* whose task it was to speak God's word to the people

2. The *priest,* who served as mediator between God and the people
3. The *king,* entrusted with the governance and protection of God's people

Normally each office was filled by one man at a time, although a man was occasionally placed in two offices at once. (Jeremiah, Ezekiel, Isaiah, Zechariah and John the Baptist were of priestly lineage and also filled the prophetic role.) But Jesus came to absorb all three offices into Himself once and for all. John Calvin wrote:

> Therefore, in order that faith may find a firm basis for salvation in Christ, and thus rest in him, this principle must be laid down: the office enjoined upon Christ by the Father consists of three parts. For He was given to be prophet, king, and priest.[2]

As we trace these three ministries in this chapter and the following two, we find that not only did Jesus unite these Old Testament ministries in Himself, but He bequeathed His threefold ministry to us, His Church, through the power of the Holy Spirit. God calls us, like prophets, to be stewards of His Word. He makes us a royal priesthood and a holy nation. And He calls us, like kings, to rule with Christ.

The Holy Spirit has been sent by God to enable us to fulfill these three ministries in the Body of Christ. Let's gaze on the splendid kaleidoscope of the Spirit's works as an extension of the works of Jesus.

Jesus' engagement in the ministry of Spirit-empowered Prophet can be summarized in three points:

1. *Jesus saw deeply into the hearts of men and women* (Luke 7:39; John 4:16).
2. *Jesus interpreted the Law of Moses and called the people to obedience* (Luke 10:25–27). Sometimes this word was geared to specific persons and circumstances (John 4:4–26).
3. *Jesus preached God's word with power and authority* (Mark 1:14–15; Luke 4:18–19, 32).

Corresponding to these points, we can summarize the ministry of prophet in three parts: seeing something as God sees it; speaking to someone else on behalf of God; and preaching or teaching under the anointing of the Spirit. Let's look at each of these in turn.

Glimpsing the Mind of God

Prophetic ministry springs from vision. The prophet is one who, if only momentarily, is given the mind of Christ—*seeing something as God sees it.*

Simon the Pharisee was sharing a meal with Jesus one day when a prostitute burst in and knelt at His feet. "If this man were a prophet," said Simon, "he would know who is touching him and what kind of woman she is" (Luke 7:39, NIV). Simon got that right. What he did not get right was that Jesus, as a prophet, had as much prophetic insight toward Simon as toward the woman of the street. So, as it turned out, Jesus had some surprising and embarrassing words for Simon.

Again, when Jesus spoke to the Samaritan woman at the well, he discerned that she had had five husbands. She responded, "Sir, I perceive that you are a prophet" (John 4:19). Today we often call the kind of insight Jesus had about this woman "a word of knowledge," but whenever we see it in the Scriptures, it comes under the heading of "prophetic insight." (Perhaps we are to regard prophecy as a large category subsuming under its heading many other gifts of the Holy Spirit.)

In any case, Jesus as the ultimate Prophet was given the insight of God toward the people around Him. He was a *nabi*, a seer. Jesus said: "The Son can do nothing by himself; he can do only what he sees his Father doing, because whatever the Father does the Son also does" (John 5:19, NIV). By prayer, Jesus always got the vision for His life from God the Father.

The apostle Paul understood his ministry in much the same way. He claimed to have "the mind of Christ" and that "the spiritual man" could make judgments about all things (1 Corinthians 2:15–16). In other words, prophetic insight—participating in the prophetic seeing of Jesus—was not only Paul's by virtue of apostolic office, but it belongs to every mature ("spiritual") Christian through the Holy Spirit.

This view must be tempered, of course, with the opposite reality— that "we see but a poor reflection as in a mirror," because during the Church age we "know in part," not "fully" (1 Corinthians 13:12, NIV).

But the Holy Spirit can and does bring glimpses into the mind of God, which is the pathway into prophetic ministry.

Joel 2:28–29 affirms that the Holy Spirit coming upon us will enable us to see as the prophets saw. The manifestations of the Spirit that Joel mentioned—seeing visions, dreaming dreams and prophesying—are means by which God gives us "a piece of His mind."

John V. Taylor clearly defines this eye-opening work of the Holy Spirit:

> The Holy Spirit is that power which opens eyes that are closed, hearts that are unaware and minds that shrink from too much reality. If one is open towards God, one is open also to the beauty of the world, the truth of ideas, and the pain of disappointment and deformity. If one is closed up against being hurt, or blind towards one's fellow men, one is inevitably shut off from God also.[3]

The gift of seeing is what distinguished Elisha as a great prophet. When he was surrounded by the army of Syria, he did not fear because he saw an angelic host protecting him, and prayed for his spiritually blind and terrified servant:

> "O LORD, I pray thee, open his eyes that he may see." So the LORD opened the eyes of the young man, and he saw; and behold, the mountain was full of horses and chariots of fire round about Elisha.
>
> 2 Kings 6:17

In the same way, the Holy Spirit opens spiritual eyes to see what God is doing. Only as we "see" can we know the way to follow Jesus Christ.

Brad: God uses divine prophecy—through which He gives us a glimpse of something as He sees it—and asks us to pray, speak and obey it into reality. We can then cooperate with God to create something new.

In December 1992, during an intensive period of intercessory prayer for the healing of wounds left from the Tiananmen Square massacre in China, the Holy Spirit gave me a glimpse of what was on God's mind. It was as though my heart would break for the Chinese people. I saw the faces of the young students being obliterated by Communist tanks and guns. I felt God's love for these youthful democracy fighters, and His yearning for them to know His peace and freedom.

This burden grew into three visions. In the first, a team of people from Taiwan, Canada and the U.S. was joined with mainland Chinese Christians in a seminary or university setting. I saw the eager faces of young students and old people alike, learning together God's ways in ministry. The focus was on leadership development so the Chinese Church could disciple new believers.

The second vision was set in the context of a sterile government office building. The place was filled with government and Communist Party workers asking questions excitedly about Christ.

In the third vision, we found ourselves in an open field with people jammed together to the horizon. It was a large-scale evangelistic meeting where, through powerful preaching, thousands were brought to Christ.

After I received these overwhelming visions, I felt the Holy Spirit say, *Get ready; you are going.*

When, Lord? I asked. *And how?*

I got no answer, only the awareness that God was birthing a vision. My role was to pray it into reality and be ready to obey.

As I write these words in 1995, three years after the visions, I am sitting on an airplane bound for Hong Kong on my way to mainland China. God has just opened a door for the fulfillment of the first vision by creating an opportunity to teach on the Holy Spirit at a government-sanctioned seminary in China. I am convinced that this is just the beginning of what was glimpsed in the vision. Prophetic vision is not just predicting the future. Rather, it invites us to share in God's creation of the future.

Speaking God's Word with Power

Doug: Those who receive divine insight may be called to speak it to someone else. The second element in prophetic ministry, then, is *speaking on behalf of God.* Sometimes this takes the form of a carefully guided word of encouragement, correction or counsel (as Jesus gave to Simon the Pharisee and the Samaritan woman).

The first time I met Brad Long was at a conference sponsored by Presbyterian & Reformed Renewal Ministries International at Montreat, North Carolina, in November 1989. The conference had disappointed me and I was not looking for much the last day. But during an introductory talk Brad gave, I felt God say, *I am going to use Brad Long to renew the Presbyterian churches.*

I felt I was supposed to tell Brad, although he was a complete stranger. Also, I rarely have such words for people, am something of an introvert and am suspicious when people have such words for me. Nevertheless, I obeyed the leading.

What I did not know was that Brad had come from a successful, fulfilling ministry in Taiwan to an American organization in decline. Once he came on board, he saw financial need, demoralization, a dwindling mailing list and a lack of vision that was being played out at the very conference we were attending. As a result he was going through a crisis of self-doubt. Though he had been invited to be executive director of PRRMI, he was thinking at that moment of telling the board of directors he had made a mistake in accepting.

I did not know these things, but, as it turned out, a prophetic word coming from a stranger strengthened Brad at an important moment and birthed a relationship between us that has prospered in ways we could never have foreseen. In particular God has used our friendship to develop the Dunamis Project, a leadership development seminar in which we teach church leaders how to rely on the power of God in ministry. And out of the Dunamis Project has come a series of books, including this present volume and our first one, *The Collapse of the Brass Heaven.* All this began when God required me to speak a prophetic and encouraging word to a man I did not know.

Events since then have confirmed the word to be true, for God has opened doors all over the world for Brad to bring renewal to Presbyterian and Reformed churches.

Brad: Several years later I had another opportunity to experience the dramatic effect of participating in the second element of prophetic ministry, speaking on behalf of God. In April and May 1995, two PRRMI mission teams went to New Zealand. Our time concluded with a conference sponsored by Presbyterian Renewal Ministries of New

Zealand prior to the annual General Assembly of the Presbyterian Church of New Zealand. Over 150 pastors and representatives from all over New Zealand attended. The evening meetings were packed.

On Saturday night the Holy Spirit, through prophecy, called the group to confess sin in the church. From my prayer journal for Saturday, May 14:

I was supposed to preach on the infilling with the Holy Spirit, and Ken was to share something about inner healing. We never got around to it, for during the worship the Holy Spirit fell on the people. First a word came saying we were to give Christ back His Church. This drove all of us to our knees for an extended period of confession for the way we had imposed our own agendas or been afraid to go forward with Christ's agenda. The silence was deep and full, and in it many wept.

Then came a series of prophetic words that told us of areas that needed to be dealt with. One sister had a vision of chains holding down the Presbyterian Church of New Zealand. Someone else discerned that this was Scottish traditionalism as well as Freemasonry. These words, spoken with an anointing of the Holy Spirit, found their mark.

In response, one of the pastors stood and shared that he had been involved heavily in Freemasonry. He had even been invited past the 30th degree to be made a "grand prince of darkness." He also told of the practice of offering adoration to "Ja Ba La," a syncretistic god whose name had apparently been composed of the names of Jehovah, Baal and the Egyptian god Rah.

He said he had seen nothing wrong with being a Presbyterian minister and a Freemason until he was baptized with the Holy Spirit. The Spirit awakened a deeper faith in Jesus Christ and showed him he could no longer be a Christian and a Mason.

Then this pastor asked all those in the room who had been or were involved in Freemasonry to stand up. To our amazement, about half the room stood. There followed powerful prayers of confession and renunciation. Then I read through Tom White's prayer for renouncing and breaking demonic strongholds.

As we went through the prayer corporately, things started to happen. Many pastors went to their knees or fell on their faces in confession and repentance. Others started to get very uncomfortable as evil spirits were driven into the light. A number of people experienced deliverance from evil spirits that night. There followed a time of silence broken only by muffled sobs.

I discerned that a *kairos* moment of opportunity had come, so out of obedience, I prayed that the Holy Spirit would come upon the group in power, then invited the PRRMI New Zealand board and the American team to come forward so they could pray for people. As they were coming forward, I spoke the words of prophecy I felt the Lord had given me: "My people, I am pouring the Holy Spirit out upon you, so that you may be empowered and equipped to be My witnesses at this General Assembly and in your churches."

While the ministry teams were still gathering at the front, the Holy Spirit fell on the whole group. It was incredible! Manifestations started all over the packed sanctuary. A wave of the Holy Spirit came over me and I found myself going down. It was so refreshing and I was so tired that I let myself go into God's grace and presence. When I got up, power ministry was taking place all over the room. Apparently, now that the counterfeit had been cleared away, it was time for God's true power to appear.

We prayed for people eager to be filled with the Holy Spirit until around midnight. There were all sorts of manifestations. Some had holy laughter; many went down on the floor overcome by the Spirit. There was a release of tongues and prophecy. Most important was the strong awareness that God was wonderfully at work empowering His people.

Prophetic Preaching

Doug: The Holy Spirit equips us not only for power encounters like that, but in a broader sense for everyday ministry in local churches. Most of us recognize inspired preaching when we hear it—and we know what uninspired preaching sounds like as well! The third element in prophetic ministry is *Holy Spirit—anointed preaching and teaching that bring the Kingdom of God to people.* In this more general unfolding of the mind of God, He reveals His nature, commands, promises and plans through pastors and teachers gifted by the Holy Spirit to fill people week after week with a vision of the Kingdom of heaven.

Donald Gee, a Pentecostal pastor, saw two of the gifts of the Spirit listed in 1 Corinthians 12, the word of knowledge and word of wisdom, as pastoral gifts. They represent the Spirit-given ability, he wrote, to convey the knowledge of the things of God and their application to human life; and they are given in particular to pastors and other disciplers—those given to oversee others by the great Shepherd of our souls.

> There come times when the Spirit of revelation is so operating through a teacher exercising an anointed ministry that we become conscious of an illumination transcending all natural ability either to gain or to impart. It is in such hours that the sheep hear the voice of their Good Shepherd speaking through human lips, even as the early Christians of Asia had heard Christ speaking and had been taught by Him at Ephesus (Eph. 4:20, 21). We know it because our hearts burn within us as surely as theirs did upon the Emmaus road when the risen Christ "expounded unto them in all the scriptures the things concerning himself."[4]

Ordinary preaching, when empowered by the Holy Spirit, can take on a prophetic quality, as though God Himself were speaking into the congregation, ministering His knowledge and wisdom to people's hearts. It is said of Jesus, "They were amazed at his teaching, because his message had authority" (Luke 4:32, NIV).

When people come to our churches, they are often looking for a word from God that will catch them up and speak to their hearts. It is, above all else, our failure to speak such words that causes the present generation to look elsewhere to satisfy its spiritual longings. We have forsaken the authenticity of the Holy Spirit in favor of the allure of philosophies that will appeal to the world. The young sense we are giving them what they already have, so they look elsewhere for what they lack.

Yet God still holds out to us the anointing of the Holy Spirit, who longs to use us as mouthpieces to invite the next generation to feast with Jesus.

The Ministry of Jesus as Priest

Brad and Doug: We have seen that Jesus Christ united three Old Testament ministries in Himself, then bequeathed this threefold ministry to His Church through the power of the Holy Spirit. We saw that the three offices of Christ as Prophet, Priest and King provide the parameters within which we may expect the Holy Spirit to work today; and that God calls us, like prophets, to be stewards of His Word.

In this chapter we find that God enables us, through the power of the Spirit, to be a royal priesthood and a holy nation.

Jesus Christ, as Spirit-empowered Priest, fulfilled four tasks that emanated from the Temple under the Old Covenant:

1. *Jesus fulfilled the Old Testament sacrificial system by giving Himself as the offering for sin* (Leviticus 1:2–17; Hebrews 9:11–14, 22). The result: Jesus forgives sin and reconciles sinners to God (Luke 7:48–50; 2 Corinthians 5:17–21).
2. *Jesus gave thanks and praise to God, ministering to God as the Old Covenant priests were to do* (1 Corinthians 11:24).
3. *Jesus heals and cleanses all who are sick* (Luke 5:12–14, 18–25; Romans 8:19–23; Revelation 21:1–4; 22:1–5).

4. *Jesus intercedes with the Father for us* (Isaiah 53:12; Romans 8:34; Hebrews 7:25, 9:24; 1 John 2:1).

Let's look at each of these tasks.

1. A Sacrifice for Sin

In the Old Testament, blood was required to atone for sin. So the first task of the priest was offering sacrifices on behalf of the people. But on the cross Jesus offered Himself as the Lamb of God, a sacrifice without blemish, the atonement for our sin.

The sacrifice of Jesus was a finished work. Neither the Holy Spirit nor you nor I can add anything to it. Yet this sacrifice would be wasted if the Holy Spirit did not bring it home to people in each succeeding generation.

Apart from the work of the Spirit, people defend themselves against the idea of sin, feeling God is likely to infringe on their freedom to do as they like. They are not convinced of their sin or their need for God's forgiveness. For them the death of Jesus is an irrelevant detail of history. But when the Holy Spirit convicts them of sin and their need for forgiveness, the atonement of Jesus finds its mark.

Normally, in the convicting work of the Holy Spirit, He leads unbelievers to places where the Gospel is being declared or shared. The speaker speaks and the Spirit convicts, in a cooperative work. The speaker becomes a mediator between a lost soul and his or her Creator. And here is where the first of our priestly tasks comes in— *pointing to Jesus as the sacrifice for sin.*

The Holy Spirit convicted large numbers of people on the Day of Pentecost in Jerusalem, when Peter stood up and invited the crowd to accept the atoning sacrifice of Jesus. "Repent," he said, "and be baptized every one of you in the name of Jesus Christ for the forgiveness of your sins; and you shall receive the gift of the Holy Spirit" (Acts 2:38). And later:

> "Repent, then, and turn to God, so that your sins may be wiped out, that times of refreshing may come from the Lord, and that he may send the Christ, who has been appointed for you—even Jesus."
>
> Acts 3:19–20, NIV

Peter, filled with the Holy Spirit, was acting as a priest, bringing the forgiveness of God to people who formerly had seen no need for it but now were "cut to the heart" (Acts 2:37).

The Conviction of Sin

The conviction of sin is one of the most consistent elements of spiritual awakenings, when large numbers of people are led to seek the redemption made available by Jesus through the cross. But the conviction of sin is the work of the Holy Spirit, not a contrivance of human oratory.

Many people believe that Jonathan Edwards' sermon "Sinners in the Hands of an Angry God," a classic of American history, was a fire-and-brimstone word delivered with eloquence and scorching condemnation. It was not. Edwards, wearing his granny glasses, delivered it in his usual scholarly, ultra-Congregationalist style. The response was as much a surprise to him as the entire Great Awakening that flowed in its wake, which Edwards recorded in his book *A Faithful Narrative of the Surprising Works of God.*

The point? Conviction of sin depends not on hellfire preaching but on the power of the Holy Spirit. During the Great Awakening the Holy Spirit used Jonathan Edwards and other preachers of the time as "priests" to reconcile a generation of Americans to their God. We have only to look to David Brainerd to see this point.

Brainerd was a contemporary of Edwards (he would have been Edwards' son-in-law if his life had not been cut short), a man of prayer intent on bringing the Gospel to the native tribes of the Eastern seaboard. No fire-and-brimstone preacher, he focused on the love of God and God's divine favor—for the members of his audience, as he wrote,

> . . . have almost always appeared much more affected with the comfortable than the dreadful truths of God's Word. That which has distressed many of them under conviction is, that they found they wanted, and could not obtain, the happiness of the godly. At least, they have often appeared to be more affected with this than with the terrors of hell. But whatever be the means of their awakening, it is plain, numbers are made deeply sensible of their sin and misery, the wickedness and stubbornness of their own hearts, their utter inability to help them-

selves or to come to Christ for help without divine assistance; and so are brought to see their perishing need of Christ to do all for them, and to lie at the foot of sovereign mercy.[1]

When the Holy Spirit does His work in answer to prayer, He is as likely to use a sermon on God's love as on His judgment. And once again, the Spirit uses human instruments to stand between people and God to bring the word of reconciliation. Here Jesus bequeaths to us His priestly ministry and empowers us to fulfill it by the Holy Spirit.

Some Christian college campuses have experienced the genuine conviction of the Holy Spirit recently. At Wheaton College, for example, during the week of March 23, 1995, large numbers of students lined up at the chapel microphone to confess personal sin. The lines were so long that the confession could not be completed in one night, so more chapel services were scheduled, each one extending into the wee hours of the morning.

In past revivals, like those at Asbury College, students involved in such a cleansing work were anointed by the Holy Spirit to bring the same spirit of confession to other groups. They had only to go and speak of what had happened to them in order to see the same profound confession of sin break out in a new place. Revival would spread like fire touching a dry field.

Wherever the Holy Spirit moves and revives people, He invites the Church into her role as a royal priesthood, drawing people into accepting the forgiveness and grace of God.

2. Praise and Thanksgiving

The priestly role, besides offering sacrifice for sin, included *praising God and giving Him thanks.* Jesus fulfilled this office many times, but especially on the night He was betrayed. As the hour approached in which His life would be sacrificed, He gave thanks and broke bread (as we remind ourselves in the sacrament of Communion). Some traditions honor this event by calling this sacrament the Eucharist. *Eucharistas* means thanksgiving. In the Upper Room with the disciples, Jesus offered the ultimate act of worship by expressing His love for the will of God as over against His will for self-preservation. He thanked God "in all circumstances" (1 Thessalonians 5:18), even that of His approaching death.

Worshiping God "in spirit and truth" (John 4:24), by which we come to love Him above ourselves, is a ministry of the Holy Spirit to God the Father and God the Son. The Spirit pays tribute to Jesus and the Father through us (John 16:14). So once again Jesus has taken the ministry of the Old Testament priesthood, drawn it up into Himself and passed it on to us by His Spirit.

This ministry of the Spirit transforms the worship of God from dry, religious duty to the daily refreshment of communicated love. Worship becomes a privilege. Thanksgiving brings transforming power, pushing away darkness and inviting the presence of God.

3. Healing and Reconciliation

The saving work of Jesus leads directly into a third priestly task: *the ministry of healing and reconciliation.* In being reconciled to God at the cross, Jesus beckons to us to treat each other like family—the way He Himself did when He said to the apostle John, "Behold, your mother!" and to His mother, "Behold, your son!" (John 19:26–27). God will not be satisfied until He has brought "all things in heaven and on earth together under one head, even Christ" (Ephesians 1:10, NIV), thus healing our divisions and strife.

Accordingly, an important dimension of the Spirit's work today is reconciliation in the Body of Christ through Christ's work on the cross. He is confronting us with racism, denominationalism and other cultural separations that have split the Church. John Dawson and Jean Steffenson of the International Reconciliation Coalition teach identificational repentance, in which representatives of one group confess the historic sins of their group to other racial and cultural groups, and find healing in the process. The Holy Spirit today is bringing about reconciliation, as Christians are called to be mediators between groups that have sinned against each other.

Brad: New Zealand has a long and dismal history of government violation of the native aboriginals, the Maoris. Whites have broken treaties, appropriated land unjustly and massacred the Maoris. To complicate matters, Maori subtribes have their own history of wars and injustice. And in the past they have participated in cannibalism of one another.

On a mission trip in 1995, at a renewal service at St. Giles Presbyterian Church in Rotorua, my co-worker, Ken Shay, taught on the need for corporate healing as a way to pull the ground out from under Satan. Conferees agreed that wherever sin remains unconfessed, the Church is struggling. In addition, New Age spirituality and traditional worship of Maori gods still provided alternatives to the worship of Jesus as Lord.

After Ken's teaching, people started making observations about their history and the nature of the demonic strongholds over their area. A woman from the Cook Islands stood up and told of the fear she felt at seeing a Maori Tiki (an object reputed to have occult power) that had been erected at one of the scenic lakes in Rotorua.

"We people from the Cook Islands are Christians," she said, her voice shaking. "Our only 'Tiki' is Jesus. Why are the Maori raising up these other Tikis? These Tikis frighten me. Each time I go by that place, I am gripped by fear. There is something evil there!"

As she said this, it was as if an evil presence moved through the room, and a shudder of fear went through the group. Both Westerners and Islanders felt we had exposed a demonic stronghold hidden behind traditional symbols that have been allowed a foothold because of past injustice.

Right afterward, a meek Scottish lady stood and confessed, with tears, that she had grown up in New Zealand despising the Maoris. Sobbing, she asked forgiveness from the two Maoris present. Then a group of whites and people from the Islands gathered at the front of the church confessing past sins and injustices toward the Maoris. The two Maoris present also came forward, confessing their people's sins of cannibalism, worshiping false gods and hating the whites and Islanders. Nearly everyone was crying; they ended up hugging each other.

After Ken offered some words of forgiveness, we began to celebrate. Everyone in the room was conscious that a spiritual transaction had taken place—one that removed fear, hostility and opposition to the Gospel. Christians were becoming mediators to bring healing among the people groups of New Zealand. We were learning to be a royal priesthood—part of the role Jesus gives us by the Holy Spirit.

A Mandate to Heal

Doug: We know from the Scriptures that "all who touched [Jesus] were healed" (Matthew 14:36, NIV; Mark 6:56). After Jesus went away, He sent the Holy Spirit in His place as an earnest or down payment toward the full and complete healing He will bring at the close of the age. Thus the Old Testament ministries of *healing* and *cleansing,* which God gave the Old Covenant priesthood, Jesus drew up into His own Person, then conferred on the Church.

Healing takes many forms because our wounds take many forms. Every pastor quickly finds that most people carry inside them many wounds and traumas that diminish their effectiveness in witness and ministry.

My wife, Carla, suffered from a fear of church people and churches—a real hindrance in her role as pastor's wife! We traced this situation back to traumas she experienced growing up as a pastor's kid. In one troublesome situation, her father suffered an emotional breakdown. She could not forget the memory of him preaching that Sunday, alternately laughing and crying in the pulpit. Although this trauma had happened many years before, the memory affected her relationships with people in the present.

I spent time with Carla in prayer and helped her lift that painful memory to Jesus. Jesus appeared in the memory and began to change it. *Go out and play,* He said to her. *This is too much for you, and it is not your responsibility. Just go out and play.*

As a result, Carla was able to surrender the traumatic event to Jesus and yield responsibility for it to Him. Today her anxieties have been vastly reduced.

My role was a priestly one. The Spirit of Christ entered with power to heal her pain, and I was the mediator, the priest of her healing.

4. Intercessory Prayer

The fourth priestly ministry that Jesus drew up into Himself and then gave the Church through the Holy Spirit was the ministry of the intercessor. Peter and John were astonished at the prayer life of Jesus; they could not understand it (see Mark 1:35–37). It was nothing like the priests at the Temple. What they came to realize was that Jesus was behaving as the true High Priest, while the high priestly dynasty headed up by the perverse snake Annas at the Temple had little if anything to do with God. It was part of a Sadduceean political party that did not even believe that God acts and moves with power.

Jesus, by contrast, was so genuine in His prayer life that the disciples eventually recognized His priestly calling and asked Him, "Teach us to pray." He did, and they responded after the dark events of Golgatha by investing much time together agreeing in prayer (see Acts 1:14).

Prayer itself is a work of the Holy Spirit—motivated, guided and brought to completion by the Spirit. One does not need to pray in tongues to pray giftedly as the Holy Spirit impels and guides. God can pour out "a spirit of compassion and supplication," as the prophet Zechariah prophesied (12:10). In other words, the Holy Spirit births in us the compassion of God for some person or city or nation that is in sin and bondage, and we cry out to God with tears for them, just as Jesus did while on earth, and as He continues to do as Intercessor.

When prayer is being birthed by the Spirit of God, it can grow into deep travail, almost like a woman in labor. We have the sense in such moments that God is birthing something important, something new, and we are standing with Jesus in the holy place in heaven, praying with the High Priest in words and thoughts given by the Holy Spirit.

The Christian churches have endured a long season of prayerlessness brought on by a Western worldview that excludes God and the spiritual realm. Today the Holy Spirit is calling the people of Jesus back into prayer. He is calling us to be a house of prayer. He is building us into a royal priesthood and a holy nation.

In the next chapter we will look at the third of the Old Testament ministries. God calls us, like kings, to rule with Christ.

Reigning with Jesus the King

Brad: When Jesus first came, according to the prophecy of Daniel, He established the Kingdom of God:

> "In the time of those kings [the Romans], the God of heaven will set up a kingdom that will never be destroyed, nor will it be left to another people. It will crush all those kingdoms and bring them to an end, but it will itself endure forever."
>
> Daniel 2:44, NIV

So Jesus, the Son of David, came not only as Prophet and Priest but as anointed King, preaching, "The kingdom of God is near. Repent and believe the good news!" (Mark 1:15, NIV). The Kingdom Jesus proclaimed is where He Himself rules (Luke 8:19–21; 17:20–21; John 3:5).

His authority as King manifested itself, while He was on earth, in three ways: by His power to call people to obey God; by His power over demons who rebel against God; and by His power to command the forces of nature. Here is a summary of these three dimensions of kingly power, which we will look at one by one:

1. *Jesus calls men and women to follow and obey Him* (Mark 1:16–20).
3. *Jesus routs the kingdom of Satan* (Luke 11:20; Matthew 12:28).
4. *Jesus exercises authority over nature* (Luke 8:22–25; John 11).

Calling People to Obey Christ

There are times the Holy Spirit calls us to follow Jesus in His kingly ministry, *inviting people to obey Him*—and our words have such power that they respond!

During the PRRMI mission trip to New Zealand that I mentioned in the last chapter, I found myself empowered to express this dimension of Jesus' kingly office. One evening I preached to a packed sanctuary to which church people had brought non-Christian friends. I preached on *kairos* moments as the key to moving into power ministry.

Then I sensed the Lord saying, *Now tell them about the greatest* kairos *moment of all—the opportunity to accept My Son, Jesus, and receive eternal life.*

Jim Wallace, president of Presbyterian Renewal Ministries in New Zealand, and I both gave a bold invitation. Our words, I sensed, had power, and I could tell they were finding a mark in the congregation, summoning people to the feet of Jesus.

During the ministry that followed, numbers of non-Christians came forward to accept Jesus Christ as their Lord and Savior. Many had seen evidence of God's power for the first time that night. As Jim put it, "When people see the power of God at work in signs and wonders, they are led right into a power encounter with Jesus. The result is salvation."

Most of these people had never been in a church and scarcely knew what to ask for when they came forward. As for me, I was aware of a mystery: God was calling to people He loved, inviting them to begin to learn how to obey His commands.

One man in particular stands out in my memory—a completely pagan Englishman responding to the inner urging of the Holy Spirit for the first time. Jim led him in a prayer for salvation. Then he asked us to pray for healing for a medical condition. We laid hands on him and began to pray. Suddenly a look of surprise and terror came across his face. He was going down. He tried to catch himself, but it was too late and he fell to the floor.

For about twenty minutes he rested in the Spirit. Upon recovering his feet, he turned to Jim and said, "Man, this is better than beer!"

Then he was surrounded by a group of young people who began to instruct him in the ways of Christ. The elders of the church invited him to a discipleship group, where over the next weeks and months he began to be discipled systematically in the ways of Christ, and taught how to obey Jesus as his sovereign Lord and King.

Routing the Kingdom of Satan

The effects of Jesus' Kingship and authority as He walked this earth could be seen through demonic manifestations and the people being set free from demonic bondage. When some accused Jesus of driving out demons by Beelzebub, He set the phenomenon in its proper kingly perspective: "If I drive out demons by the Spirit of God, then the kingdom of God has come upon you" (Matthew 12:28, NIV).

Through us Jesus continues the second dimension of His kingly work: *setting the captives free from Satan's kingdom and claiming them for His own.* In a day when New Age spirituality fascinates more and more young people in Western nations, there is a corresponding need for deliverance from demons. Churches must acquaint themselves with spiritual warfare in general and with deliverance ministry in particular.

One Sunday morning I was preaching at St. John's Presbyterian Church in Palmiston North on the North Island of New Zealand. The sanctuary was packed with young people. During the service a young man started to thrash around and grimace horribly. As I approached him and started to pray, his face contorted with rage and his hands twisted and went for my throat. If he had not been restrained, I think he would have tried to strangle me. He told me afterward that as the evil spirit manifested itself, he was overcome with a murderous hatred of Jesus Christ and of me.

I began to command the spirits to leave. An intense struggle followed while the young man writhed on the floor. The pastor and I called the group of people who had gathered around to quit gawking and start praying. As we all prayed for deliverance, we could feel the power and presence of God filling the place and the demonic power giving way. Finally, in the name of Jesus, I commanded the spirits to leave. They gave a final shriek. The young man retched violently and the spirits left.

Soon he was in his right mind. In great joy he went jumping around the church (yes, a Presbyterian church!) shouting that he was set free.

Needless to say, this manifestation of the power of God over Satan had a significant effect on most of the young people in the sanctuary. All glorified Jesus that day with fervency, and many, including the once-demonized man, were brought to a new level of commitment to Jesus Christ.

Asserting Jesus' Kingship through casting out demons from afflicted individuals is not just an isolated act of compassion, but the visible result of battles in the spiritual realm, as the Kingdom of Jesus routs the kingdom of Satan.

Higher-Level Warfare

The Body of Christ has also been given the power to do battle with demonic principalities over larger areas, such as churches, towns or cities. Here we are battling not private demons but strongholds that create industries out of sin and the perversion of justice.

Binding the Strong Man

The power of the Christian community to hinder satanic strength is reflected in the words of Jesus in Luke 11:21–22 (NIV):

> "When a strong man, fully armed, guards his own house, his possessions are safe. But when someone stronger attacks and overpowers him, he takes away the armor in which the man trusted and divides up the spoils."

If deliverance ministry is "dividing up the spoils," then binding up the strong man so his house may be plundered may be called higher-level spiritual warfare. Both levels of warfare reflect Jesus' kingly work. We are called and empowered by the Holy Spirit to share in both levels, and the gates of hell cannot prevail against us.

In recent years, through the work of Peter Wagner, Tom White, George Otis, Jr., Ed Silvoso, Cindy Jacobs and others, the Church has become more aware of higher-level spiritual warfare. Often this warfare is needed to prepare for the advancement of the Gospel. Experience from the front lines of missions reveals that until demonic strongholds are crushed by prayer, the people in an area cannot truly hear the Gospel. This recognition has led to spiritual mapping— research that uncovers spiritual obstacles to revival in a particular place—and intentional actions by Christians to pull the rug out from under evil spirits by confession and reconciliation.

Although this form of high-level spiritual warfare is invisible and takes place, for the most part, in the heavenly realms, it yields very tangible, earthly results.

The Sins of People Groups

Pastor Jim Logan has a vision of building an interracial church in Charlotte, North Carolina—a city notorious for its murder rate in the black community—as a testimony to God's reconciling love. Yet in the fall of 1995, the vision seemed to be blocked.

About this time, Peterson Sozi from Uganda and I joined Jim in conducting a special evening service at his church, South Tryon Presbyterian in Charlotte. I was the only white person present.

At the end of the worship service, the Holy Spirit led us into strategic intercessory prayer for the neighborhood. I received a spiritual impression that something about the land in the past had given ground to strongholds of racial hatred. I spoke this out to the group.

Jim had felt the same thing, he said, and added that the area in which the church was located had been "for whites only" in the Old South.

As we started to pray against this stronghold, a disconcerting realization came to me: My ancestors in colonial days had received a large land grant from the king of England that had at one time included a large portion of the county in which this church was located. Furthermore, my mother remembers rows of cabins on our family farm that had once housed slaves. While I could not be certain of a direct connection with this exact area, the spiritual connection could not be denied.

I sensed the Holy Spirit saying, *You must confess the sins of your ancestors who helped build the stronghold of racial hatred in North Carolina. This is a strong man and he must be bound. The way to start is through identificational repentance.*

The Holy Spirit was leading me to identify with a people group, white Southerners, and repent on their behalf in the presence of another group, the descendants of black slaves.

I fought an inward battle, not wanting to face up to my family's responsibility. But finally I asked Jim (an African-American) and Peterson (an African) to come lay hands on me. As they did, I told the congregation of my family background. Then I asked for forgiveness. It was humiliating yet liberating.

A number of people gathered around me, weeping and saying they forgave me. Then they asked forgiveness for their hatred of white people, which I extended. Then we moved back into spiritual warfare prayer. And as we did, we felt something begin to break.

It is too soon at this writing to evaluate the results in Jim's church, but we expect to see it grow in numbers and also to become increasingly interracial.

Exercising Authority over Nature

Doug: In, through and for Jesus all things were made. He is Master of the universe, involved in its creation from the start. And as the disciples learned (to their astonishment), He commands even the wind and sea.

From time to time this same King Jesus, who rules over creation, invites us to participate, through the Holy Spirit, in the third dimension of kingly ministry: *seeing the power of God over nature manifested in the midst of believing and praying Christians.*

Danny Peck, a Sunday school teacher in my church and the father of two, is loved by children and adults alike. Six years ago Danny was diagnosed with testicular cancer. I assembled the church to pray for him, seeing a crisis like this as an opportunity, not a tragedy, and the cancer as a challenge to our faith.

Danny went through a long struggle with chemotherapy and was subjected to many fearsome visits to the hospital and doctor's office. In this God was dealing with a basic weakness of fear in Danny's life. After many months, whether from the chemotherapy or massive doses of prayer, the "markers" revealed no trace of cancer remaining in Danny's body. His doctor made it very clear, however, that he would never have any more children.

A year later Danny announced that his wife was pregnant with their third child. Under the circumstances it was clear to all of us that God did not want us to attribute Danny's healing to chemotherapy. God had reversed the decision of nature to show that He, not the doctor, was in charge.

Today Danny, still free from cancer, and little Benjamin are evidence of Jesus' power over nature. We wonder if there will not be some very special calling on Benjamin's life.

Brad: Sometimes on the mission field, God alters the course of nature in order to advance His Kingdom.

An evangelism team from Youth With A Mission accompanying Dr. Charles Kraft to Taiwan in 1987 reported an incident that had occurred on their recent crusade in Hong Kong. The crusade had been planned for months and was expected to draw large crowds. Yet the day of the event was threatened with cancellation because of a typhoon headed directly toward Hong Kong.

That afternoon, as the winds built to gale force, the ministry team struggled to the top of a hill, where they prayed in the Spirit, asking God to intervene so the crusade could go forward and the Gospel of Jesus be proclaimed.

Then came the Holy Spirit's command, *Now rebuke the winds just as Jesus did in the boat.*

The leader of the group, a carpenter from Portland, stood into the wind and, in the name of Jesus, commanded the typhoon to turn away. As he did so (he told the team later), he sensed something strange, as if a malignant force that was more than wind lashed out at him. He felt a shot of terror go through him as he realized he was in a face-to-face confrontation with demonic power. Boldly he continued to rebuke the winds in the name of Jesus Christ.

Several hours after this power encounter, the winds subsided and the typhoon turned out to sea.

The crusade went on as planned and provided an occasion for the powerful preaching of the Gospel with signs and wonders that brought many to salvation. Once again Jesus the King had worked through Spirit-empowered Christians to advance His Kingdom.

In Summary

Jesus' fulfillment of the offices of prophet, priest and king in the power of the the Holy Spirit provides us with the possibilities as well as parameters for how the Spirit will also move in us today. In understanding these offices, we gain the freedom to move in power ministry and the basis for discerning what may or may not be of the Spirit.

In the next chapter we deal with what blocks the Church from moving in ministry empowered by the Holy Spirit.

Breaking Tribalism in the Body of Christ

Doug: As we see all the ministries that the Holy Spirit brings to the Body of Christ, we are astonished at their variety. Prophet, priest and king? We could spend the rest of our lives investigating the fascinating facets and fullness of these ministries!

Yet we have shown in Parts 1 and 2 of this book that the Holy Spirit does not force on us gifts we do not want. We receive from His abundance mostly what we choose to accept and ask for. God gives us the right to keep a closed mind and spirit to any of His gifts.

Surely the Holy Spirit is one of the treasures Christ gave His disciples at His departure—the treasure to which He referred in His parable in Luke 19. A nobleman gave ten pounds to each of his servants before he went away: "Trade with these till I come," he said (Luke 19:13).

But the Body of Christ has been reluctant to trade the treasures of Christ. We have more often kept to ourselves the one or two gifts we have already received from the King. Proud of what we have, we have seen little need for what He has given other Christians.

Breaking Out of Narrow Liberalism

How well I remember my days in a liberal seminary, taking pride in my liberal Presbyterian credentials! In the halls and dorm rooms, we aimed many potshots of ridicule against evangelical schools and churches, and against the even worse people we called fundamentalists. In the mid-1960s we were barely aware of charismatics, but we would have been against them if we had known more.

One thing we were sure of: We were the mainstream and all those other groups were the fringe. Sometimes we called them the "lunatic fringe." To us, *mainstream* meant politically liberal, orderly in worship, no funny business in our theology. (The God-is-dead theology of those years did not seem like funny business to us.)

Then in 1972, when I asked Jesus to baptize me with the Holy Spirit, He threw open my narrow boundaries. I happened to attend a worship service at the Word of God Community in Ann Arbor, Michigan. Here was a profoundly exciting community full of power and love, manifesting both the inner and outer working of the Holy Spirit. The worship service was orderly, but the order seemed to flow from something other than human control or tradition. It was an orderliness of the Holy Spirit. This intrigued me.

And they were Catholics! I subscribed to *New Covenant* magazine and began to read Catholic charismatic writings. I did not need to accept Catholic beliefs about Mary or the Mass to get from these Christians the good gifts God was giving them.

Afterward I decided to explore other avenues—the evangelical, the independent charismatic, the conservative Reformed, the "fundamentalist" and the Christian traditions of other denominations, including black Pentecostals—reserving for myself the right to "test all things" and to take what I believed the Lord wanted me to learn. In all these explorations, the Holy Spirit was my teacher.

Not everything has been helpful in my search for a broader experience of Christ, and in all my searches I have been faithful to my own tradition. But on balance I have been enriched by virtually every corner of the Christian community I have explored.

The Holy Spirit, I believe, is fueling the openness I feel toward other believers in the Body of Christ. He has helped me understand where these believers are coming from and that we indeed have Jesus

Christ in common. The vast majority of what I now value in my walk with the Lord I received through people outside my Presbyterian heritage. If the Holy Spirit takes what belongs to Jesus and gives it to us, He gives to them differently than He gives to me. So I have to come to them to get what He has given them.

Incidentally, I find another surprise in this broader experience in the Church. When we stand together as Christians, we are better able to discern unhealthy influences that are not of Christ—the New Age, neo-pagan counterfeits growing up everywhere around us and seeping through the pores of the Body of Christ.

When Tradition Becomes an Idol

Many today seem caught in a rut, reluctant to "trade with these." We exercise a sort of natural discernment based on familiar tradition. Whatever accords with our tradition, we open ourselves to. Whatever does not, we do not.

Let me use my own denomination as an example. At its inception the Presbyterian Church stood for the Word of God and the importance of the Holy Spirit working on the conscience. Presbyterians believed that "God alone is Lord of the conscience"—meaning we Christians must never allow chain-of-command structures to replace the voice of the Spirit speaking within our hearts. This conviction was birthed amid profound struggles against a chain-of-command system in Britain, when the Holy Spirit was bringing Reformed faith to thousands of people independent of a harsh, overbearing church system.

But with the passage of years, our tradition changed. Most people today believe that the Presbyterian Church stands for a very different principle: "Let all things be done decently and in order" (1 Corinthians 14:40, KJV). In fact, we Presbyterians, while paying lipservice to the historic principles our denomination used to stand for, often cherish this admonition as our greatest gift. Presbyterian churches *are* orderly and decent—of that we are sure. Any church that is not orderly or decent surely is not Presbyterian, and we avoid those places.

Only by my association with other traditions can I look back and see the idolatrous nature of this faith in decency and order. We have taken it out of the context of 1 Corinthians 14, in which Paul was speaking of gifts of the Holy Spirit like tongues, prophecy and healing. He was describing a decency and order such as I experienced at the Word of God Community—an order produced when we maintain a balance between Holy Spirit love and Holy Spirit power.

Love? Power?

As for love, we Presbyterians have gained a reputation for being "the frozen chosen." On top of that, the Enlightenment descended on our seminaries so that our leaders became bogged down in "analysis paralysis." So now Presbyterians are both frozen and paralyzed! We have a hard time expressing love toward God or toward other people. When visitors come to our churches, no one speaks to them. We are too busy being decent and orderly. We have a greater commitment to Roberts Rules of Order than the law of love. On Sundays our vocal cords seem paralyzed and our limbs frozen as we move into what we call "divine worship." We chuckle among ourselves about our icy reputation, but we do not repent of the lovelessness that has earned it.

As to Holy Spirit power, American Presbyterians have resisted the gifts of the Holy Spirit for years, even though our guiding philosophy ("Let all things be done decently and in order") appears smack-dab in the middle of a discussion of spiritual gifts. Nevertheless, we have chosen to filter spiritual gifts out of our worship life and ministries. We are professionals. Professionals rely on their professional training, not on the Holy Spirit. The professional model of ministry is different from the biblical model. It does not follow Jesus so much as Sigmund Freud, Carl Rogers and other Western intellectuals who developed it.

So we cling to the one part of 1 Corinthians that we can still accept, "Let all things be done decently and in order," and we use it to justify our lack of love and power. But when we take this passage out of the context of the power gifts of 1 Corinthians 12, and out of the love context of 1 Corinthians 13, the result is bone-chilling.

Orderly decency has become our one food group. We suffer from scurvy because we are not getting a proper diet. In proper amounts, order is a necessary dietary ingredient. But by the truckload, it becomes a poison that stanches our appetite for the other food groups.

Like so many North American churches, we must move outside of our narrow tradition to discover the gifts God has given to people of other traditions. If we will learn to trade gifts with the others in the Body of Christ, we can have a time of refreshing. And this is the very thing the Holy Spirit is challenging us to do.

The Call to Christian Unity

The Holy Spirit is once again inviting unity in the Body of Christ, calling us out of our denominational cubbyholes. What's more, this seemingly impossible task suddenly does not look impossible.

Unity is one of the watchwords of the Promise Keepers movement, attracting men of mainline, evangelical, conservative and charismatic church traditions—men from diverse racial and cultural backgrounds. They are discovering it is possible to be one in Jesus. The quest for unity also fuels the Concerts of Prayer (identified with David Bryant) and the Pastors' Prayer Summits (identified with Joseph Aldrich). It impassions the International Reconciliation Coalition, whose founders, John Dawson and Jean Steffenson, work to heal historic wounds between white and Native peoples and whose ministry now extends to people of other races. It empowers the Harvest Evangelism ministry of Ed Silvoso, whose experience in Argentina is based on large numbers of Christians in a city coming together to seek the heart of Christ amid deep Christian unity and prayer evangelism.

I could give dozens of examples of this Spirit-inspired call to unity—the March for Jesus or the frontier missions movement that pulls diverse Christians together. In all of them, the Holy Spirit is offering an "earnest" of what Jesus will do when He returns—unite all things in heaven and on earth.

Yet the forces that drive us apart are still real and powerful. Why are we Christians so reluctant to trade with each other the treasures Jesus has given? Brad and I continue to see Christians hurting each other with words. We argue. We get proud. We build our own kingdoms and pursue our hidden agendas. In the light of all this, we *have* to remain separate to protect ourselves from one another's careless and cruel words.

But the apostles warned again and again of the danger of divisiveness and quarreling in the Body of Christ. For example:

> ". . . pursue righteousness, faith, love and peace, along with those who call on the Lord out of a pure heart. Don't have anything to do with

foolish and stupid arguments, because you know they produce quarrels. And the Lord's servant must not quarrel; instead, he must be kind to everyone, able to teach, not resentful. Those who oppose him he must gently instruct, in the hope that God will grant them repentance leading them to a knowledge of the truth, and that they will come to their senses and escape from the trap of the devil, who has taken them captive to do his will.

2 Timothy 2:22–26, NIV

Paul does not demand that we accept every teaching that presents itself to the Body of Christ—far from it! Some teaching, he said, is demonic. But we *are* responsible for the way we behave toward other Christians, even if the teaching they bring is outright demonic. By gentleness we can lead some people out of deception. If gentle love does not accomplish this, then prayer (not divisive argument or political maneuvering) is our alternative. The fruit of gentle and patient love is necessary to keep the Holy Spirit in the midst of the Church. Without love, the Holy Spirit is grieved and His power disappears from the Church. Holy Spirit love and Holy Spirit power are connected because they both come from the same Spirit and flow from the nature of the same God.

A Powerful Move of the Spirit

I have pastored many students involved in InterVarsity ministries over the last decade. Recently one InterVarsity chapter bumped its way through an intense Holy Spirit controversy. I asked Kim and Kevin Greene, campus staff members for the University of Richmond and Virginia Commonwealth University, to share the story of the intense struggle they went through and the way God resolved it:

> In the fall of 1993, the InterVarsity chapter at the University of Richmond faced great turmoil over the issue of the role of the Holy Spirit in our individual and corporate lives.
>
> During the summer several students were stirred by the idea of revival. They came to school with a great desire to see God move as He had through other seasons of revival. Several had been baptized in the Spirit and received the gift of tongues. To them this experience seemed to be integrally connected to revival, so they began to preach

the need for the baptism and tongues on campus. A group of four men began to call the InterVarsity group to repentance.

At the beginning of the semester, these four came to every Inter-Varsity event, standing on the sidelines looking displeased and praying for our repentance. To them, we were relying not on the Holy Spirit in our ministry, but on worldly strategies. The proof of this, they said, was the absence of signs and wonders at our meetings. They believed our commitment to relational evangelism and a Gospel of grace was watering down the message of Christ. They rebuked us in prayer.

So we began to use our prayer times to preach against each other in prayer. A spirit of defensiveness and oppression began to pervade every meeting.

The leadership met with the four men to see if there was a way we could work through our differences. They were cordial but spoke against us afterward—that we did not believe in the Holy Spirit, that we were instruments of Satan, that we were false prophets.

The issue of the baptism with the Holy Spirit became critical. One of our key leaders, a good friend of mine, asked for the baptism and received the gift of tongues. Then she told us we were sinning by not preaching the baptism with the Holy Spirit with tongues for everyone. I [Kim] believed her experience was real and valid, but that we could not mandate it for everyone. Eventually she told me she believed that God wanted her to have no further contact with me because I had "the form of godliness but was denying its power." This devastated me.

We had no contact for thirteen months. She urged all 25 men and women on our leadership team to be baptized with the Holy Spirit. Thoroughly confused, they began to leave InterVarsity to join up with a new group of students. The experience of the baptism in the Holy Spirit was elevated as a cure-all for any spiritual struggle, including personal temptation. Students who spoke with tongues were filled with pride; those who did not questioned their salvation. For a few days following their experience, they were filled with peace and joy, but when struggles crept back, they were often disillusioned.

We were deeply wounded. We disagreed with these students less for their theology than for their approach. They asked few questions but spent much time talking and preaching. Assuming none of us had the Holy Spirit, they never inquired about our spiritual lives. To them we seemed powerless, while they longed for power. They made us feel joyless, confused and afraid. Also, the prospect of revival was laid on us as a heavy yoke.

Ultimately they began fighting among themselves about who was sold out for God and who was not. By April the group disintegrated. Our own InterVarsity group was severely weakened and demoralized.

For our part, we saw we had much to learn. As evangelical Christians, we had a very developed theology and vocabulary about Jesus, but a limited understanding of the Holy Spirit. Part of the reason the tongues issue jarred our students was that they had had little teaching about the role of the Holy Spirit, either from us or from their home churches.

So this difficult year taught us that we needed to understand more about the Holy Spirit. We had put too much confidence in our theology and were unwilling to search the Scriptures because we thought we knew them already.

A turning point in this struggle for me was the day I quit trying to defend myself and decided my only defense was Christ's grace and love for me. This opened me to hearing what the Lord was saying in this struggle. I called several pastors who knew more about the Holy Spirit than I did.

(At this stage I became involved, along with several other pastors from the community. I gave some of the teaching that appears in this book.)

Their loving, gentle words made me hopeful and erased my fear. From that point on I asked God to fill me daily with His Spirit and teach me how to rely on the Spirit in ministry, giving me whatever gifts would please Him.

Though in the short term this struggle was difficult, God used it for good in the long term as we humbled ourselves and kept listening to Him. Often when the leadership came together, we were so sad and confused that all we could say was, "Jesus, Jesus." We didn't know how to pray. In conversation it took great effort for us to keep from defending ourselves. We had to die daily to our desire to be right and to appear successful. Eventually we and the students who remained with us became grounded in the promises of God's sufficiency in all things. We were learning to wait on Him.

God was faithful. The next fall one of the men involved in the core group that had broken away came to us and asked us to forgive him. He had spent the summer in Estonia and been so humbled by the Estonians' love for him that he realized all he had been doing was cursing people, whereas Jesus had commanded him to bless, not curse.

We prayed together. Then he joined our leadership team, confessing to the whole group of 25 leaders. He joined us to pray for reconciliation with the other students who had broken away.

This began an influx of those students, including my friend who had left the previous year. She asked forgiveness publicly at a leadership meeting. Many of our leaders confessed to her their hardness of heart. There was much weeping and laughter as we experienced the sweet joy of reconciliation. That night we thought, *These people will be key instruments of power and peace in the Church because of what they have experienced tonight. Few people in their lifetime get to experience this kind of reconciliation.* Every one of us had been brought to repentance by the humble, gentle love of someone we respected, mostly mature pastors in the Richmond community who modeled for us true humility and love.

It is ironic that the most powerful move of the Spirit any of us have ever seen came as we were reconciled and knelt together to pray in unity.

Breaking Strongholds of Separateness

Others before us have had to learn difficult lessons about disagreeing with other brothers and sisters in the Body of Christ.

During the Great Awakening the Holy Spirit was working overtime. But the two most anointed leaders of that Awakening, George Whitefield and John Wesley, instigated a public controversy over the issue of predestination. After several years they recognized the harm they were doing to the cause of Christ, repented of the sin of speaking evil against each other and patched up their quarrel publicly. They did not have to feign theological agreement. They just had to agree with what Jesus and the apostles told them to do with their disagreements.

In his book *Healing America's Wounds,* John Dawson analyzes the spiritual deception behind Christian disunity. He outlines Satan's strategy for wasting the power of the Church, so that the Holy Spirit is grieved and the Church remains ill-equipped for her work:

The Nature of Strongholds
Instructions to a Demon

1. Take some truth.
2. Polarize the people with different sides of that truth.
3. Tempt them to unrighteous judgment.

4. Watch them wound each other with rejection, harsh words and injustice.
5. Now that they are alienated, resentful and feeling guilty, bring them under condemnation by accusing them and tormenting them with remorse. Recruit other demons. Attempt to establish a permanent stronghold.
6. In the midst of their pain and confusion, offer them a way out through a cover-up deception, religion or philosophy that covers guilt through transferring blame to nature, matter or society. They can't live without hope. Give them a false hope.
7. Attempt to close the prison door by permanently damaging their knowledge of God's character. Above all else, bring accusation against God.[1]

As we look back at the renewal movements of the past, we see the accuracy of this assessment. When God pours out the Holy Spirit, some get the fruit of the Spirit. Others get the power of the Spirit for ministry. Then the two groups fight each other.

If the coming revival of the Holy Spirit is to last, we must learn to appreciate one another's gifts, overlook one another's faults, give each other the benefit of the doubt and trade the treasures of Christ back and forth, so that no good gift in the Body of Christ is lacking.

May the ????? Be with You

Doug: There is a limit to unity. That limit is Jesus Christ Himself. God prepared for the revelation of Jesus by teaching His people Israel not to bow down at the altars of pagan idols. God revealed Himself and His ways to free the world from the curse of paganism. Yet pagan teaching surrounds us still. A defeated Satan remains in the world to lure us away from Christ. Paganism offers its own form of satanic spirituality. We must get clear about the difference between the two or we will be forever muddling about.

During the modern era we did not have to deal with this issue. As to spirituality, we called it superstition and moved on. But ever since Dr. Raymond Moody wrote his best-selling book *Life after Life,* scientists themselves have staked a claim on the spirit realm. That science would abandon its addiction to materialism is a sign of these postmodern times.

All the more urgent it is to know the difference between God's teachings and the doctrines of demons mentioned in 1 Timothy 4:1: "The Spirit clearly says that in later times some will abandon the faith and follow deceiving spirits and things taught by demons" (NIV).

Star Wars or Spiritual Battles?

Pagan religion looks at the spiritual world as a swirling soup of powers that can be manipulated mentally or placated to serve us. Luke Skywalker, like the Pied Piper, led a generation of Western children into clouds of pagan belief when he said, "May the Force be with you." George Lucas' teaching, enhanced by Hollywood gizmo-magic, sparked the Western imagination. Children of the *Star Wars* generation grew up with the doctrines of the Force planted in their minds so firmly that Sunday school teachers could scarcely uproot them.

Why do pagan and New Age teaching so attract Westerners trying to relocate their spirits?

For three generations we modern Westerners wanted to take our destinies into our own hands, to manipulate the material world by science and technology and to prove we did not really need God after all. Brad and I have already discussed the rise and fall of modernism in *The Collapse of the Brass Heaven.*

Now that our spiritual hunger has reached unavoidable intensity, everyone is talking about spirituality. But most people looking for spirituality still want to retain control over their own lives and destinies. The idea of surrendering our lives to a sovereign God with a will of His own makes us nervous. "Surrender theology" seems un-American. Paganism has this advantage: In it we retain control of the spirit realm. We "use" spiritual power and knowledge just as we "use" material power and knowledge.

Paganism does not require the conversion of the will. George Lucas' New Age teaching, therefore, has great attraction for Westerners who, ninety years ago, began to forget how to surrender their lives to God. Now the main issue in the Western world is, Who is in control?

The control issue has a direct bearing on how we think about the Holy Spirit. Ninety years ago, as the modern era was just getting under way, R. A. Torrey wrote in *The Person and Work of the Holy Spirit:*[1]

> If you think of the Holy Spirit, as many even among Christian people do today, as a mere influence or power, then your thought will constantly be, "How can I get hold of the Holy Spirit and use it?" But if you think of Him in the biblical way, as a person of divine majesty and glory, your thought will be, "How can the Holy Spirit get hold of me and use me?"
>
> p. 14

Among Christians at the turn of the century, R. A. Torrey was finding an incipient paganism. Even then the central issue was, Who is in charge? Am I using God or is God using me? Which one of us is Lord and calling the shots?

If Americans are to avoid descending into the pit of paganism, we must confront this issue.

A Person or a Force?

The charismatic movement brought great spiritual renewal to the West and still has a lingering impact. Charismatic churches have grown and prospered (as Brad and I showed in *The Collapse of the Brass Heaven*), in contrast to the conservative and evangelical denominations, where growth has leveled off, and the mainline churches, which are losing life rapidly.

But in the last decade, something deadly happened to charismatic renewal. It welcomed teaching that began to treat God like a set of laws that could lead us to health and wealth. The so-called "prosperity gospel" repudiated Paul's virtue of being "content . . . in plenty or in want" (Philippians 4:12, NIV). His absolute surrender to the will of God did not fit this "name-it-and-claim-it" gospel, which is a form of paganism with a thin Christian veneer.

Our culture has been built on the idea that we should be able to take control and achieve what we want, especially when it comes to material prosperity. God ought to be an American. We did not like the prospect of surrendering our wills to a God who might want us to be poor, either temporarily or permanently. We preferred to think of Him as a set of laws to make us rich and successful, and to turn the name of Jesus into a sort of mantra.

But if God is personal, He has a will of His own. In fact, the Personhood of God is essential to our Christian faith: "God in three Persons, blessed Trinity." Nor is the Holy Spirit a force to be manipulated. We must learn to listen for His will and respect His judgments.

Brad: Yet there are times the Holy Spirit does not seem like a person. Sometimes, to be honest, He seems more like a force.

It was the last night of a Dunamis Project conference at Hendersonville, North Carolina, and people were coming forward for prayer. Suddenly the Holy Spirit fell on a young pastor, who was overcome with heavenly joy. He began to laugh almost drunkenly and fell to the floor shouting for joy.

I had seen this kind of behavior before, but here, where many decent-and-orderly Presbyterians were likely to be offended by such goings-on, it seemed out of place. Feeling responsible for keeping a lid on what seemed a disorderly outburst, I sidled over sternly to calm down the laughter.

But as I drew close to the man, it was as if I had stepped into a river of swirling, sparkling joy. I could no longer stand, but ended up on the floor with the pastor overcome with delicious, cleansing laughter.

What was this power? I knew it was the Holy Spirit. But it felt more like a river than a Person.

On other occasions the Holy Spirit resembles another kind of force.

At a service at Reynolda Presbyterian Church in Winston-Salem, North Carolina, a couple brought their ten-year-old boy forward for prayer. He was overweight, and the walk of a few yards to the front of the church left him huffing and puffing. His face reflected resigned sadness.

He suffered from a rare heart condition, his parents told me, and was not expected to live more than a year. The father wept quietly as he described how his boy could only sit by the window and watch other children play. They wanted me to pray for his healing.

I felt totally inadequate. But I laid hands on the boy and cried out to Jesus to show His love and power so that this child could have a chance at normal life. My words seemed insufficient, so I prayed in tongues. During none of my prayers did I feel any particular faith or inspiration.

Yet suddenly the boy looked up in surprise and said, "My chest is so hot, it feels like someone is lighting a fire inside me!"

We all gave thanks, though we were uncertain of what might be happening.

The heat apparently intensified. Soon the boy took several deep breaths, stood up and said excitedly, "I feel like I can run now."

He broke from our hands and bolted out the door to run around the parking lot.

The parents were astonished and frightened. Apparently their son had been unable to do such a thing for several years.

The boy returned even more excited than before.

"Look, I can run!" he shouted.

Off he went again.

They wrote a year later to thank me and give praise to Jesus for the healing. Not only had the boy not died, but he had continued to gain strength as God healed his heart.

In this case, too, the Holy Spirit felt more like a force—light, power, electricity—than a Person. Is it little wonder people sometimes characterize the Holy Spirit in that way?

This ambiguity about the Holy Spirit is also found in Scripture. The prophet Isaiah spoke of the Spirit of God as water and as "streams on the dry ground" (Isaiah 44:3). The Hebrew word *ruach*, taken literally, means "breath" or "wind."

New Testament descriptions of the Holy Spirit are more personal than the Old, but even Jesus called the Spirit "rivers of living water" flowing out of our hearts (John 7:38). And in Acts 2:2–3 the Spirit is pictured as wind and fire. So even in the New Testament we see a scriptural basis for "river of joy" and "healing heat" kinds of stories.

But the Holy Spirit Is a Person

In spite of biblical images that describe the Holy Spirit as wind, fire and streams, Scripture teaches clearly that God is personal—and *God* includes the Holy Spirit.

The New Testament presents two major lines of evidence for the Personhood of the Holy Spirit.

The Holy Spirit Possesses Personal Attributes

First, the New Testament attributes to the Holy Spirit characteristics that belong only to persons, as the table on the following page indicates (borrowed from R. A. Torrey, pp. 11–16).

Let's take a sampling of three of these personal attributes. Perhaps we can see the relevance of the Personhood of God.

The Love of the Holy Spirit

The Holy Spirit reflects the nature of God, and the beloved disciple tells us what part of that nature is: "God is love" (1 John 4:8).

Reference	Text	Attribute
Romans 15:30	". . . and by the love of the Spirit. . . ."	*Love*
1 Corinthians 2:10	"The Spirit searches everything, even the depths of God."	*Discernment, reason*
1 Corinthians 2:11	"No one comprehends the thoughts of God except the Spirit of God."	*Understanding*
1 Corinthians 12:11	"All these are inspired by one and the same Spirit, who apportions to each one individually as he wills."	*Will, ability to make decisions*
Ephesians 4:30	"Do not grieve the Holy Spirit of God, in whom you were sealed. . . ."	*Grief*

Yet people often do things in the name of the Holy Spirit that do not reflect love. Doug and I have both heard "prophecies" that claim to have come from God yet are confrontative to the point of being dark and condemning. The Holy Spirit may well chasten us through a word of prophecy, but when He does, He does not threaten, shame or condemn. Instead there is a sense of grief, pleading, invitation and promise. "In him is no darkness at all" (1 John 1:5).

Many people who move in the gifts of the Holy Spirit forget that the Spirit wants to love people. It is His nature to love. Both Doug and I have seen far too many examples of people burning bridges with other Christians "because," they said, "we are Spirit-filled now."

David du Plessis gave a memorable talk in Portland during the height of the charismatic renewal. The man known as Mr. Pentecost said, "Do not speak so much of power. Speak, rather, of love."

The power of the Holy Spirit is the power to create love and to minister the power of God lovingly to people who are hurting. Even when confrontative words are given, the motivation of love comes through when the word is from the Holy Spirit.

A Will of His Own

The Holy Spirit has His own agenda and gives gifts and ministries as He chooses. While we are given the right to ask and pray with authority, our role is to submit to Him and flow with what He wants to do in and through us. God's greatest power is given to those who are submitted and surrendered to Him.

Once, at a Prayer Mountain event in Taiwan, one of the students from the Presbyterian Bible College in Hsinchu announced that she had one desire: to receive the gift of tongues.

"I am not leaving this Mountain until God gives me this gift!" she declared. "For three years I have prayed for this, and now I must receive it."

I explained to her that tongues was a good gift but not the only sign that one had been baptized in the Holy Spirit. I assured her that she could receive the empowering of the Holy Spirit without this particular manifestation.

"No!" she cried. "I must have tongues."

"O.K.," I said. "I'm delighted to join you in asking for this gift. Let's just ask the Holy Spirit and see what He does."

I gave her some instruction about how to keep from blocking tongues. Then I gathered four students and a co-worker, Grace Lo, to pray for her. Of the six of us, only Grace had received any infilling with the Holy Spirit, and I was the only one who had received the gift of tongues.

As we prayed for the young woman seated in the middle, suddenly the Holy Spirit began to work among us. Grace began spontaneously to speak in tongues. Then, quite contagiously, the Spirit began to urge the others in the circle to pray in tongues. Each student, with a look of surprise and wonder, began to receive the gift the woman in the middle had asked for.

As for the woman herself, she began to shake all over and weep, experiencing the Spirit's power. That day she received peace in her heart and was equipped for a ministry as a teacher of children. But she did not speak in tongues.

The Holy Spirit has a will of His own.

Doug: In February 1991, at a Dunamis Project retreat at Silver Bay, New York, a team of people, including Brad, prayed for my chronic back problems. As we prayed, Brad began to feel heat and healing energy flowing through his hands. I felt heat in my back.

Then, mysteriously, the power stopped. No reason given. It just stopped. It was as though God was saying, "No," or, "Not now."

We were confused over this inexplicable cessation of God's power. To this day I have received no clear explanation for it. But I am forced to acknowledge that the Holy Spirit has a will of His own. He is not a force that we can "make happen" whenever we want, but a Person.

He Grieves

The Holy Spirit is deeply grieved by sin and communicates that grief to us. And we may grieve the Holy Spirit through our disobedience and sin that block His gracious work in the world.

On Father's Day 1991, about four months after the prayer with Brad and the others, I was having dinner in Branson, Missouri, and praying with some friends, Jim and Nancy. The Holy Spirit began to give Nancy a mental picture of my back. Since my problems are not visible to other people, there was no way she could have known about my back pain except through a word of knowledge.

Hoping this would be the first step in healing, I asked for prayer for my scoliosis. But a day or two later, as we were praying earnestly about it, God began to give Jim a sense that somehow my back pain was connected with an ancestor of mine who had committed grievous sins against Native Americans. I was instructed to pray for healing and forgiveness between whites and Natives.

The moment I obeyed (although I know of no one in my ancestry who committed sins against Native Americans), I was overwhelmed with the grief of God for the sins of the white race against the people who first inhabited this continent. The emotion came as a surprise, especially since I am not at all an emotional person, but it just about broke my heart. I have never experienced such grief either before or since—as if to confirm that Jim's word to me had validity.

I am not sure it was correct. But God did something in my life that somehow utilized my back pain to communicate His grief.

Many times since then I have been touched by a compassionate grief when in the presence of Native Americans or people who minister among them. That Father's Day incident grew into a continuing prayer burden. My back pain reminds me of the pain of Native peoples, because God seems to want to use it that way. So this pain tells me, all at once, of the love, independent will and grief of the Holy Spirit.

Perhaps one reason the Church has been powerless is that we have preached against one another, thus grieving and alienating the Holy Spirit. Bitterness, wrath, anger, clamor and malice cause God pain and weaken the Church because they "grieve the Holy Spirit of God" (see Ephesians 4:30–31). And when the Spirit is grieved through infighting and divisiveness, His power in pushing back the evil one (Ephesians 6:10–18) is weakened.

The Holy Spirit Fulfills What Only a Divine Person Can

The second compelling reason for affirming that the Holy Spirit is a Person is that *to Him are ascribed positions or offices that only a person can fulfill.* Again we borrow from the teaching of R. A. Torrey (pp. 16–20):

Reference	Text	Position
John 14:16–17	"He will give you another Counselor . . . even the Spirit of truth. . . ."	The Holy Spirit replaces Jesus as our *Counselor.*
John 14:26	"The Counselor, the Holy Spirit . . . he will teach you all things, and bring to your remembrance all that I have said to you."	The Holy Spirit serves as our *Teacher* and knows all that Jesus has said.
John 15:26	"When the Counselor comes . . . he will bear witness to me."	The Holy Spirit is a *Witness* to Jesus.
John 16:8	"He will convince the world concerning sin and righteousness and judgment."	The Holy Spirit is our *Judge.*
Romans 8:14	"All who are led by the Spirit of God are sons of God."	The Holy Spirit is our *Leader.*
Romans 8:27	"The Spirit intercedes for the saints according to the will of God."	The Holy Spirit is our *Intercessor.*

In these Scriptures we find that the Holy Spirit has been sent to fill the office that Jesus filled while on earth. He is our Counselor and Friend—the One who stands beside us. Only another divine Person could take His place.

Worth the Risk?

If we see the Holy Spirit as a Person—in fact, the third Person of the Trinity—we have a bulwark against the deception of New Age teaching to keep us from "using" the Spirit for our own purposes.

And if the Holy Spirit is a Person, He cannot be manipulated. It can be a little frightening to be in His presence and recognize He could do things that are beyond our control. We may, in quiet and honest moments, wonder whether we really want Him in our lives. "Is it worth the risk?" is a valid and thoughtful question that many a Christian has asked.

Yet with our backs against the wall, our country in profound moral decline, our churches failing, our institutions in disarray and our families falling apart, we cannot get along without Him. Our powerlessness drives us at last to take the risk and abandon ourselves into His keeping, to seek His gifts and cast care to the wind.

We can be secure in the belief that God will not give us a stone if we ask for a loaf of bread.

Discerning Signs and Wonders

Brad and Doug: Many people are trying to interpret the spiritual phenomena (including laughter in the Spirit) that have broken out at the Toronto Airport Christian Fellowship and in other parts of the world. They want to know, Are these from God or not?

The same quest for evaluation pursued the charismatic renewal decades ago, when believers tried to arrive at a simple conclusion: Are tongues from God or the devil? Others asked, "If I've received the Holy Spirit, do I have to speak in tongues?" What we were seeking then was a paradigm—a doctrine to fit our belief systems. Some of us were not interested in knowing the truth about glossolalia, especially if it might be complicated or require searching the Scriptures. Most of us, uncomfortable with complexities, develop paradigms to resolve them or reduce them to manageable size. But in the case of tongues, we needed deeper discernment about the way the gift was being used in the Body of Christ and some instruction about its potential dangers.

This was what the apostle Paul offered. He did not say, "Tongues are of God," or, "Tongues are of the devil." He knew his readers needed pastoral discernment, not mere paradigms or doctrines.

The same is true of revival phenomena today—shaking, healing, laughing in the Spirit, dreams, weeping in the Spirit, deliverance from demons, resting in the Spirit and so on. So in this chapter we will look for a biblical pattern against which we can measure signs and wonders.

The Biblical Context

First we must see signs and wonders in their biblical context as expressions of the Kingdom of God actually advancing on earth. In the ministry of Jesus, proclaiming the Kingdom included both preaching and accomplishing signs and wonders. The Lord sent the Twelve (Luke 9:1–6) and later the 72 (Luke 10:1–24) not only to preach but also to heal the sick and cast out demons. At one point Jesus commanded the disciples to heal sick people and tell them, "The kingdom of God is near you" (Luke 10:9, NIV).

Manifestations of power came first, in other words; then the preaching that explained the meaning of the miracle. So the Kingdom of God was validated by the sign, which in turn derived its value from the coming of the Kingdom.

We Westerners have a hard time living out this basic truth. Evangelicals, on the one hand, tend to focus on Jesus' preaching and pass over the signs and wonders that nearly always accompanied the preaching. The result: Bible-centered churches that are closed, for the most part, to manifestations of the Holy Spirit. An overemphasis on preaching and teaching accommodates the Western rationalistic worldview that took over our culture in the first half of this century (but which is on its way out). It advances the Kingdom of God in word only, lacking the full power and authority of Jesus Christ.

A corresponding error is found among those touched by the third wave or Pentecostal or charismatic renewals. Such proponents, while they appreciate the manifestations of the Holy Spirit, may see signs and wonders as ends in themselves. But miracles alone do not lead people into the Kingdom of God when they are not exhorted to obey Jesus as King, or helped through biblical preaching to see the broader context of promise and commandment under the New Covenant of Jesus. Some charismatics have developed a reputation for being off the wall—unreliable, unstable, unfaithful. Some divorce spiritual gifts from the basic love and justice God wants to break through into the world.

The coming of the Kingdom of God, by contrast, combines the reality of God's power with the preaching of His character. Promise and commandment under the New Covenant go hand in hand. It is futile and dangerous to divorce them.

As we think about signs and wonders in their biblical context, we can best understand them according to the two motifs of the Holy Spirit's work that we explored in Part 1—"the Spirit upon" and "the Spirit within." Manifestations like holy laughter, resting in the Spirit, tongues, prophecy and healing belong to the motif of the Spirit upon. They reflect neither sanctification nor salvation. They may even happen to people who are not yet converted. In such cases they become a bridge to salvation, inviting a response to the preached Gospel. They can lead unbelievers, through a direct experience of the Holy Spirit, into a saving relationship with Jesus Christ. Herein lies much, if not most, of their value.

Apostolic teaching about signs and wonders is not simply "for" or "against" them.

On the one hand, Jesus referred to signs and wonders as evidence of His Messiahship: "I have testimony weightier than that of John. For the very work that the Father has given me to finish, and which I am doing, testifies that the Father has sent me" (John 5:36, NIV). Hebrews 2:4 nails down these works as "signs and wonders and various miracles and . . . gifts of the Holy Spirit distributed according to his own will." The apostle Peter described Jesus as "a man attested to you by God with mighty works and wonders and signs which God did through him in your midst" (Acts 2:22).

But on the other hand, Jesus offered two warnings regarding the manifestation of spiritual power.

Warning #1: Embezzled Power

First, Jesus warned that signs and wonders do not necessarily come from God or lead people to God. Satan performs signs and wonders, too.

"Many will say to me on that day, 'Lord, Lord, did we not prophesy
in your name, and in your name drive out demons and perform many
miracles?' Then I will tell them plainly, 'I never knew you. Away from
me, you evildoers!'"

Matthew 7:22–23, NIV

Jesus was not describing sincere believers who serve Him all
their lives, but "false prophets" (Matthew 7:15) who would deceive
Christians with a false gospel. Apparently these prophets would be
gifted with counterfeit gifts of the Spirit and have power to do "lying
wonders."

With the New Age movement spearheading its way into mainline denominational churches, we need Jesus' first word of caution
more than ever. John White, in his book *When the Spirit Comes with
Power,* described an example of lying wonders ministered by false
prophets:

Among the Family of Love movement, once known as the Children of God, are documented healings, along with false spiritual
gifts such as tongues and prophecy. The source of many of them
was diabolical. In her book *The Children of God,* Deborah Davis (formerly Linda Berg, daughter of Moses David Berg, the founder of
the movement) gives her father's colorful description of how at the
age of fifty he received something he had longed for all his life—
the gift of tongues.

"I was lying there between Martha and Maria [his illicit wives] praying like a house afire, and all of a sudden before I even knew what
happened I was praying in tongues. . . . It was probably Abrahim. I
was finally desperate enough to let the Lord really take over and take
control. Abrahim was praying through me in the Spirit."

Abrahim was a spirit guide Berg had picked up at a Gypsy camp,
reputedly the spirit of a former Gypsy king. At that point, if not before
then, dark powers had invaded the movement called the Children of
God, and iniquity was soon to abound more and more. Pride and fear
had opened the movement to deception. It was prepared neither spiritually nor intellectually to distinguish between dark powers and divine.[1]

John White goes on to interpret satanic counterfeits as power stolen
from God:

There is one source of supernatural power, and one only. Satan's power is power once entrusted to him by God. God was the Creator of the power just as, being the Creator of all that is, he created Satan himself. The power was meant for use in God's service. It is what we might call embezzled power. And that is exactly what magic is—stolen power, used for the user's delight. Whenever anyone, Christian or non-Christian, angel or demon, uses power for selfish ends (for the love of power or for the justification or glory of the self), the power can be called magical power. It is the same power with the same characteristics put to a wrong use and subtly changed by that use.[2]

John White's comments are anchored in Scripture. For example:

In [Jesus] all things were created, in heaven and on earth, visible and invisible, whether thrones or dominions or principalities or authorities—all things were created through him and for him.

Colossians 1:16

So spiritual power is the creation of God in Jesus Christ, intended to glorify Jesus and lead people to Him. The Colossians needed this reminder because that church was already discovering Gnostic teaching and demonic power, which came from spirit guides or "archons" (rulers, powers). Those spirit guides claimed precedence over Jesus; the teaching they whispered into the Church apparently had enough power behind it to attract serious attention. (More about this in a moment.)

Doug: I became aware of embezzled power in 1973, when I was first exploring the manifestations of the Holy Spirit and had seen genuine healing take place in answer to prayer. Then I happened to see *Nicholas II.* The film tells the story of the demise of the last of the Russian czars and of his wife's relationship with the "monk" Grigori Rasputin, who in the name of God ministered healing throughout Russia at the turn of the last century. Rasputin, a wanton and depraved man, bragged of his power over women (especially the czar's wife, Alexandra) and of his sexual exploits. He also healed people by the laying on of hands and prayer. The private journals of the czar's family record many instances of this healing power in their household.

As I watched the film, I grew more and more confused about the healing power of the Holy Spirit. My mother had been wonderfully healed of a back disability, a brain hemorrhage and an ulcer all in a single day, through prayer and anointing with oil. Yet here was a profligate ministering the same kind of healing power—a man many suspect to be a major occult figure at the turn of the century.

As time passed I began to sort out the truth—that power can be either legitimate or illegitimate. The latter is what the Bible predicts for the end of the age (Matthew 7:15–23; 24:23–24; 2 Thessalonians 2:9; Revelation 13:13–14; 16:14). Satan wants to "lead astray, if possible, even the elect" (Matthew 24:24). Should we not be concerned about this in the Church as we prepare for the twenty-first century?

In the wake of the Welsh revival ninety years ago, Jessie Penn-Lewis wrote:

> It is probably true that the psychic, or soul-powers, require supernatural power for their full development, and that since the Fall this power is not of God but Satan. If so, much that has been unaccountable in the influx of satanic workings in the supernatural experiences of many of God's children during recent years, becomes clear. It also explains why a "baptism of power" which was supposed to be of God, could result in the development of a "selfhood" with *strong personal powers manifestly in exercise*, instead of deep humility, brokenness of spirit, tender love of souls, and effacement of self.[3]

The Seduction to "Use" the Holy Spirit

Brad: People in power ministry are, as Jessie Penn-Lewis warned, uniquely susceptible to corruption, and need to guard against subtle temptations and abuses of spiritual power.

This danger confronted me early in my participation in this dimension. I was leading a power ministry meeting in Taipei in 1985 attended by several hundred Christians, as well as a number of nonbelievers. We were all on our feet, praying and waiting on the Lord.

Suddenly I felt the Holy Spirit hovering over me. I had a sense of tingling power moving through my hands. In the next moment came a strong nudge from the Lord: *Go and lay hands on the senior pastor. I want to show My power and glory by resting him on the floor.*

Nothing like this had ever happened through me and I was startled at this guidance from God. I was also dismayed at the forbidding, staunch, ice-cold, Presbyterian demeanor of the man I was supposed to lay hands on. I asked the Holy Spirit to find someone a little more amenable to the laying on of hands. But He persisted in directing me to this pastor.

Out of sheer obedience, without expecting anything to happen, I walked across the room and lifted my hand to pray for him. Before I even touched his head, a sort of liquid love surged through me. The next moment the frozen exterior of this pastor melted into joyful astonishment, and he fell to the floor with a thud.

Immediately, as I looked around, I knew the Holy Spirit wanted to bless six other people in the same way. I skipped from one to the other. Each went down under the same blissful power.

This was a heady and invigorating experience for me.

What a blast! I thought to myself. I wanted the feeling of divine love and power to continue, so more people would be blessed. I was being blessed, too.

But just as suddenly as it came, the anointing lifted and I knew the Holy Spirit was finished.

The trouble was, by this time the atmosphere of the place had become charged with expectation. Other people were coming forward, wanting me to lay hands on them. They had accorded me great authority and were, I sensed, in my "power." All I had to do was go push a few people on the head, and they, too, would go down.

Perhaps the Holy Spirit would honor my prayers and bless the people, I thought, or perhaps the power of suggestion would have a positive influence on them. At least, so I began to rationalize as I considered the pros and cons of continuing.

I sensed a voice whispering to me: *Go ahead, just push a few of them with your hand. The power is yours. If you keep going, they will love you. They will see you as a great servant of Christ.*

But I sensed God saying, *I no longer desire to keep working through you like this. Obey Me.*

Sometimes Satan seems more loving than God!

I hesitated. An inner battle raged. I wanted the heady power, yet saw that the integrity of the Holy Spirit was at stake—and my integrity, too.

I broke free of the struggle and blurted out the words, "O.K., everyone, please sit down. Let's give praise to Jesus Christ for these wonderful manifestations of His presence. I believe that the Holy Spirit is finished doing this kind of work for the moment."

Their disappointment was obvious and cut me to the heart. Yet today I believe that if I had given in to the temptation to abuse the power of God, I would have failed Jesus and disqualified myself from further service.

What Does God Want from His People?

Doug: After I asked Jesus to baptize me with the Holy Spirit, I was enamored of the idea that maybe I could build a charismatic church where everyone would be baptized in the Holy Spirit. So I dedicated my first few years as a solo pastor to teaching on the Person and work of the Spirit and helping people open up to His power.

The same Holy Spirit who was making tongues, prophecy and healing real to me was opening up the Scriptures to me as never before. As I pored over the Word of God, I began to ask, *Lord, what is it You want from me and from Your Church? We want charismatic signs and wonders, but is that what You want?*

This question became more urgent when several families came into my church who were zealous for manifestations of the Holy Spirit. They had heard I was charismatic and wanted to help me build a charismatic church.

All of us were sincere. We had been baptized with the Spirit and wanted others to be, too. Yet bad things began to happen:

> Prophetic words were given that never came true.
> Dark, condemning prophecies sometimes came forth purporting to be from God.
> Demons were discerned in people who had no demons.
> An arrogant spirit developed against people who were not "Spirit-filled."

Certain external manifestations, such as raising hands and speaking in tongues, became badges of spirituality.

Speculative preoccupation simmered about when Jesus was coming back.

"Chain of command" teaching imposed "shepherds" between new believers and the Holy Spirit.

All these trends disturbed me profoundly, for they seemed to take place in the congregation whether I liked it or not. They were part of a movement identified as coming from the Holy Spirit. Many in the church automatically labeled everything identified "charismatic" as good, while others labeled everything "charismatic" bad. As for me, I was trying to find some way of discerning what was from the Holy Spirit and what was not.

As I sought an answer to this question, God led me back repeatedly to one issue (the same one Brad has to face every time he moves into power ministry): What is it God wants from His people?

The Pattern: What God Wants

God's answers to this question were clear and unequivocal, a valuable means of discerning the genuine from the phony, and they have been at the center of my ministry ever since.

He has given a pattern—the same one found all through the New Testament, remarkably uniform and clear-cut. This pattern becomes our basis for discernment. We can hold it, like a dressmaking pattern, against what we are making to see if our creation fits. This is how we discern spiritual things and how we know we are getting off track.

What is God's pattern? Faith working through love. It is as simple as that. Here are the Scriptures God led me to during those important days early in my ministry (emphasis added to each):

Through the Spirit, by faith, we wait for the hope of righteousness. For in Christ Jesus neither circumcision nor uncircumcision is of any avail, but *faith working through love.*

Galatians 5:5–6

We always thank God, the Father of our Lord Jesus Christ, when we pray for you, because we have heard of *your faith in Christ Jesus* and of the *love* which you have for all the saints.

Colossians 1:3–4

The aim of our charge is *love* that issues from a pure heart and a good conscience and sincere *faith*. Certain persons by swerving from these have wandered away into vain discussion.

1 Timothy 1:5–6

Follow the pattern of the sound words which you have heard from me, in the *faith* and *love* which are in Christ Jesus; guard the truth that has been entrusted to you by the Holy Spirit who dwells within us.

2 Timothy 1:13–14

This is his commandment, that we should *believe in the name of his Son Jesus Christ* and *love one another,* just as he has commanded us. All who keep his commandments abide in him, and he in them. And by this we know that he abides in us, by the Spirit which he has given us. Beloved, do not believe every spirit, but test the spirits to see whether they are of God. . . .

1 John 3:23–4:1

Many New Testament writings—especially Colossians, 1 Timothy and 1 John—were written to refute early Gnostic teaching. This teaching promoted negative, dark ideas about the Creator, denied the incarnation and encouraged Christians to put their confidence in those "archons," or angelic principalities, that were supposedly more intelligent and good than Jesus Himself. Gnostic teachings also promoted severe asceticism, fasting and religious ritual, and (by contrast) loose morals. The apostles John and Paul taught that Gnosticism drew people away from the pattern of sound teaching, which includes both faith in Jesus and love in the Body of Christ, and was demonic in its origins.

As a pastor searching for God's heart, I began to get a feel for what He was looking for: people learning to believe in Jesus, especially the power of the cross, and people learning to love one another because Jesus loves them.

How Do Signs and Wonders Fit the Pattern?

Brad: There are two ways that signs and wonders build this pattern. First, they can encourage people to believe in Jesus. And second, they can remove barriers to love.

They Can Encourage Belief in Jesus

It is difficult for people who have no evidence from their senses to step out in faith. God knows this and accommodates Himself to us by manifestations of His power. So the first way signs and wonders fit the biblical pattern of what God wants is this: They can help people believe in Jesus.

Often the most visible, awesome manifestations happen among unbelievers. These are God's way of drawing non-Christians to make their initial decisions for Jesus. Displays of spiritual power that draw people to believe in Jesus, therefore, are genuine works of the Holy Spirit. That is what the power of God *should* do. The Holy Spirit comes to glorify Jesus, and to take what belongs to Jesus and give it to us. (Notice that the counterfeit gift of tongues given to David Berg was designed to glorify the spirit guide "Abrahim" that had taken over that man's life. It did not lead him closer to Jesus.)

Signs and wonders can draw believers along with unbelievers to a deeper faith in Jesus.

In July 1995, on the final night of the Congress on the Holy Spirit and World Evangelization in Orlando, hundreds of young people responded to an altar call to commit their lives to Christ and to Christian service. At the end of this part of the service, the leader prayed a prayer of dedication for them.

He was about to send them back to their seats, since the front of the convention center was choked with young people and would block the parade of banners that was to follow. But suddenly I heard the Lord say, *In addition to calling them to follow Jesus, I also want to pour out My Spirit upon them for power to fulfill the mission they have given their lives for.*

I rushed forward and said to the leader (a good Pentecostal friend with whom I have the freedom to do this kind of thing), "Don't dismiss them! The Holy Spirit isn't finished yet." I asked him to announce that Jesus wanted to fill them all with the Holy Spirit to equip them to follow Him.

"Yes," he said, "but the program calls for a banner parade."

"Please don't miss this *kairos* moment just because of some banners. If these kids are baptized in the Holy Spirit, it's going to make a lot more difference for the Kingdom of God."

So he turned and prayed into the microphone, "Come, Holy Spirit, and fall upon each of these young people, that they may be empowered to do Your work."

At that, many of the young men and women began resting in the Spirit or exhibiting other manifestations of the Spirit's power. The banner parade proceeded, but participants had to step carefully over the many young people resting all over the floor. Ministry was taking place everywhere. I watched all this with a jolt of joy.

Then a young woman started to shriek, and fell writhing to the floor. A large crowd gathered around her and started shouting at the demons that were manifesting. The girl appeared frightened and confused. The more the people shouted at the demons, the more terrified she looked. Then Vernon Stoop of Focus Renewal Ministries and I were called over to help. We calmed the young woman and started to engage the demons. After a considerable struggle, which included discernment and shutting the doors the evil spirits had used to get in, she was set free. She got up, exhausted and crying but saying over and over, "Thank You, Jesus, for setting me free."

The impact was immediate. I could see fear and wonder in the eyes of the young people all around who had witnessed this dramatic power encounter.

"Evil spirits are real," I observed. "Sin really does open the door to them. But Jesus is our Victor. Do you want to reaffirm your faith in Him and be filled with the Holy Spirit in order to do His work?"

A number of them dropped to their knees and accepted Jesus Christ for the first time as Lord and Savior. Others reaffirmed their faith. We spent the next few moments praying that the Holy Spirit would fill everyone present for power ministry.

What was happening here? Power ministry had led directly into evangelism. The Lord was reminding me that the purpose of the manifestations of the Holy Spirit is to set people free to know Jesus

Christ. Signs and wonders encourage faith and can help people dedicate their lives to Him.

They Can Promote Christian Love

The second way signs and wonders fit God's pattern for the Church is that they open us to a deeper love for Him and one another by sweeping away barriers: sin, guilt, self-doubt, false concepts about God, spiritual deception, deep wounds. Not that the signs and wonders themselves remove these barriers. But they point to an invisible work of the Spirit of God, who is cleansing and rebuilding us on the inside. We will say more about this in the next chapter.

Distracting Patterns

Doug: In key discernment passages in the New Testament, the writers contrast the pattern of "faith working through love" with other patterns that distract believers. Some (but not all) of these distractions are:

> Religious observances that have nothing to do with faith or love (Galatians 5:6; Colossians 2:16–23)
> Unprofitable speculation that leads nowhere (1 Timothy 1:4)
> The accumulation of knowledge, especially *gnosis,* secret knowledge (2 Peter 1:8)
> The lust of the flesh, the lust of the eyes and a prideful spirit (1 John 2:16)

Surely satanic deception moves in many other ways, too, to destroy a work God is doing by His Spirit. But we can hold up any fresh movement in which spiritual power is manifested to the biblical pattern of "faith working through love" and ask, Is this movement drawing people to "know [Jesus] and the power of his resurrection" (Philippians 3:10–11)? Is it opening the door to "let love be genuine" (Romans 12:9)? The pattern gives us confidence. It helps us see with God's eyes. And it provides a pastoral way of handling spiritual phenomena.

Signs and wonders are rarely discerned just by looking at them. The first three signs that God gave Moses to perform before Pharaoh were duplicated by the court magicians. Satan's stolen power can look identical to God's original item. Signs and wonders can be from God or Satan, and can lead people in either direction. That is why Jessie Penn-Lewis wrote that our attitude toward signs and wonders, after the first flush of excitement, must be "a settled position of neutrality toward all supernatural workings, until the believer knows what is of God."

> If any experience is accepted without question, how can its Divine origin be guaranteed? The basis of acceptance or rejection must be knowledge. The believer must know, and he cannot know without examination, nor will he "examine" unless he maintains the attitude of "Believe not every spirit" until he has "tested" and proved what is of God.[4]

Warning #2: What You See Is Not What You Get

Jesus had a second warning—following His first warning that Satan has power, too—that can help us evaluate signs and wonders.

Early in His ministry Jesus said, "Unless you people see miraculous signs and wonders, you will never believe" (John 4:48, NIV). We can sense disappointment behind this statement, which increased to divine wrath when Jesus confronted the scribes and Pharisees:

> "A wicked and adulterous generation asks for a miraculous sign! But none will be given it except the sign of the prophet Jonah. For as Jonah was three days and three nights in the belly of a huge fish, so the Son of Man will be three days and three nights in the heart of the earth."
>
> Matthew 12:39–40, NIV

Jesus was referring to Himself as the greatest of all miracles—one stashed away in a tomb. His bodily resurrection was a hidden miracle, revealed quietly to a small number of women and men who were then required to go tell about it.

When Jesus comes back, things will be different. His return, He said, will be like lightning, obvious in a way that will require no one to testify, "Look, here is the Christ" (see Matthew 24:23–27, NIV). But in the meantime we have the resurrection, which does require testimony. It was a work of the Holy Spirit but not a manifestation of the Spirit.

Most of the important works of the Kingdom of God during the present period are, like the resurrection, hidden. Jesus multiplied the loaves and fishes, yet "the kingdom of God is not food and drink but righteousness and peace and joy in the Holy Spirit" (Romans 14:17). Righteousness, peace and joy in the Holy Spirit are works of the Holy Spirit but they do not qualify as manifestations. Still, they are the "meat" of the Kingdom. Everything else is a side dish, including signs and wonders—which, being visible, also tend to be external and temporary.

"We fix our eyes not on what is seen, but on what is unseen. For what is seen is temporary, but what is unseen is eternal" (2 Corinthians 4:18, NIV). Clinging too closely to visible manifestations can keep us in an adolescent stage in our walk in the Spirit. Again, Jessie Penn-Lewis:

> Depending upon supernatural things given from outside, or spiritual experiences in the sense realm, checks the inward spiritual life through the spirit. By the experiences of the senses, instead of living in the true sphere of the spirit, the believer is drawn out to live in the outer man of his body; and ceasing to act from his centre, he is caught by the outer workings of the supernatural in his circumference, and loses the inner co-operation with God.[5]

God wishes to draw our attention away from visible signs and point us toward the unseen realm for which we are being prepared:

> Since, then, you have been raised with Christ, set your hearts on things above, where Christ is seated at the right hand of God. Set your minds on things above, not on earthly things. For you died, and your life is now hidden with Christ in God.
>
> Colossians 3:1–3, NIV

Paul is exhorting us to depend less on manifestations of the Holy Spirit than on what we know of Jesus Himself. Yes, Jesus showed Thomas His visible wounds, but then He said, "Blessed are those who have not seen and yet believe" (John 20:29). He especially appreciated those who believed in Him without signs and wonders—people who could accept *Him* as the greatest supernatural intervention of all.

We appreciate this same spirit and maturity in the Toronto Airport Christian Fellowship, whose pastor, John Arnott, writes:

> . . . While the physical manifestations that have accompanied the Spirit's outpouring in our midst are abundant and varied, we have endeavoured to shift the focus off them, and appreciate rather the inward work of grace and empowering that is always the result.
>
> We are thrilled with the worldwide impact of this move of the Spirit: thousands of pastors and leaders have come from so many different countries around the world and have been touched by the power of the Spirit. Upon returning home, they have not only discovered that their own lives are transformed, but also that of their churches, as the Holy Spirit has come and been poured out upon them afresh. Our constant prayer is that this time of refreshing will increase both in depth and in breadth until the earth will be filled with the knowledge of the glory of the Lord as the waters cover the sea (Habakkuk 2:14). This has already started—it is so life-giving that denominational differences have melted into obscurity, as a fresh love for Jesus has become pre-eminent; leaders of every denominational persuasion have come and drunk deeply of this fresh outpouring. The Holy Spirit is the only true unifier![6]

People are drawn to Jesus to put their trust in Him. People are learning to love one another as Jesus loved them. This is what revival is all about.

And for it to happen, signs and wonders must find their proper place in a balance between the inward and outward working of the Holy Spirit.

Is "Holy Laughter" Holy?

Doug: Now let's test the spirits, as the apostles advised, related to the phenomenon of laughing in the Spirit. We are seeing this kind of laughter all over the world—people entering into bubbly joy and sometimes exploding into mirth that consumes whole rooms full of people. This manifestation transcends geographical and cultural boundaries.

Luke tells us that Jesus "rejoiced in the Holy Spirit" (10:21). Unfortunately we do not know what this rejoicing looked like. But we do know that the concept of rejoicing in the Spirit is biblical, and it would be hard to imagine that it does not include laughter and shouting for joy—an expression we find often in the Psalms.

The pattern for discernment given in the last chapter, faith working through love, can help us discern this phenomenon.

Laughing in the Spirit can be done, like everything else, in a good or bad way. It can become soulish and carnal, depending on whether it is handled with love. Pastoral guidance is needed from situation to situation. "Laughing in the Spirit" can be a means of drawing attention to oneself and away from Jesus. And these days it can become a badge of spirituality, a passport to the company of the truly "Spirit-filled." Yet Brad and I are convinced that holy laughter is a great gift with a variety of hidden purposes in the heart of God.

A sign, by nature, is supposed to draw attention not to itself but beyond itself to a deeper reality. The sign assures us that God is doing a deeper and enduring work in our hearts. That work carries more importance than the sign.

Again we remember Jessie Penn-Lewis' warning about getting too wrapped up in "the outer workings of the supernatural in [our] circumference." We ask instead: Does this sign point to deeper Kingdom realities? What is God saying to His Church today by means of this sign? What is He doing in the hearts of people who are laughing in the Spirit?

At least five things.

A Sign of Inner Healing

Brad: First, holy laughter may be connected with deep inner healing and the restoration of a person who has been wounded emotionally or spiritually.

In Taiwan I often saw wizened old Chinese ladies at our power ministry meetings. Their joyless faces were etched with lines of care, their shoulders slumped as though carrying a heavy load. But when the Holy Spirit fell on them, they would drop to the floor in fits of holy laughter that sometimes lasted an hour or more. When they finally walked out of these meetings, we could see that a transformation had taken place. Their shoulders were straight, their eyes sparkled, their faces looked almost young. Testimony often confirmed that during these times of holy laughter, God had worked deep healing and restoration or lifted the weariness of being a woman in a male-dominated society.

At a Dunamis retreat in Alaska in 1995, a woman seated alone in the back of the church suddenly let out a wild, giddy laugh of erupting joy. I looked at the conferees, including many pastors I hoped to draw into the work of PRRMI. I could see they were irritated. Some had checked out completely.

O God, I prayed, *please shut this lady up.*

The laughter spread, our prayers came to an end and the meeting concluded in disarray. The woman was terribly embarrassed and voiced to me the fear that she had been out of order. She looked as though she could feel the disapproval of the pastors—and, I am afraid, my irritation as well.

The only way to deal with the situation was to have an honest debriefing, so we reviewed the day and evening meetings. When we got to the interruption that had come from the laughter, one of the pastors expressed his discomfort, said the whole thing had been out of order and that he had decided not to come back for the rest of the conference.

Then I asked if the woman would be willing to share what had happened to her. By this time she was in tears—embarrassed, apologetic and asking for forgiveness for interrupting the meeting.

"No!" I said. "We have evaluated this manifestation only from the outside and not from the inside. It's true that the laughter didn't seem to be in sync with what the Lord was doing in the group, but it may have been consistent with what He was doing in you. So what was going on inside of you?"

Then she told us her story. Just before the retreat, she had been at her wit's end and was contemplating suicide. Her image of herself had been shattered through a number of urgent circumstances and she had fallen into a deep depression.

"I was desperate," she said, "and decided this conference was my last chance at life. When we started praying for the gifts of the Holy Spirit, I was too numb even to pray. Suddenly it was as if Jesus was right there. I felt His love envelop me. Something inside of me that had been dull and dead was being brought back to life. Waves of joy came over me like a sparkling stream, and the next thing I knew, I was caught up in this laughter. It's the first time I've laughed in a couple of years."

On hearing this story, the attitude of the pastors began to change. Once they could see what the Lord was doing, they realized it was more important than their own preconceived ideas of how the meeting should flow. Healing laughter was a vital part of God's grace for this woman—grace that was extended to her afterward by the other conferees.

This story reminds us of a comment by American evangelist Charles G. Finney:

Revivals of religion are sometimes accused of making people mad. The fact is, men are naturally mad on the subject of religion; and revivals rather *restore* them than make them mad.[1]

A Means for Pointing to Jesus Christ

Second, holy laughter may, like all manifestations of the Holy Spirit, be a powerful witness to the reality and love of Jesus Christ. It can (as we said in the last chapter about signs and wonders in general) help the unbeliever believe in Jesus.

This has certainly been true with the multiplying numbers who are coming to faith through the current renewal movement sweeping the world.

When manifestations result in a witness to Jesus, surely that is the work of the Holy Spirit.

A Kingdom of Children

Doug: Many Christians are self-conscious, stiff, opinionated, guarded and concerned not to leave a bad impression, especially in church. But in the face of such stiffness, God says He wants us to enter His Kingdom like little children. So the third thing God may be doing through the gift of holy laughter is inviting you and me to become like children.

My very first experience with laughing in the Spirit occurred in Oregon in a small group one evening. During a serious time of prayer, we asked Jesus to baptize us with the Holy Spirit. Various manifestations of the Spirit resulted.

One of the persons present was a young lawyer who often played the devil's advocate and enjoyed nothing so much as a good argument. Toward the end of the evening, this young man, in his gray suit and button-down manner, began to break into laughter. Of all the people we might have expected to begin laughing, he was the very last!

But first he giggled. Then he laughed more assertively. Then he roared. Pretty soon everyone in the room was laughing with him. The side-splitting hilarity spread to everyone in the room. When the group broke up soon after, he was still laughing. He told us later that he laughed all the way home, laughed his way to bed and kept his wife awake half the night with his irrepressible giggling.

What was God doing? I believe he was turning a lawyer into a little child, so that he could be fit for the Kingdom of heaven.

A Foretaste of the Great Feast

Some church people act dignified and a little grim. Others look downright sour, as though God hated laughter and fun. "If some people prefer to be unhappy," reason outsiders, "let them go to church. But that's not the way I choose to proceed through life."

But God is showing us that He does not necessarily agree with our churchly philosophy. Could it be that He Himself despises our solemn assemblies, as He did in the time of Isaiah (1:13) and Amos (5:21)? In any case, here is a fifth thing God is doing through the gift of holy laughter—giving us a joyful foretaste of the great feast to come.

I know what some say about this. God has to convict us of sin. Preachers have to tell their people the hard truth. And I admit it: God had to deal firmly with sin in Israel, as with sin in us, too. This cannot be a joyful experience; it is more likely to produce tears than laughter. James is right some of the time when he says, "Be wretched and mourn and weep. Let your laughter be turned to mourning and your joy to dejection. Humble yourselves before the Lord and he will exalt you" (James 4:9–10). Agreed.

But there is room for both weeping and laughter in the course of God's dealings with us.

Irrepressible, Holy Joy

Few people have been as serious-minded or as mature in revival phenomena as evangelist Charles Finney. His face was carved in stone and he knew the value of the conviction of sin. But solemnity was not his only response to repentance.

Finney was preaching to a room full of irreligious people in Antwerp, a town in western New York that was called "Sodom" because of its immoral reputation. Without warning, his hearers began to fall on the floor under the power of the Holy Spirit. Under a deep conviction of sin, many cried out for mercy. Soon such a noise of weeping and wailing filled the room that the revivalist could no longer make himself heard.

Finney described in his *Memoirs* what happened next:

I said to them: "You are not in hell yet; and now let me direct you to Christ." For a few moments I tried to hold forth the Gospel to them;

but scarcely any of them paid any attention. My heart was so overflowing with joy at such a scene that I could hardly contain myself. A
little way from where I stood was an open fire-place. I recollect very
well that my joy was so great, that I could not help laughing in a most
spasmodic manner. I knelt down and stuck my head into that fire-place,
and hung my pocket handkerchief over my head, lest they should see
me laugh; for I was aware that they would not understand that it was
irrepressible, holy joy that made me laugh. It was with much difficulty
that I refrained from shouting, and giving glory to God.[2]

Keeping the Feast with God

Even when God convicts people of sin and leads us through a
wilderness, He purposes to exalt us in due time. His ultimate will is
not humiliation and weeping, but happiness in His presence—"righteousness and peace and joy in the Holy Spirit" (Romans 14:17).

After God led the people of Israel into exile, He brought them
back to the Promised Land. Ezra and Nehemiah reintroduced the
Word of God to the residents of Jerusalem. On the first Feast of Taber-
nacles after their return, Nehemiah surely read how God had called
His people to bring tithes and offerings to Jerusalem and consume
them in His presence: "You shall eat there before the LORD your
God and rejoice, you and your household" (Deuteronomy 14:26).
The tithe, more than just a way of supporting priests, widows and
orphans, was a way of celebrating the harvest with God at least once
a year. God was saying, "Have a party, but don't leave Me out of
your celebration."

The people wept openly as they heard about God's good plan for
them and saw how perverse their forefathers had been. Perhaps the
ashes of the babies in the Valley of Hinnom still blew in their faces.

But Nehemiah's instructions to the returned exiles, in the middle
of all the weeping and conviction of sin, remind us of Charles Finney
with his head in the fireplace:

> Then Nehemiah the governor, Ezra the priest and scribe, and the
> Levites who were instructing the people said to them all, "This day is
> sacred to the LORD your God. Do not mourn or weep." For all the
> people had been weeping as they listened to the words of the Law.

Nehemiah said, "Go and enjoy choice food and sweet drinks, and send some to those who have nothing prepared. This day is sacred to our LORD. Do not grieve, for the joy of the LORD is your strength."

The Levites calmed all the people, saying, "Be still, for this is a sacred day. Do not grieve."

Then all the people went away to eat and drink, to send portions of food and to celebrate with great joy, because they now understood the words that had been made known to them.

. . . From the days of Joshua son of Nun until that day, the Israelites had not celebrated [the Feast of Tabernacles] like this. And their joy was very great.

Nehemiah 8:9–12, 17, NIV

Nehemiah had unusual insight about God. Punishment, he recognized, was not God's ultimate heart, but grace, kindness and joy. His first and best will for us is to throw us a feast—not just so we might make merry with our friends (Luke 15:29), but so we might celebrate deep fellowship with Him.

A Teaching Turns into a Party

At a week-long conference in Minnesota recently on prayer, I was scheduled to teach the final evening on the nuts and bolts of prayer—topics like prayer posture, prayer journals, prayer partners and the like. But I was concerned that this final evening would be anticlimactic. And when the conferees seemed unusually groggy from late-night prayer sessions the previous two evenings, I became even more concerned that this last meeting would finish the job and put everyone to sleep.

After a time of worship and before the teaching started, I felt the Lord saying, *Start your teaching by singing "I've Got the Joy, Joy, Joy, Joy Down in My Heart."*

Given the solemnity with which we had ended our worship time, it seemed an inappropriate selection. Still, I obeyed. And when we sang the song, an inexplicable hilarity entered the room and began to overwhelm us.

As I began to teach, I found unexpected jokes coming out of my mouth. Soon others were responding in repartee. Everyone was laughing, even in the back row. Within fifteen minutes I was laughing so hard, I had to stop teaching and sit down. It took another fifteen minutes to get the room under control.

I believe God was giving us a party. In some ways we were behaving as though we were drunk. (We could certainly see why the first disciples were accused of this on Pentecost!) The hilarity lifted our hearts. And the most important thing was, Jesus was at the center of it, and it drew us together in Him. All of us present will remember that day as a rewarding culmination to a week of prayer.

I wonder if this is what the Marriage Supper of the Lamb will be like. A God like the one we experienced that night is a God I can love. He is a God who has my best interests at heart. His laughter is clean, pure and wholesome.

A Revelation of God

In holy laughter the secret gets out: Out of our God flows mirth, joy unspeakable that fills the cosmos. And here is the fifth purpose of holy laughter: to give us a deeper revelation of the character of God Himself.

G. K. Chesterton, the British writer and critic in a day of stern, joyless Victorian religion, pointed to mirth as part of the nature of Jesus:

> Christianity is itself so jolly a thing that it fills the possessor of it with a certain silly exuberance, which sad and high-minded Rationalists might reasonably mistake for mere buffoonery and blasphemy, just as their prototypes, the sad and high-minded Stoics of old Rome, did mistake the Christian joyousness for buffoonery and blasphemy.[3]

In holy laughter we experience full-blown the joy that lies within every person being recreated in the image of Jesus Christ. Such joy seems a little ridiculous in a world full of tragedy, and it is still something of an offense. Yet it reflects the true nature of God Himself, who is showing us the mirth of heaven.

PART 4

Advancing the Kingdom of Jesus

18

Bringing the Next Generation to Jesus

Doug: But it is not time yet for uninterrupted parties. There is work to be done. Satan is all around us and has his eyes on the next generation. A powerless Church cannot surmount the onslaught of satanic doctrines and influences that are appealing these days to the young. The Western world is in danger of losing an entire generation to the most profound spiritual darkness imaginable, and this darkness is closing in.

The Swiss psychiatrist Carl Jung sensed more than anyone the desperate emptiness of what the Enlightenment produced in the first half of this century. He succeeded in reintroducing the West to a spiritual quest. Jung rejected Sigmund Freud's most basic presuppositions—his faith in science and the rational mind—because he saw that our lives become shallow, meaningless and empty when we fail to recognize that we are at heart spiritual beings. Many people born after 1950 now look to Jung to provide answers to the most basic questions of life. He was a true pioneer, calling to a future generation to seek fulfillment in the spirit realm, not in the materialism of science.

Yet his voice, so effective and influential, has not led this present generation to be grounded in the things of Jesus, but in clever satanic deception.

Lessons from Carl Jung

As I look at the vast number of American churches and at the relatively powerless ways we try to present the Gospel, I am reminded of Jung's early life growing up in the late nineteenth century in the Swiss Reformed church pastored by his father. As a boy he was profoundly aware of the spiritual realm—but nobody else in his church was, nor could he get anyone to talk about spiritual matters with him. He wanted to tell his father about certain dreams he had had that he thought came from God. But he felt that his father, along with the rest of the church, would not understand him, so he kept mum.

With the approach of confirmation, he was instructed by his father in preparation for his first Communion. But his initiation into church membership by means of the sacrament was so devoid of genuine spiritual experience that he began to doubt the reality of Christian promises.

Carl Jung did not meet God in the Church, as he wrote in *Memories, Dreams, Reflections:*[1]

> To be sure, there had been talk about Him, but it had all amounted to no more than words. Among the others I had noticed nothing of the vast despair, the overpowering elation and outpouring of grace which for me constituted the essence of God.
>
> pp. 54–55

Jung's father was sinking into a depression that would end up destroying his faith. Members of the church, Jung saw, were incapable of helping him, for they looked at Christianity as a matter of correct doctrine, not ministering power for healing. "They had blocked all avenues by which he might have reached God directly," wrote Jung, "and then faithlessly abandoned him" (p. 93).

In contrast to the emptiness of his church experience, which was represented by his father, Jung drew strength from his mother, who was rooted in deep, invisible ground, though it never appeared to me as confidence in her Christian faith. For me it was somehow connected with animals, trees, mountains, meadows and running water, all of which contrasted most strangely with her Christian surface and her conventional assertions of faith. . . . It never occurred to me how "pagan" this foundation was.

p. 90

In his student years, Jung had many conversations about God with pastors and professors of theology. From those conversations he recognized that the Church, clinging to Christ alone, had abandoned her inheritance in the Holy Spirit, as though the Spirit had never been given. "To me this [view] absolutely belied Christ's own view that the Holy Ghost, who had begotten him, would take his place among men after his death" (pp. 97–98).

Doorway to the Demonic

Because the Christian Church could not demonstrate that Jesus, the One from above, is uniquely able to teach about the spirit realm and baptize with the Holy Spirit, Jung threw away the Christian framework by which he might have evaluated his spiritual experiences—a framework he considered naïve because in his experience it was unproven. He decided to explore the spiritual world as an aspect of nature, part of the "unconscious mind" that Freud had exposed. "To me," he wrote, "dreams are a part of nature, which harbors no intention to deceive, but expresses something as best it can . . ." (pp. 161–162).

Jung was an exceedingly optimistic man who believed that nothing in nature could harm him, and that simple truth would reveal itself to him if he opened himself to anything and everything. So he began to explore the spiritual realm through the doorway of the unconscious. Whatever spirit he met there, he accepted as being "part of nature" that would have "no intention to deceive."

By this time he had thrown away all remnants of personal Christian faith, while (unlike Freud) retaining the sense that Christianity is an important and generally positive ingredient in Western culture.

By means of dream and fantasy, Jung made contact with what was more than dream or fantasy—spirit guides, whom he frankly recognized as demonic. Yet he was not afraid of these demonic powers because of his conviction that they were friendly.

> But there was a demonic strength in me, and from the beginning there was no doubt in my mind that I must find the meaning of what I was experiencing in these fantasies. When I endured these assaults of the unconscious I had an unswerving conviction that I was obeying a higher will, and that feeling continued to uphold me until I had mastered the task.
>
> p. 177

Jung invited the spirit guides to come and speak to him, and they did. Two spirit guides appeared to him who called themselves Salome and Elijah.

> Elijah assured me that he and Salome had belonged together from all eternity, which completely astounded me. . . . They had a black serpent living with them which displayed an unmistakable fondness for me. I stuck close to Elijah because he seemed to be the most reasonable of the three, and to have a clear intelligence.
>
> p. 181

Another spirit being calling himself Philemon came to Jung to guide him into truth: "Philemon was a pagan and brought with him an Egypto-Hellenistic atmosphere with a Gnostic coloration" (p. 182). Philemon taught Jung that many thoughts do not originate with people but are given to them from outside themselves. Jung called Philemon his "guru."

Jung wrote down some of the thoughts of Philemon in a self-published work, *The Seven Sermons to the Dead*. From that time, during World War I, his house began to be haunted. Yet compared to the spiritual dryness and powerlessness of the church he had grown up in, his occult experience was more real and fascinating by far.

Alchemy and Gnosticism

This fascination lured Jung into a study of alchemy (medieval chemical philosophy) and, beyond that, of the Gnostic writers of the early years of the Christian era. The first Christians regarded Gnosticism as a subtler deception than old-line paganism because it presented itself as a higher form of Christianity, whereas it was not really Christianity at all, but a falling away from Christ.

Carl Jung was fascinated with Gnosticism and alchemy, however, and so convinced that everything that came out of his unconscious would be beneficial and truthful that he jumped in where the apostles had feared to tread. He did not want to be trapped in the same experience of death as his father—the death of traditional religion and dry doctrine. So, guided by a dream, Jung collected a library of occult books.

In *The Collapse of the Brass Heaven*, Brad and I trace how the occult "wisdom" and "knowledge" being discovered among German-speaking people during Jung's lifetime were not as healthful and benign as Jung believed them to be. Medieval occultism going back to the Rosicrucians and other ancient searches for occult knowledge (or "Gnosis") generated immense evil—evil that produced both world wars that boiled up out of Germany during Jung's life.

It is a great tragedy that Carl Jung, who experienced a genuine hunger for God in his early years, ended up rejecting Jesus Christ as having any relevance to fill his spiritual emptiness. He sought and found in medieval alchemy and Gnosticism a more "genuine" spiritual experience that, by any biblical standard, would be called doctrines of demons (see 1 Timothy 4:1).

Searching for Authentic Spirituality

We Christians must ask some hard questions about cultures that have been immersed in the Gospel of Jesus Christ, yet have turned to demonic spirit guides. Why was Jung's experience of the Christian Church so shallow, his experience of Jesus Christ so empty? Why could he not have discovered Christ as the conclusion of his search for spiritual reality?

Brad and I can only say, by way of reply, that the Western Church has willfully drained herself of the power of the Holy Spirit and rejected the insights of her own mature teachers. Jessie Penn-Lewis, writing out of vast experience in spiritual discernment, wrote in *War On the Saints:*

Why the Church in the twentieth century has not recognized the existence, and workings, of evil supernatural forces, can only be attributed to its low condition of spiritual life and power. Even at the present time, when the existence of evil spirits is recognized by the heathen, it is generally looked upon by the missionary as "superstition" and ignorance; whereas the ignorance is often on the part of the missionary, who is blinded by the prince of the power of the air to the revelation given in the Scriptures, concerning the Satanic powers.[2]

Europe experienced a brief revival of spiritual life and power during the world tour of R. A. Torrey. But most European churches (including Jung's Swiss Reformed Church) and the churches of Canada and the U.S. rejected that power as normative for Christian experience. Again, the Pentecostals had the motor car; the Protestants had the instruction manual. The latter saw no need for the former, nor the former for the latter.

What a tragedy! It is the Holy Spirit, after all, who brings the power of Christ to bear upon the real needs of human beings. The Spirit makes Jesus real, confirms His message "with signs following" (Mark 16:20, KJV), makes the Word "living and active" (Hebrews 4:12), and fills our inner nature with "the breadth and length and height and depth" of the love of Christ (Ephesians 3:18).

The keys to the Kingdom are still given today to the Church, and the Holy Spirit is still the power of God given exclusively to those who follow Jesus. Meanwhile, Generation X is searching, just as Carl Jung was, for an authentic experience of God. Will the Christian Church at the end of the twentieth century be better able to minister the grace and love of Jesus than the Church in Jung's day?

Part of her role is to guide people away from spiritual counterfeits and deceptive teaching. The best way to oppose unholy spirits is by presenting the Holy Spirit—which the following story shows.

Lessons from Marie

In December 1994 I was preaching about the seven steps of R. A. Torrey. Marie White (not her real name), a visitor that day on a quest for spiritual reality, took an interest. The message was different from anything she had heard in other churches she had tried. So after the service that morning, she handed me a visitor's card indicating that she wanted to talk to someone about God.

Later that week, during a get-acquainted time, I heard her story:

I was raised Roman Catholic. During my early years, God entered my life and I gained a vibrant faith in Jesus. My upbringing created in me a desire to do some good with my life, so I signed up for the Peace Corps and ended up in Cameroon from 1983 to 1987. My experience there exposed me to a blend of Islam, animism, ancestor worship and Communism. As a Westerner I did not know how to evaluate these ideas and philosophies. I just took them all in, and they lodged in my heart along with my faith in God.

At the end of my first year in Africa, my faith was shattered one day when I was raped. I could no longer believe in a God who takes a personal interest in our individual lives. After that, the God I was able to believe in was a remote Creator God who has backed off from His creation, waiting with His infamous patience for us to destroy ourselves. I searched among the other philosophies that swirled around me, looking for meaning in my life.

These searches led nowhere. I married an African Communist. After four more years I became severely depressed. My husband kept giving me the line that "God" was a social invention to keep the masses in line. Having nothing with which to combat these ideas, I tended to agree with them. At least Communism was a search for a more just world, and that hope was better than nothing. Still, I was profoundly unhappy, and my marriage was a mess. My continuing search led me into the financial industry in the U.S. I divorced, then remarried, but still did not have a clue how to have peace or joy. My second husband and I fought constantly.

One thing I couldn't understand: Three times I came very near death, and each time I was miraculously spared. *Why,* I kept wondering, *was I spared? Why am I alive? Is there something or someone protecting me?*

Sheer desperation forced this young woman (who now had a small son) to keep up her quest for deep meaning that would fill the emptiness of her life. She still wanted to devote her life to doing good for others, so she became a massage therapist in addition to her job in finance.

One day, while preparing to do massage for her sister, who was a Christian, she saw six angels surrounding her sibling. This vision shook her worldview, which had ruled out spiritual reality. A question began to nag at her: If there are personal angels, perhaps there is also a personal God who created the angels.

Soon afterward she was invited to visit a friend in Europe who had been converted from Taoism to Christ. While packing for the trip, she threw some books into her bags, only to discover later that each book was about God. As she read them and talked with her friend, she began to sense God healing the pain of her past.

"I call that my week of tears," she says, "for every day would bring forth more pain, yet along with it a quiet peace."

New Age Discoveries

Marie's quest for God and meaning led her to Richmond. There her five-year-old son, after conversations with other children at school, began talking about church. For his sake she visited several churches. None helped her in her search.

In 1994 she attended a workshop on "healing touch." She became acquainted with a self-described "spiritual" woman who helped her see that "spiritual energy" would greatly increase her effectiveness as a massage therapist. So Marie began to explore New Age feminist spirituality.

Attending various goddess-feminist workshops, she encountered teaching about the Hindu goddess Kalri, a three-thousand-year-old maiden mother, Crune, and a six-thousand-year-old Minoan snake goddess of Crete. These spirits claimed authority from the fact that they were "older than Christ." Marie opened her life to a spirit guide who presented himself at a healing touch seminar and called himself Elijah.

Because these spirits seemed genuinely interested in healing and helping people, Marie assumed they were from God, just as Carl Jung had in an almost identical experience. Even the name *Elijah* was the same. (Demonic spirits sometimes use Bible names when dealing with people from Christian backgrounds.) She trusted both the humans and the spirit guides coming into her life, looking to them to lead her to God. New Age feminist seminars became her place of spiritual nurture.

Messages

Marie was severely shaken one day when she woke up to find a black mark mysteriously and unaccountably inscribed on her arm.

A friend from Trinidad claimed that this mark was of the devil, who had marked her for his own. Marie began to wonder if she was getting into something she would eventually regret.

Then she had a dream. She knew it was the Holy Spirit warning her of danger. In the dream she was standing behind a pickup truck alongside a lawn. A large truck came out of nowhere and smashed into her, destroying her. What was unusual was that the truck came not from down the street but from across the lawn, where she least expected it. She told the dream to her feminist friends, but no one was able to interpret it.

After several months this young woman began to feel an inner pull to go to church again, although she was still involved in New Age feminism. In fact, the Sunday after she attended our worship service, she attended a "Women's Spirituality Solstice Service" in which the "Mother's Ministry Order of Worship" included an invocation to the "sacred" elements of fire, air, earth and water, a "Goddess Dance for the Great Cosmic Mother" and a homily on "The Ancient Mystery of Eleusis: A Path to Wisdom and Healing from the Cosmic Mother." The service culminated in a "Sacred Rite of Holy Eucharist to the Holy Uterus." (This kind of teaching, full of Jungian psychology and goddess feminism, is creeping into Christian theological seminaries as a way of showing empathy with women's issues.)

During those days of profound spiritual search, Marie could not forget the dream she had had several months earlier about being blindsided by the truck.

Then she recounted it to me, and God gave me the interpretation, which immediately struck her as true. The spirit guides in whom she was placing her confidence were really out to destroy her. If she kept going to them, rather than to Jesus Christ, her life would be demolished, as she had been by the pickup truck in her dream. And because she had learned to place her confidence in them, the disaster they would bring would come from the last place she expected.

God began to woo her through other dreams, too. In one she was giving her life to Jesus with a jalapeño pepper crammed into her ear. God's Word as she heard it was burning its way into her heart through her ears.

In another dream she was on her way to a meeting when she was confronted by a woman on a stretcher who looked just like her. The woman said, "It's time for me to die," and handed her a gun. Marie shot her in the back of the head. As she did so, she was filled with peace. Later, during a counseling session, she saw that the woman on the stretcher was the "old, unbelieving Marie." God wanted to give birth to the real Marie, the Marie He had created her to become.

Surrender to Jesus

A week or two later, my wife had an opportunity to pray with Marie to accept Jesus Christ as her Lord and Savior. This was a critical time of decision for her, because it placed her will on the side of Jesus and against the spirit guides. Marie was blessed with a deep sense of inner peace as a result of this prayer of surrender to Jesus. But it was the beginning of warfare over her soul.

Marie joined a small discipleship group I was leading full of other young people seeking healing and redemption in Jesus Christ. Each week, it seemed, some fresh dream or exciting evidence of the Holy Spirit reached out to draw Marie to Jesus and away from the spirit guides. For make no mistake: There was no place for both the spirit guides and Jesus.

Marie was struggling with this issue and asked me often, "How do you know when the spirit powers are of God?"

The Holy Spirit in Marie was struggling with unholy spirits masquerading as holy. Who would gain the victory?

Deliverance from Demonic Strongholds

As Marie continued to attend church and group meetings, her faith in God increased. Through the revelations of the Bible, she began to discern for herself that the spirits she had invited to befriend her and help her minister healing were anti-Christian spirits—angels of darkness masquerading as angels of light.

Now they blocked Marie's mind when the Scriptures were read, and they spoke to her from within her mind—scorning, arguing against apostolic teaching, ridiculing me and other ministers of the Gospel. It was, she told me, as though the left side of her head were full of goodness, the other side full of evil and darkness.

This reminded me of two things. First, Carl Jung had ministered to a woman like this but was never able to heal her from the voices in the left side. He concluded that at least the patient had been "half cured" (p. 127). I also remembered an almost identical situation in a woman a dozen years before. That woman had tried obsessively to destroy the left (evil) side of her body by tearing out body parts. But after deliverance from evil spirits, this manifestation ceased, to the astonishment of her neurologist.

So when Marie began to describe this pattern, I recognized it as a serious demonic affliction.

One night Marie was thrown physically out of bed by the spiritual powers controlling her. God protected her from banging her head on her computer table. He was showing her that, though she had opened herself to destructive forces, He would protect her if she continued to trust the name of Jesus. This experience also gave Marie the courage to face those powers and ask for deliverance.

"It took a conscious decision and an act of my will," she says, "to cooperate with what God wanted to do to get me free from my past."

Demonic powers are not expelled automatically through the preaching of the Gospel or normal prayers to God. Jesus did not use these methods in dealing with them and neither should we. These beings are bitterly resentful of Jesus, who has more power than they do. They do not like to be reminded of His Lordship, but they must respect it; and they can be addressed and commanded to leave in His name.

Christians ministering deliverance must be armed with the power of the Holy Spirit, rather than with mere self-confidence or professional aplomb. In fact, it is in deliverance ministry that we see most clearly the divine power given to those who have learned to trust Jesus and have asked to be baptized in the Holy Spirit.

At Marie's request, another experienced Christian and I set about to bring her deliverance from the powers to which she had opened her life. My partner was Robson Gomes, a Brazilian with much experience dealing with spiritism in his own country. (Often Americans inexperienced in spiritual warfare can learn much from Christians of other nationalities who have not been hemmed in by our Western worldview.)

During the next three weeks, we identified three spirits that had made their home in Marie. She knew their names herself and described them to us. The first, a familiar spirit, had come in by invitation when she was a child. The second had entered during an ancestral ceremony in Africa to which she had submitted herself. The third was the spirit guide Elijah, whom she had invited in during her naïve foray into goddess-feminist spirituality.

Each of these spirits had to be forced out by strong application of the word of the cross. I discovered afresh the apostolic truth that

> now, through the church, the manifold wisdom of God should be made known to the rulers and authorities in the heavenly realms, according to his eternal purpose which he accomplished in Christ Jesus our Lord.
>
> Ephesians 3:10–11, NIV

The result: Marie was fully delivered of the influence of the spirit guides (demons), and has become a delightful and productive part of our church.

Freedom, Life and Peace

Marie's response after weeks of spiritual struggle was, "I'm finally becoming the person I'm supposed to be." During all her exploration of Communism, atheism and New Age feminism, she explains, she kept hoping she would find herself. Yet each time she put her hope in these faiths, she was eventually disappointed and felt she was becoming less and less the person God wanted her to be. Only the power of God in the Holy Spirit leading her to Christ delivered her from counterfeit hopes that had led her to be false to God and to herself.

"Only Christ," she says, "has the power to birth a person 'in water and the Holy Spirit.' No other spirituality can do this for people. In Christ I discovered true, lasting satisfaction and inner peace. The other promises were counterfeit and ultimately disappointing."

Out of Marie's experience of Christ and the Holy Spirit, she has at last received an answer she can give to other people—an answer that will be of help in their struggles and turmoil: Jesus Christ.

We Need the Holy Spirit

The earnest of our inheritance in Christ is the Holy Spirit, the power of God on earth until Jesus comes back. It is this power alone that can win the young to Jesus the King, who alone deserves their full allegiance.

> For in him all things were created, in heaven and on earth, visible and invisible, whether thrones or dominions or principalities or authorities—all things were created through him and for him.
>
> Colossians 1:16

In the urgency of this hour, and especially for the sake of the young, is it not time for the Western Church to rediscover the truth first revealed by John the Baptist: that Jesus baptizes us with the Holy Spirit? Can we seriously hope to win young people to Christ without the realities promised and power gained in the Person and work of the Spirit of God?

The Spirit Brings the Kingdom

Brad: Despite the spiritual vibrancy of Ashbel Green Simonton, founder of the Presbyterian Church in Brazil, that church has been as bound by tradition and spiritual powerlessness as most congregations in North America. In the past, Presbyterian missionaries have met great resistance when Brazilians discovered they had had an experience of the Holy Spirit. And Brazil has seen considerable tension between the mainline denominations and Pentecostals.

In September 1995 I took part in a PRRMI mission trip to Brazil. There I experienced an extraordinary move of the Holy Spirit among Brazilian Presbyterians, which demonstrates the empowering work of the Holy Spirit and places it in its proper framework: the advancement of the Kingdom of God. Reflecting on what happened among these mainline traditional Christians will, we hope, serve as a fitting conclusion to this book.

First Signs

Eight of us went to Brazil by invitation to conduct a Dunamis Project retreat (or, in Portuguese, "Projecto Dunamis") for leadership training at a church camp an hour outside the capital city, Brasília. In the daytime 180 people attended the five-day teaching event, including, amazingly, all the ministers and many of the elders from the local presbytery (the Presbyterian governing body in a particular locality). In the evenings the outdoor meeting area was packed with people from nearby towns.

The first night was an incredible beginning, with two hundred or so people present. The worship team from Central Presbyterian Church of nearby Anapolis, Goias, started off with some powerful songs exalting Jesus. Then the moderator of the presbytery gave a talk about his experience of being filled with the Holy Spirit and how it had changed his ministry. For years, he said, he had prayed that God would send a Holy Spirit revival on the Presbyterian Church, and he urged all the pastors and elders present to seek the same empowerment so they could be effective in their pastoral work.

Then this moderator started to weep. Other pastors gathered around him. The place was filled with intense expectation, although on the faces of some I read reserve and apprehension. Suddenly the Lord gave me a vision of fire falling on this place and each person taking a torch of the Holy Spirit's fire and igniting renewal throughout Brazil.

Then God said something to me that brought me to tears.

You are here, He said, *and this revival is going to take place because of the prayers and obedience of Ashbel Green Simonton.*

Doug and I have already told the story of Simonton, founder of the Presbyterian Church in Brazil in the mid-nineteenth century, and of his search for empowerment for ministry. He, too, prayed for an outpouring of the Holy Spirit on Brazil.

More than a century later, in 1995, came an outpouring of prayer by pastors of that presbytery in Brazil. And the arrival of our PRRMI team that fall was preceded by a remarkable five-week, 24-hour-a-day prayer vigil conducted at Central Presbyterian Church of Anapolis (which was also leading us in worship). The plea of the people had been, "Lord, send Your Spirit."

Laying a Teaching Foundation

The next morning I taught on worldview and the Person of the Holy Spirit. American and British missionaries have brought to Brazil a Western scientific worldview excluding spiritual realities that are vital to the biblical worldview. Because of the pervasive presence of spiritualism in that country, missionaries armed with a Western world-view have often been ineffective in dealing with spiritual bondage.

As I reached the end of my teaching, I knew we needed to break for lunch. At the same time, I was aware of a brooding sense of the holy presence of God.

"Let's get off British time that says it's time for lunch," I suggested, "and go to Brazilian time. Let's wait on the Holy Spirit. I think He's about to do something."

The silence intensified. I could see expressions of awe, joy and wonder on the faces around the room. Then I had a vision of Jesus walking in our midst, touching each of us and beckoning us to follow Him. No sooner had I described this vision than people started to weep, confess sin and recommit their lives to Jesus.

I received words and images revealing what the Lord was doing. Every time I called out what I heard or saw, those things happened all over the room. One of the most beautiful was when I heard God say He was blessing the marriages of those present. Instantly couples began to hug one another and weep in each other's arms. This wonderful *kairos* moment enabled me to relax and turn the event completely over to the Holy Spirit.

An excellent teaching by my co-worker Ken Shay that evening on inner healing led into an extended period of healing prayer.

An Unexpected Act of God

All the next morning I taught on the inner and outer work of the Holy Spirit. I could sense light being shed in the thinking of these pastors, and problems being resolved. Some hurried up to me after the lecture to say they had struggled for years to put together an understanding of the Holy Spirit that made sense of their experience and was consistent with their Reformed understanding of Scripture. Several said they could go home now because their questions had been answered.

That evening I summarized the three concepts of the Holy Spirit's work—the Pentecostal view, the evangelical view and the neo-evangelical, "within-and-upon" view that has already been presented in this book. Then I shared the seven steps of how to receive the Holy Spirit for power in ministry.

As I concluded, I struggled for guidance from God. It was obvious that the people had been moved deeply. I started to go right into prayer but got a strong check in my spirit. *I should release them from the emotional atmosphere,* I thought, *and give them space to make cool, rational choices.*

"Let's take a break," I said. "Go out and seek God's face as to whether now is the time for you to pray to be filled with the Holy Spirit."

I could sense disappointment so I explained that if some of them still had questions or unresolved issues, tonight might be too soon for this prayer.

After thirty minutes we regathered. As the worship team led us into worship, people started to weep or shake uncontrollably. The awesome presence of God filled the place. American and Brazilian prayer leaders came together and began to pray for each other. Many people fell to the floor in the Spirit. Others began speaking in tongues. Then we scattered the prayer teams around the room. People surged forward. All over the room came a release of the gifts and power of the Holy Spirit. Almost all the members of the presbytery were baptized with the Spirit. Everywhere people were calling on Jesus and giving Him glory.

Toward the end of the evening, a retired, greatly beloved pastor stood and said that thirty years ago he had tried to introduce the renewing work of the Holy Spirit to the Presbyterian Church, but he had been ridiculed.

"Today my prayers have been answered," he said. "I am seeing the power fall on this Church that I have loved and grieved for, for so many years. This Church will never be the same. We are now being empowered to extend the Gospel to the whole area."

Then he gave a powerful prophecy about what the Holy Spirit was going to accomplish in the presbytery and throughout the Church of Brazil.

Debriefing and Discernment

I could tell, as glorious as this experience was, that some of the pastors were concerned about some of the manifestations. One pastor's daughter who was filled with the Holy Spirit had fallen on the floor, where she had shaken all over and gotten a small dose of holy laughter. Throughout it all she had smiled radiantly, but this did little to set her father at ease. He had never seen anything like it.

So after midnight I called everyone together for debriefing. About a hundred people, including many of the pastors, stayed until past one in the morning.

Many of those who had rested in the Spirit told us what had happened to them on the inside. And I offered some principles of discernment as to how to sort out what had been of the flesh, what had been of evil spirits and what had been truly of the Holy Spirit. Whenever there is such an outpouring, I explained, there is always a mixture of things going on. Some of the weeping, for example, was not a direct manifestation of the Spirit, but a human response to the working of the Spirit. At other times we were dealing with demons that had been forced into manifesting their presence when Jesus had shown Himself so powerfully. But some people present had been frightened that these demonic manifestations were from the Holy Spirit.

This was all very instructive and helped to nurture the gift of discernment.

We experienced this incredible outpouring of the Holy Spirit, I believe, for several reasons:

- The sovereignty of God in His plan for world history
- The persistent prayer of Brazilian Christians
- Our obedience, at great expense, to take our team to Brazil
- Clear, balanced teaching on the Holy Spirit
- The Brazilians' thirst to ask for and receive the Holy Spirit

What was the purpose of this outpouring? It aimed to deepen the faith of these church leaders and prepare them for the advancement of the Kingdom of God. The challenge in the future will be to keep the inward and outward working of the Holy Spirit in balance.

Encounter with Poverty

More happened at those meetings, but before I share one final experience, I want to jump ahead to another portion of the trip, where we saw long-term results from a previous outpouring of the

Holy Spirit in Brazil. Here we could see how the Spirit works to bring the Kingdom of Jesus on earth.

In the tropical oceanside city of Fortaleza, members of the PRRMI team were distributed to three local churches to preach the Sunday evening service. I was to preach, accompanied by a team member and a missionary translator, in a Presbyterian church in one of the slums—an experience for which I was unprepared.

The houses there were little boxes made of whatever materials could be scrounged up—flattened tin cans, strips of tarpaper, cardboard and wooden crates. At times I nearly gagged from the smells that filled the place, from cooking aromas and garbage to open sewers.

People were everywhere. Entire families sat by the side of the road. Dirty children ran hither and yon. Shirtless men in shorts stood or squatted in knots. Wretched children begged. Prostitutes lounged in the doorways of their hovels. About the whole place hung the atmosphere of life at its most basic level. And beyond the visible human structures of oppression and poverty, I could feel the presence of demonic strongholds that fed on and perpetuated this human misery.

But I observed all this with a detached unreality—until we walked past a barefoot, hungry-looking girl of about twelve. She wore a dirty, torn top and baggy shorts. Her teeth looked half-rotted. Her blonde hair, blue eyes and freckled face reminded me of my own twelve-year-old daughter.

If the Holy Spirit cannot minister to a person like this, I thought, *what's the purpose of the Holy Spirit? This girl needs to enter the Kingdom of God!*

Her face smashed through my comfortable fortress of detachment, caught and held me. I had a strong impulse to give her a hug and unload all the money in my pocket. But I rushed on, fearing that if I lingered for just a minute, I would slip into the same abyss that had already consumed her.

I felt stupid in my suit and tie (standard dress for a Presbyterian minister) and utterly unprepared and unworthy to preach anything to people who lived in such misery. What could I say to them? I prayed urgently for guidance.

Then the word came: *Tell them about Jesus and how He continues to work in your midst through the Holy Spirit. Tell them that My Kingdom has come.*

We reached the church and were welcomed warmly by the pastor, who showed us the building. It was a large cinderblock structure, its tin roof just now nearly completed. It had been built by the church people themselves and was the center of all kinds of ministry in the area, including daycare, education and a feeding program for children.

The pastor told us the remarkable history of the church. It had been founded in the area nearly twenty years before but had done little beyond survive. Then, three years before, renewal in the Holy Spirit had come to the church. Traditional Western worship had been replaced by guitars and praise songs in the language and style of the people. They had moved into power ministry. They had begun to take a compassionate interest in the surrounding community. Soon the church was growing so fast that it was spawning other congregations.

The service began. After a time of praise, the missions committee presented a report on their activities in the neighborhood, and a second report on the plight of persecuted Christians in Iraq. Their concern for Iraqis blew my mind. Wherever the Holy Spirit is working, I realized, He calls people to pray for the advancement of Christ's Kingdom worldwide.

One of our team members, Jeanne Justiss, shared her testimony of healing from sexual abuse. Then I followed the guidance I had been given and preached about Jesus' continuing work through the Holy Spirit, and that God's Kingdom has come.

Afterward they came forward and laid hands on me, praying that I would be empowered to share the Gospel in the U.S. Clearly these people felt they had gotten hold of something they wanted me to export to people they believed were poorer than they were! In spite of their abject poverty, they considered themselves rich in the things of God.

I left the meeting dumbfounded and humbled. In this slum, with its concentration of humanity, spiritual darkness, broken relationships, degrading immorality, drug abuse, sickness, hunger and economic and political oppression, I had seen the light of Jesus shining more purely and brightly than I usually saw in my own country. What these poor Christians had was the Kingdom of Jesus—a Kingdom begun in the inner work of the Holy Spirit, extended by signs and wonders and healings, and leading to compassionate ministries flowing from the Body of Christ. Behind the ministries I saw a relationship with Jesus and obedience to Him that brought peace, joy and satisfaction, even in the midst of the kingdom of darkness that raged all around.

I could see the Kingdom of God more clearly here for two reasons. First, the contrast between those who knew Jesus and those who did not was more obvious than in North America. Light shines more brightly in a dark place. Second, there were no signs of external success to confuse the picture of what a successful church looks like. Faith and love for Jesus and for one another were all these people had—the treasures of the Kingdom of God. They knew the abundant life of Jesus because they were obeying Him. He had become their King.

Lessons of the Kingdom

So I saw more clearly than I ever have, in an impoverished city in Brazil, why God gives the Holy Spirit. He is the power of God who brings people into an obedient relationship with Jesus the King. Jesus keeps blessing and rewarding the obedience of those who take steps of faith. These blessings, too, come from the Holy Spirit. The Kingdom of God comes not through bureaucracies, political structures, power-mongering or mere moral precepts, but through the power of the Holy Spirit ministered through the Church.

"If it is by the Spirit of God that I cast out demons," Jesus said, "then the kingdom of God has come upon you" (Matthew 12:28). In this little verse we see that it is Jesus who ministers the Holy Spirit, and that the Spirit is the power who brings the Kingdom of God among us.

This same Jesus has given the Church the power to "tread upon serpents and scorpions" (Luke 10:19). He says, "The gates of hell shall not prevail" against His Church (Matthew 16:18, KJV). And by the gentle, beckoning power of the Holy Spirit, the Church stands amid poverty, satanic systems, violence, prostitution and tragedy and says, "Here is where you can find abundant life. Here is where you can find Jesus. Obey Him and see what will happen."

The Holy Spirit brings the Kingdom of God by changing the reality of people's lives, beginning on the inside and working out to the externals. Specifically, He brings the Kingdom in these ways:

> He introduces us to Jesus and the Father (John 14:15–20; Revelation 5:6).
>
> He adopts us into a relationship with God (John 1:12–13; 3:5; Romans 8:14–17; 1 Corinthians 12:3).
>
> He transforms us into the image and character of Jesus (2 Corinthians 3:17–18; Galatians 5:18–23).
>
> He instructs us to be obedient to Jesus daily (Romans 8:14; Galatians 5:25).
>
> He empowers us to do the works of Jesus (Luke 3:16; 24:49; John 14:12).
>
> He builds us in fellowship and love with one another (Acts 2:37–47; 2 Corinthians 13:14; Ephesians 4:4–16).
>
> He guarantees eternal life (Ephesians 1:13–14; 1 John 5:6–12).

Tension between Two Kingdoms

The slum church in Brazil was a disconcerting picture of contradictions. Among those Christians I saw the Kingdom of God breaking into the world. They had been born again and were living in a new reality. While poverty, hunger, death and oppression raged all around them, they had received eternal life and were walking in love, joy and peace. Like seeds planted in manure, gifts from God were sprouting up everywhere, not by human contrivance but by the Holy Spirit.

Although the people were oppressed by human power structures, they were experiencing a higher authority that was very real to them. Though they confronted the results of demonization, sickness and death all around them every day, they had received limited power to set captives free, bind up the wounded and be a compassionate presence to the hungry. Yet the existence of the appalling conditions around them demonstrated that the Kingdom of God had much yet to do against the prince of darkness, king of the manure pile.

Scripturally there is an incompleteness to the Kingdom of God as shown in the following chart:

We live in a world where there is still much rebellion against God (Romans 1:18–23).

Even among Christians, the power of sin is still at work (Romans 7:21–25).

The natural order is not fully set free from its bondage (Romans 8:19–23).

Though Satan was defeated by Jesus on the cross, he still holds sway over the earth through deception (Luke 4:5–7; 2 Corinthians 10:3–5; Ephesians 2:2–3; 6:10–18).

Be Obedient!

Our job in the midst of human need is not to come up with grandiose schemes (à la Karl Marx, Mao Tse-tung or Adolf Hitler) for solving all the world's problems. It is simply to learn to obey God when He calls us to represent Him, to bring some sign of the Kingdom into some corner of the world He made. Our obedience is an essential ingredient in the process of fulfilling the Kingdom of God.

May I tell one more incident from my experience in Brazil? Let's go back to the Dunamis Project conference near Brasília. Quoting from my prayer journal:

The day after this most extraordinary outpouring of the Holy Spirit, the Spirit started to call people out into the work of the Kingdom. That night the building was packed to overflowing. People had come in from everywhere. There was eager expectation that God would work. The worship team from Central Presbyterian Church led us in an extended period of worship, after which I was asked to share the vision of PRRMI's worldwide ministry.

Then I invited prayers for people who were yet unsaved, and the focus was directed outward into the world. After praying for many young people who came forward to give their lives to Jesus, the Lord began to birth ministry through the prayers. Soon the Holy Spirit began calling people out and appointing them to ministries such as intercessory prayer, evangelism, spiritual warfare and healing. Each time guidance was given, a number of people sensed the Lord confirming what most people already knew was their calling. The Brazilians were now praying for one another; the pastors were moving into leadership among themselves. The torch had been passed from us to them. I felt that our mission there had been completed.

That night I lay awake for a long time. It seemed as though a river of the Holy Spirit was still rushing through me, and in it was mingling all the faces of the people who had been in the meetings. I guess I must have been partly dreaming, but it was as though I were surrounded by a great host of people all connected together by Jesus, and joining others at a great feast with dancing and celebration in many tongues.

As I looked at this throng of people all dancing and celebrating the Feast of the Lamb, I saw some who, in the mystery of God's sovereignty, were there because I had been obedient to the leading of the Spirit.

This was not a self-exalting vision. Rather, it presented the sobering reality that our obedience and faithfulness are part of advancing the Kingdom of God. And it put the work of the Holy Spirit in its proper context—bringing the Kingdom of God. In this vast, eternal work, the Spirit calls, directs, gives gifts and empowers us. But we must receive and use His gifts obediently. When we do, each one of us can make an eternal difference in someone's life that may include every dimension of reality—spiritual, psychological, economic, political and social. The Kingdom of God is an all-encompassing vision of release, healing and practicing God's righteous order in a world that has been His from the beginning.

Teaching on the work of the Holy Spirit finds its true meaning and balance only when placed within the context of the Kingdom of God. Otherwise we will distort the Gospel of Jesus Christ. When you look into the eyes of a poverty-stricken little girl who does not have enough to eat, the gifts and power of the Holy Spirit take on a different perspective. What are they really for? Why has God the Father poured out the Holy Spirit? Who is Jesus, really? The answer to these questions in this total context is the Kingdom of God.

The goal of Christ's coming is not just to get us into heaven; rather, it is to bring a new heaven and a new earth. The Holy Spirit has been sent to bring a revolution—the revolution of God's Kingdom, which is the first step to the new heaven and earth.

God is sovereign, but His sovereignty includes our participation in His work. He has destined us to rule with Christ on earth, to pray, "Thy Kingdom come, Thy will be done on earth as in heaven." So the Kingdom of God is advanced against the evil one by means of the only power greater than he is—the power of God.

At the end of the age, at the Marriage Feast of the Lamb, there will be dancing in the Kingdom because we saw an opportunity to receive the Holy Spirit and minister the power of God to others, so that they could know Jesus Christ the King.

Notes

Chapter 1: A New Movement of the Holy Spirit

1. Don Dunkerley, "Fire and Light," a leaflet of World Outreach Committee (P.O. Box 12268, Pensacola, FL 32581).
2. Leadership training conferences called the Dunamis Project are sponsored by Presbyterian & Reformed Renewal Ministries International (P.O. Box 429, Black Mountain, NC 28711–0429), of which Brad Long is executive director.

Chapter 2: Healing the Wounds

1. J. Edwin Orr, *Full Surrender* (London: Marshall, Morgan & Scott, 1951), p. 115.
2. John T. Nichol, *The Pentecostals* (Plainfield, N.J.: Logos, 1971).
3. Orr, *Full Surrender*, p. 110.
4. Manual of the Pentecostal Holiness Church (Oklahoma City, Okla.: 1991).
5. Dennis and Rita Bennett, *The Holy Spirit and You* (Plainfield, N.J.: Logos, 1971), pp. 64–65.
6. Larry Christenson, *Speaking in Tongues* (Minneapolis: Dimension, 1968), p. 53.
7. Charles G. Hummel, *Fire in the Fireplace: Contemporary Charismatic Renewal* (Downers Grove, Ill.: InterVarsity, 1978), p. 49.
8. We describe this trend in our book *The Collapse of the Brass Heaven* (Chosen, 1994). Virtually all mainline denominations in the West decided that we must adapt the biblical message to the tenets of modernity, a widespread philosophy or worldview that overtook Western cultures during the first half of the twentieth century.
9. Edward D. O'Connor, *The Pentecostal Movement in the Catholic Church* (Notre Dame: Ave Maria, 1971), pp. 215–216.

Chapter 3: The Power of God

1. C. Peter Wagner, *The Third Wave of the Holy Spirit* (Ann Arbor, Mich.: Servant, 1988), p. 18.
2. Roger Martin, *R. A. Torrey, Apostle of Certainty* (Murfreesboro, Tenn.: Sword of the Lord, 1976).
3. J. C. Pollock, *Moody: A Biographical Portrait of the Pacesetter in Modern Mass Evangelism* (New York: Macmillan, 1963), p. 82.
4. Ibid., pp. 90–91.
5. R. A. Torrey, *The Person and Work of the Holy Spirit* (Grand Rapids: Zondervan, 1910, 1974), p. 211.
6. The other sermon Moody referred to was "Why I Believe the Bible to Be the Word of God."
7. Torrey, *Person and Work*, p. 108.
8. Ibid., p. 123.
9. These steps are summarized by Roger Martin, *R. A. Torrey*, p. 117.

Chapter 4: The Holy Spirit "Upon"

1. Archer Torrey, "The Holy Spirit and You: On or In?" *Christian Life*, April 1983: p. 33.
2. Kenneth Scott Latourette, *A History of Christianity* (New York: Harper & Brothers, 1953), p. 1387.
3. Andrew Stewart, quoted by Iain H. Murray, *The Puritan Hope* (Edinburgh: Banner of Truth, 1971), p. 30.

Chapter 5: Three Prophetic Hopes Fulfilled in Jesus

1. Frank Worthen, "From Being Different to Making a Difference," *Lifelines of Love In Action,* Vol. 21, No. 4 (April 1995), pp. 4–5.

Chapter 7: Is There a Baptism with the Holy Spirit?

1. R. A. Torrey, *What the Bible Teaches about the Holy Spirit* (New York: Revell, 1898). The other quotes from Torrey in this chapter are from the same book.
2. Thomas Smail, *Reflected Glory: The Holy Spirit in Christ and Christians* (Grand Rapids: Eerdmans, 1976), p. 143.
3. Jessie Penn-Lewis, *War on the Saints* (New York: Thomas E. Lowe, 1973, 1991), p. 50.
4. Joseph M. Wilson, "Ashbel Green Simonton," *The Presbyterian Church in the United States (O.S.), The Presbyterian Historical Almanac and Annual Remembrance of the Church for 1868,* Vol. X (*Philadelphia: Joseph M. Wilson, 1868),* p. 136.
5. Ibid., p. 137.
6. Joao Marcos Pacheco, *Brazil Presbiteriano,* April 1994, trans. of journals of Ashbel Green Simonton from the Portuguese by William L. Bryant (no page numbers). Italics added for emphasis.
7. Ibid.
8. Conversation with author, August 1991, Black Mountain, N. C.

Chapter 8: How to Pray for the Empowerment of the Holy Spirit

1. We have found the seven fundamentals of R. A. Torrey (notwithstanding our addition of one step) to be sound, scriptural, practical, nondivisive and fruitful. Again, our purpose is not to introduce new teaching about the Holy Spirit but to showcase the teaching of Torrey, which we believe timely for the 1990s. Now is a fit time to rediscover the soundness of his teaching—not for the sake of abstract debate, but as a practical way of discovering the power of the Holy Spirit in ministry.
2. Torrey, *Person and Work.*
3. Penn-Lewis, *War,* pp. 10–11.
4. John Calvin, *Institutes of the Christian Religion,* III.XX.2.
5. R. A. Torrey, *The Holy Spirit: Who He Is and What He Does* (Old Tappan, N.J.: Revell, 1977).

Chapter 10: A Summary: Three Views of the Holy Spirit

1. John R. W. Stott, *Baptism and Fullness: The Work of the Holy Spirit Today* (Downers Grove, Ill.: InterVarsity, 1964), pp. 25–26.

Chapter 11: The Ministry of Jesus as Prophet

1. Penn-Lewis, *War,* pp. 46–47.
2. Calvin, *Institutes,* II.XV.1.
3. John V. Taylor, *The Go Between God* (Oxford: Oxford University Press, 1979), p. 19.
4. Donald Gee, *Concerning Spiritual Gifts* (Springfield, Mo.: Gospel, 1972), p. 40.

Chapter 12: The Ministry of Jesus as Priest

1. Jonathan Edwards, *The Life and Diary of David Brainerd* (Chicago: Moody, n.d.), p. 178.

Chapter 14: Breaking Tribalism in the Body of Christ

1. John Dawson, *Healing America's Wounds* (Ventura, Calif.: Regal, 1994), pp. 106–107.

Chapter 15: May the ????? Be with You

1. Torrey, *Person and Work*. The other quotes from Torrey in this chapter are from the same book.

Chapter 16: Discerning Signs and Wonders

1. John White, *When the Spirit Comes with Power* (Downers Grove, Ill.: InterVarsity, 1988), p. 140.
2. Ibid., p. 141.
3. Jessie Penn-Lewis, *Soul and Spirit: A Glimpse into Bible Psychology* (Poole, Dorset, England: Overcomer Literature Trust, 1968), p. 79.
4. Penn-Lewis, *War,* p. 237.
5. Ibid., p. 221.
6. Guy Chevreau, *Catch the Fire* (Toronto: HarperCollins, 1994), p. viii.

Chapter 17: Is "Holy Laughter" Holy?

1. Charles Finney, *Memoirs* (New York: A. S. Barnes, 1876), p. 107.
2. Ibid., p. 102.
3. G. K. Chesterton, "The Blatchford Controversies," *G. K. Chesterton: Collected Works* (San Francisco: Ignatius, 1986), Vol. 1, p. 374.

Chapter 18: Bringing the Next Generation to Jesus

1. Carl G. Jung with Aniela Jaffe, *Memories, Dreams, Reflections* (New York: Vintage, 1961, 1963). The other quotes from Jung in this chapter are from the same book.
2. Penn-Lewis, *War,* p. 29.

Index

For more information, write to

Presbyterian & Reformed Renewal Ministries International
P.O. Box 429
Black Mountain, NC 28711–0429